Baby Birds

AN ARTIST LOOKS INTO THE NEST

Baby Birds

AN ARTIST LOOKS INTO THE NEST

Julie Zickefoose

HOUGHTON MIFFLIN HARCOURT

BOSTON NEW YORK 2016

For information about permission to reproduce selections from this book,
write to trade.permissions@hmhco.com or to Permissions, Houghton Mifflin Harcourt Publishing Company,
3 Park Avenue, 19th Floor, New York, New York 10016.

www.hmhco.com

Library of Congress Cataloging-in-Publication Data is available.
ISBN 978-0-544-20670-0

Book design by Martha Kennedy

The author is grateful for permission to reprint the text on pp. 261–275 originally published in *Flight Lines*
by Keith Corliss, and text on pp. 206–220 by Cynthia L. Routledge.

Printed in China
SCP 10 9 8 7 6 5 4 3 2 1

To Ida. Thank you for letting me bring all those baby birds into the house,
for letting me turn my bedroom into a jungle aviary, and for allowing me to disappear
into the woods and down country roads. Thank you for cultivating excellence in your children
without ever once begging, bribing, or rewarding. You were the best mom. And DOD: Thank
you for knowing a lot about anything I could come up with, for spinning stories both mundane
and astonishing, and for challenging me to think. "What good is a warthog?" you'd ask.
I know now you just wanted to hear what I'd come up with.

Piper
on the farm
hose bell 7/14/12

Contents

Acknowledgments

My dear friend Donna, in trying to cheer me up, once said, "Julie, you have your own gravity. People are drawn to you." True or not, working on a project for thirteen years will pull a lot of good people into one's orbit. I've made a taxonomy, dividing them into those who brought me baby birds; those who made and loaned images of birds; those who helped in some other capacity; those who helped bring the book to publication; and those who, in many capacities, fed my creative fire along the way.

There's nothing like being a bird's mama to acquaint you with how it behaves, looks, and thinks. Four hummingbirds came in two different nests on July 9, 2003, one nest borne by Lori Hall. Rosetta Dalison brought me five chimney swifts on June 24, 2004, and Gwen Kelby added five more on July 6 of that year. Kandy Matheney and Sandy Fredenburg came bearing two eastern phoebes on June 8, 2006, and Don and Deana Noland gave me a lovely orphaned mourning dove on April 21, 2010. Milford and Fran Fore, directed to me by my redneck pal Jeff Warren, did a fine job raising three eastern bluebirds, leaving them with me on July 7, 2013, to ready them for release. I am indebted to these kind people for the life-changing presents that came chirping, packed in cardboard boxes for me to open.

I prefer drawing from life, and hands-on experience with baby birds, but when I can't get that, photographs are indispensible. Images flowed in from far-flung places as friends answered my call for assistance. Nina Harfmann's photographs of early hummingbird development in southwest Ohio made it possible for me to paint that sequence, while Dan Kaiser contributed some vital images of later development and of hummingbird and tree swallow parental care. Shila Wilson patched in two days of tufted titmouse photos when I was called away; Phoebe Thompson did the same with house wrens. Bruce Di Labio shot chimney swift nests in his homemade Ontario nesting tower, augmenting my life studies, while Keith Corliss braved parental wing-slaps to record the daily development of West Fargo mourning doves. Connie Roman made comprehensive daily portraits of New Jersey house finch nestlings when asked nicely. Cyndi Routledge went above and beyond the call in photographing and ferociously protecting prothonotary warblers in her Tennessee nest box, and also teetered on a ladder to photograph barn swallows, which I ran out of time to paint. Diane Tracy and Shannon McNeil kindly loaned yellow-billed cuckoo photos from their studies of endangered California birds. BeaAnn Kelly provided a cuckoo threat display shot. Tim Shreckengost and Alan Poole greased some skids for that chapter. It is no coincidence that most of these people were already friends; they're curious and brave, the same kind of crazy as I am.

In a quest to provide a solid scientific background for my observations, I turned again and again to Birds of North America (a joint project of the American Ornithologists' Union, Academy of Natural Sciences, and Cornell Lab of Ornithology). Running across my own drawings in its species accounts makes me smile. I thank editor Alan Poole for caving when, upon viewing the first few species accounts to be published in 1992, I wrote and essentially demanded to be engaged to illustrate it. I recall saying, "You need me." Now I need a daily dose of BNA; the electronic version is always open on my laptop. There are few questions about North American birds that BNA can't answer, and most of them have to do with cuckoos. I thank Bob Mulvihill for illuminating the subject of molt and setting me off on avenues of inquiry, and Dr. Janice Hughes for cheerfully lighting my way through the tangle that cuckoos have made of their own breeding biology. Thanks to Dr. Terry Whitworth for identifying the bird blowflies I tweezed out of house wren nestlings, grew in a jar, and sent to him.

I am indebted to the dedicated wildlife rehabilitators at the Ohio Wildlife Center for standing ready to receive several thousand birds and animals each season, for doing their best to save as many as they can, a good number of them referred by me. My fiddling with the few that I'm able to help is but a drop in the ocean of need in this state. Private wildlife rehabilitators, who give their time, money, and energy trying to fix what people and their cars, windows, and free-roaming cats break, are my heroes. Thanks to Lee Hermandorfer for transporting broken birds, and to avian rehabilitator Astrid MacLeod for essential advice on raising swifts, hummingbirds, and others.

Throughout my career as an artist and writer, I've been nurtured and buoyed by the friendship of The Artists' Group, a loose confederation of bird painters, some of whom are recovering and have gone on to landscape. Some of us, after all these years, are still painting birds. All of us hold a net of loving mutual support. Larry Barth, John Baumlin, Robert Braunfield, Jim Coe, Mike DiGiorgio, Al Gilbert, Cindy House, Debby Kaspari, Sean Murtha, David Quinn, Barry Van Dusen, and the indomitable and dearly missed Brenda Carter all inspired me with their passion for their work, and helped me realize that these baby bird paintings were unique and largely unrepeatable works that deserved a wider audience. My agent, Russell Galen, flipped out over the first few paintings I showed him back near the turn of the century, and his enthusiasm and faith were twin midwives for the book's birth.

Houghton Mifflin Harcourt continues to dignify my art and writing with unparalleled production. For that, I am forever indebted. Lisa White edits lightly, always clarifies, makes me laugh, and goes to bat for my always bigger-than-anticipated books. You can't ask more of an editor than that. Designer Martha Kennedy is a gift. It's an honor to have her showcase my work. Copy editor Liz Pierson lovingly bore down to make sure, among other things, that myriad dates jibed with the nestlings' ages, making this both a better scientific document and a better book. Publicist Taryn Roeder somehow got *The Bluebird Effect* under Oprah's nose for a 2012 Book of the Week, which hasn't hurt at all.

I am blessed to have four siblings, each uniquely talented, wise, and kind. As the one who went west, I miss you every day. Barbara, Bob, Nancy, and Micky, it's a privilege to be your sister, and to watch your amazing families grow.

It is the support I've received at home, though, that has made this project possible. Robert Braunfield first showed me how to care for birds in nest boxes, and the bluebirds we housed in the mid-1980s sparked my fascination with nestling development. Shila Wilson keeps me looking up in myriad ways, always following the butterfly. In the electronic age, "friend" has a newly nuanced meaning, and I am amazed every day as I am able to interact with far-flung, seldom-seen but deeply cherished people. Community and support are where you find them, and that's usually many miles from Whipple,

Ohio. My beloved friends—you know who you are—inspire me every day with lives well and bravely led. And I thank my brilliant songwriting and performing partners in The Rain Crows for the creative release our music provides.

Bill Thompson III and the amazing staff of *Bird Watcher's Digest* keep my work in front of the nicest people I know: *BWD* subscribers. Bill's vision helped make this book what it is. He's fielded my eccentricities, whoops, and wails for twenty-four years, knowing just when to encourage and when to duck and get out of my way. Our children, Phoebe and Liam, who have showered orphaned birds with love and stood in for me in many a feeding session, are fledging even as this book takes off. For them, summer has always meant answering wildlife calls and stuffing food into baby birds. Much as I miss them as the bigger world draws them away, seeing them lift themselves on strong wings is a great and gratifying consolation. A lifetime spent raising and rehabilitating wild birds turns out to be helpful for knowing when to let them go, and being glad about it.

Sandhill cranes
with their colt—a
high-investment baby.

Introduction

FROM THE MOMENT we're old enough to go exploring in our backyards, we're told not to touch bird nests. "The mother bird will smell you on the babies and then she'll abandon them, and we don't want that." A sort of magical protective shield springs up between child and bird. This fable, while untrue, is probably mostly good for the birds. For people, though, I've noticed that a drilled-in parental admonition can result in reticence about approaching birds and sometimes progresses into a full-blown phobia. Birds flying about our heads or birds in our hands can be too scary to contemplate. We may not exactly recall where or how it started, but a lot of people are skittish about handling birds. I am not one of them.

Over thirty years as a bird rehabilitator and bluebird nest box landlord, I've gotten good at handling, reviving, doctoring, and feeding fragile nestlings, and in the process I've gained a deeper understanding of the parent birds' behavior. Songbirds have one, two, or, if they're lucky, three chances to raise a brood in a given nesting season, and they don't give up easily on this investment. They won't desert their eggs or young just because a person has handled them. Not only is a songbird unable to detect human scent on its young, but it will closely watch its nestlings being handled and go right back to feeding them when the person

Starling nest with narcissus, last fall's mushy jalapeño pepper, and the promise of five eggs. April 23, 2006

leaves. If their offspring are alive and well and still begging for food, the parent birds will resume caring for them without hesitation.

As a natural history illustrator, it was an inevitable and unconscious progression for me to move from studying the development of nestling bluebirds to depicting it in pencil and watercolor. It was all happening in a nest box just 200 feet from my front door. In 2002 it occurred to me: Why not go out, borrow a hatchling, paint its portrait, and then replace it in its nest? And then go back and do the same thing at the same time the next day? I could make a record of its daily development, drawing it from life, documenting changes big and small. Having been an avian rehabilitator since 1984, I held the proper state and federal permits to handle migratory birds. I knew from years of experience that the parent bluebirds would not desert their nest. There was nothing to stop me.

I'm not sure what compelled me to start the project, other than a burning desire to understand more of how baby birds are put together, how they grow and develop. As I learned in a college botany class, to draw is to see, is to understand. If you would know how something is built, draw it. Try it with a flower sometime. Pick one and start drawing it. You'll fall into the corolla and the ring of stamens around the pistil and become fascinated by how it's all constructed, and at the end of this simple exercise you'll understand something of that blossom that would never have impressed you, had you not attempted to draw it. I wanted to understand how baby birds blossom. And in executing the drawings, I might come closer to grasping the central miracle of their development. Some of the birds I would come to study and draw metamorphose from a writhing pink hatchling no bigger than your thumbnail to a flying bird in eleven days.

Back up, if you would, and think about that for a moment. How much does a newborn human baby change in eleven days? Her eyes clear up; she becomes more alert, more attuned to voices and faces around her; she gains some strength and a few ounces of weight. But eleven days out, can she get up and dash after you to the nearest woodland border? If she had them, could she spread new wings and fly?

As much as I've drawn it, as much as I've witnessed it, the transformation of a nestling

Butterfly Weed
Asclepias tuberosa

each twenty-four hours is still the most astonishing yet underappreciated phenomenon I know of. Once I'd witnessed it in eastern bluebirds, I was all afire to see how other species develop. I was off, looking for more subjects, hoping to compare and contrast, to learn—loving the quest and most of all the process of drawing these sweet writhing blobs of protoplasm throughout their infancy.

Altricial birds are born blind and helpless; all the songbirds of the order Passeriformes fall into this category. Precocial birds, by contrast, hatch with open eyes and strong legs, and pick up their own food from the start. Galliformes (grouse, turkeys, and pheasants) and shorebirds are precocial. Of course, there are shadings and gradations, with some precocial birds being fed for a while by their parents, and some altricial birds that hatch better developed than others. Carolina wrens are a good example of the latter. Both eastern bluebirds and Carolina wrens are technically altricial, but the Carolina wren can fly at eleven days of age, while bluebirds must wait until Day 18. And then there's the yellow-billed cuckoo, with an arc all its own, the most amazing one of all.

Compare altricial nestling development, generally with a two-week span between hatching and mobility, with that of the truly precocial ruffed grouse, which can walk as soon as it's dry. It's born with fully emerged feathers, and can make short flights on its fifth day. I'll never forget opening an egg left behind in a Connecticut grouse nest and finding a downy chick with fully feathered wings, dead in the shell. No amount of warmth and massage could bring it around. I was sad, but understood the hen grouse's need to quickly take the ten new hatchlings away from the nest, now richly scented with pipped eggshells and a great lure to predators. It was cold and rainy, and the last egg probably got chilled before it could hatch. I remember turning the chick over and over in my hand, unable to believe that something so beautiful, so perfect, could be dead before it ever saw daylight.

Why are some birds altricial and others precocial? The simple answer is that big birds can lay big eggs with bigger yolks. A precocial chick needs a well-provisioned egg if it is to hatch ready to walk and even flutter a few feet. Think of grouse, turkeys, and shorebirds, which lay big eggs with large yolks. Even thrush-size shorebirds such as the piping plover lay eggs that are enormous proportionate to their body size. From these outsize packages emerge bright-eyed, downy, fleet-footed chicks. They'll follow their mother, picking up their own food, in a lengthy apprenticeship to becoming a self-sufficient bird.

Small songbirds, with their explosive adaptive radiation and exploitation of many specialized niches, pay the price for their small body size in smaller, comparatively poorly provisioned eggs. Songbird eggs have higher water content and less protein in their yolks than do the eggs of precocial species. As a result, songbird chicks are born blind, weak, and helpless. It's the catching-up time—that two-week period when a songbird is growing like kudzu—that fascinates me.

A two-day-old ruffed grouse teeters 15' up in a balsam fir, having flown there under its own power.

That this thumb-sized bird can fly on Day Two astounds me.

If they can't be mobile, it behooves songbird chicks to grow fast. The period when they must lie stationary in the nest is the most vulnerable of their entire lives. Jays, crows, grackles, squirrels, mice, rats, opossums, skunks, raccoons, housecats, snakes—everything that eats live food relishes eggs and chicks. From the moment it is laid, an egg is racing to produce a chick, and from the moment it hatches, the chick is racing to become a bird. It's trying to beat predators, parasites, wind, and cold rain—all the things that can kill it, racing to make it to the sky.

I know of two bird artists who have painted individual portraits of baby birds. Connecticut painter Albert Earl Gilbert made exquisite studies of young cracids for a landmark volume, *Curassows and Related Birds.* Over the course of a long career, Oklahoma ornithologist George Miksch Sutton executed thirty-six watercolors of the downy precocial young of sandpipers and gallinaceous birds, as well as individual portraits of newly fledged songbirds, beautifully gathered in Paul Johnsgard's *Baby Bird Portraits by George Miksch Sutton: Watercolors in the Field Museum.*

Neither of these artists, however, methodically painted nestlings as they develop every day, and it was Al Gilbert who, on viewing some of my early plates, helped me understand that I was breaking new artistic and scientific ground, and urged me to paint as many species as I could get my hands on. Over the next thirteen years, I did.

A group of fellow bird painters to whom I was showing my work asked me if anyone has ever done this. I replied that I was sure no one had. If they had, I'd know about it. "Why not? It's so amazing, it seems like someone would have attempted it before!" I thought about it and answered, "Well, in order to do it, you'd have to be able to draw birds from life. But you'd also have to know how to access their nests, and feed and care for them. That narrows the window of possibility that anyone else is doing this or has done it. It's a rather specialized set of skills."

George Sutton, another artist who worked with nestlings, put it well in the March/April 1949 issue of *Audubon Magazine*: "Baby birds of all sorts make wonderful models. Some of them are excitable and restless and will no more 'stay put' than a healthy child would, but others will, when properly fed, stay in one position and allow an artist to study them carefully as he draws." Sutton's words have the ring of experience. As a new mother, I never expected my toddlers to ride contentedly in a grocery cart without handing them a cup of something good to eat. Likewise, I won't ask naked nestlings to pose for me without a warming lamp, soft tissues, and a steady supply of newly molted, tender mealworms or other species-appropriate food. In return, they rest quietly, allowing me to turn them this way and that, and rarely move a muscle while I do my work. Because I take pains to select the same nestling to work with each day, the individual becomes accustomed to the drill, and seems to anticipate the food reward that goes with being temporarily removed and transported away from its nest. Thanks to these positive associations, just as my children loved to go to the grocery store and generally behaved beautifully, the nestlings seem to enjoy serving as models and settle down comfortably in their odd role. I can tell immediately when I've accidentally picked out a nestling that doesn't know the drill!

I draw and paint the nestling, usually in two poses, as quickly as possible as it rests on a bed of tissues directly on my oversize sheet of hot-press watercolor paper. The studies are generally completed in less than forty minutes, during which time I might feed the bird three times. I then replace it in its nest and come back for it around the same time the next day. Over the next ten days to two weeks, painted studies snake around and eventually fill the sheet with a life-size record of the chick's development from pipping egg to

fledgling. Where I've had the opportunity to make follow-up studies post-fledging, I've painted as many older juveniles as possible.

For its part, the nestling I select to paint from—the same bird each day, if I can get it—prospers by its unsought position as artist's model, being visibly larger and fatter than its nestmates by virtue of my supplemental feedings. Just three or four extra feedings a day can make a visible difference in a nestling's vitality. How do I know I am painting the same bird? Just as puppies and kittens select and stick to (and often fight for) the same teat on their mother, I have noticed that young birds tend to keep the same seat in the nest throughout their infancy. It may be that this allows the adult birds to keep track of each individual chick's development—which ones have been fed in a round and which haven't. Patricia Gowaty's studies of eastern bluebirds revealed that male bluebirds preferentially feed female over male offspring. They most likely do this through both voice recognition and position in the nest, though how a bluebird determines the sex of naked chicks in a dark box will remain a mystery for the ages. Do female nestlings sound different from males? Or do the white-edged outer tail feathers of female bluebird nestlings serve as a visual cue for the parents? Pondering on a mystery opens the door to more mystery.

From the start, I had a notion that the paintings that piled up in my flat file would someday find their way into a book. I certainly wasn't executing such detailed portraits for their commercial appeal. Nobody commissions paintings of naked baby birds. I've never seen paintings of larval birds on a gallery wall. Curiosity and passion drive the enterprise. Having painted seventeen species, I want only to paint more.

There are several things stopping me. I can't study just any wild bird's nest that I happen upon. Foremost in my mind is the Hippocratic oath: *Primum non nocere* (First, do no harm). To have any of these wild, free-living birds suffer or die for my art is unacceptable. The danger is that, in beating a trail to a wild bird's nest, I'll lead nest predators such as raccoons and black ratsnakes to the hidden treasure. And so I work only with nests whose safety I can virtually guarantee. At first, that meant nests inside the birdhouses I managed, which were mounted on galvanized pipe and protected with 2-foot-long stovepipe baffles, to ensure that no climbing predator could reach them.

I started, then, with the cavity nesters on my bluebird box trails, which gave me not only eastern bluebirds but tree swallows, Carolina chickadees, and tufted titmice. After that, I painted nestlings that came in as orphans to my modest avian rehabilitation facility. Later, I branched out to paint some open-cup nesters in highly protected situations. And at my daughter's urging, I realized that there were subjects waiting in species that I generally evict from my nest boxes: house wren, house sparrow, and European starling. Phoebe helped me realize that all birds are deserving of study, and in doing so sent me on a wonderful journey. Through various safeguards taken to protect my study subjects, I'm happy to say that, with the exception of some mite incidents and a phoebe nest raided by a snake-genius despite my best efforts to baffle it, every other nest I've worked with has gone on to fledge young; some of the nestlings have survived *because* I was there to help when they got into the kind of routine trouble that plagues all wild nesting attempts.

Thirteen years later, I've almost exhausted the possibilities of birds I can study without endangering them, painting every cavity-nesting bird that could inhabit my nest boxes save white-breasted nuthatch. Oh, how I would love to have white-breasted nuthatches to paint. But each species I have been able to depict seems like an extravagant gift.

Tufted titmice nested in one of our boxes in 1992, the very first year we put them up and well before this project germinated; it took twenty years to attract another pair. My rehabilitation efforts have brought in gems like ruby-throated hummingbird and chimney swift. Taking serendipitous photos of some open-cup nesters in protected places around our sanctuary rounded out the total. And a few I've painted from photographs sent to me by friends who were up for taking them and just as excited about the project as I am. With this multipronged approach, I've been able to document the natal development of seventeen species over the past thirteen years. I dream of a second volume, depicting whatever birds fate sends my way. Top of the list: white-breasted nuthatch. The possibilities are delightful, if not endless.

These paintings were done on 20 × 30 inch sheets of 140-pound Fabriano or Winsor & Newton hot-press watercolor paper. There's something about the smooth, quiet surface of hot-press paper that helps me relax and keeps me from noodling too much detail into the paintings. Detail, obviously, is called for, but speed is of the essence; I don't want to keep a nestling away from its parents too long. I also want these to look like watercolors, not rendered photographs. Pencil and brush glide smoothly over hot-press paper, leaving stray lines, accidental hard edges, and puddles. They speak of the immediacy of the moment, of painting a live, wriggling creature from life.

Another virtue of 140-pound hot-press paper is that it is thin enough to be rolled under my drawing table as I work. That's necessary for me to be able to reach every corner of the oversize sheet. It's hard to draw well when you're spread-eagle over your paper, trying to reach its upper right corner. Because I depict them life-size, larger species such as the mourning dove presented the challenge of fitting all their images on the same 20 × 30 inch sheet. I was reminded of Audubon's American flamingo, bent and folded to the dimensions of the elephant folio paper; of the golden eagle, flying diagonally upward, the only way it would fit. The mourning doves nearly flew off the plate before their final, fully feathered portraits on Day 21.

Though the bulk of my work has been done direct from life, I have resorted to drawing from photographs when I couldn't get the reference any other way. I've never lived near enough to nesting prothonotary warblers to be able to paint them daily, but I couldn't resist the chance to press a talented Tennessee friend into service to create a daily photographic document of these tiny firebrands for me to work from. Being a cavity nester, prothonotaries are the only warbler species I can ever expect to safely work with, and I wasn't going to let a few hundred miles get in the way.

After the Google search engine, the cell-phone camera, I believe, is the twentieth century's greatest gift to natural history inquiry. That any person can carry in his or her pocket a camera capable of any shot from macro to wide angle is a modern miracle. The fidelity of these tiny cameras is remarkable; I could make out individual filaments of down in the high-resolution photos. To have them sent by friends, and arrive daily in my e-mail inbox, felt to me like a miracle.

There are challenges in working from photographs, most having to do with scale. Unless an object of known size such as a ruler or a quarter is in the frame, it's hard to know when the image is life-size. In many cases, lacking anything else for size reference, I measured eggs depicted in the photos and sized the photos according to known egg dimensions in the species. After the chicks hatched, I then measured bits of nesting material against the eggs and used them for size reference in subsequent photos. Sometimes I had nothing but a person's finger or a corner of a paper towel in the photo as size reference: tricky, but surmountable.

Once I had the photos properly sized, drawing from them was a snap compared with working with wriggling nestlings. The paintings done from photographs reflect a certain tranquility and are more lavishly detailed than the rest in the book, for the camera picks up more than the eye can in a lightning life drawing session. What the mind and heart pick up from working from living birds falls into the realm of the intangible, but I can see it reflected in the dashier, dribblier paintings. As grateful as I am to have been given the chance to draw a few nestlings from photographs, I greatly missed the interaction and the unique story I get from visiting a nest, interacting with the adults, and caring for a live nestling.

Although I would love to be able to explain some of the hormonal and physiological changes behind the stunningly rapid development of nestling songbirds, I'm not sure much is known about it. We know a great deal about the growth and development of domestic chickens because it behooves us to know about it: we want to eat them as soon as possible after they hatch. But studying the development of nestling songbirds is a little like waking up in Oz. The rules are different here. A nestling that was naked and pink the afternoon before looks back at me, prickling with blue quills the next day. And the day after that it's reinvented itself again. There's magic in the nest, and there's really no explaining what's happening. There's looking and wondering, drawing and painting, all in hope of conveying the unfathomable.

What results from all this is an odd sort of book, like a Victorian-era curiosity. It's a throwback to the days when ladies of means and high upbringing might spend their days wandering the meadows, plucking flowers, and collecting birds' nests and eggs to add to their collections and paint in their journals. I've had neither means nor a particularly high upbringing. What I've had is a lust to understand the mystery of baby bird development and an inordinate fondness for small, helpless young things—and for watching and drawing them as they change, grow, and thrive.

As each fandling is released, wild swifts
swoop down to flank it, following its every move.
I never expected that! July 19, 2004

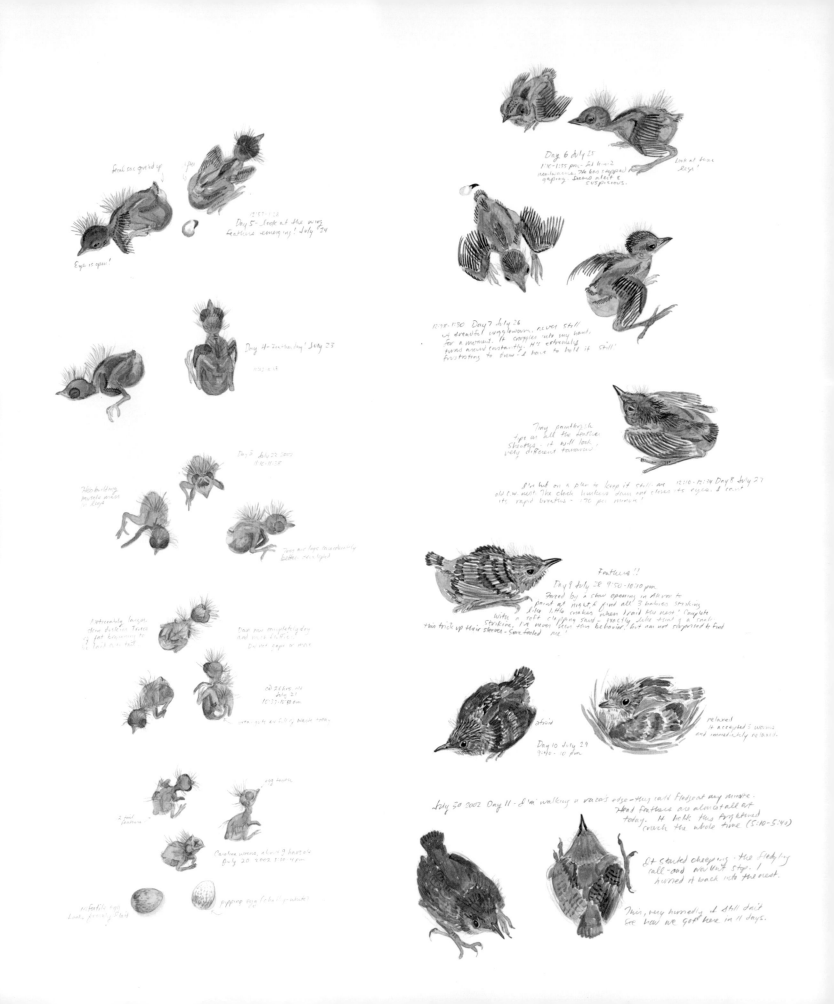

Carolina Wren, 2002

July 31 Day 12

I reach to get one at dark—it's 9:20pm—
and it shrieks, and all three explode from
the nest. I hold them in it with one
hand while Bill fetches a plastic box.
These sketches done until 10 pm. They're popping like corn all
over the place, squawking constantly. I'll take them in at dawn
and release them to their parents' care. Pride goeth before
a fall—I thought I'd get away with it!

Skveet! A new fledgling
eyes a camel cricket.
Looks like a bit much.

Carolina Wren, 2002

OF THE BIRDS with which I interact on a daily basis, only the Carolina wren rivals the eastern bluebird in the intimacy of our relationship. The wren's propensity for infiltrating our living spaces invites rich interaction. It likes to build its bulky, intricate nests in garages, toolsheds—any of the myriad crannies it finds in our structures. But its ability to make eye contact with me and seemingly hook into my thoughts is what I find most interesting. I've written a number of essays about these encounters. A female Carolina wren started a nest in a potted bougainvillea in my small greenhouse one warm early spring week when I'd propped the door open. The weather turned cold, as it will in spring, and I was forced to close the door. The wren scolded and fussed. While she watched, I knelt and removed a small round vent screen near the ground. "You can enter here," I said, and stepped back, the screen in my hand. The wren bobbed as if curtsying, hopped directly to the vent, entered, and wound up fledging a brood of four from the friendly confines of the greenhouse. One Carolina wren, trapped in a carpet warehouse, allowed me to walk behind it, guiding it with hand gestures and slight nods of my head, from one enormous room to the next until we reached an open door through which it could gain its freedom.

Another wren, accidentally shut in our house for four winter days while we were away, explored the house from top to bottom until it found the mealworm bin in the basement. It made its way in and out through a 2 × 6 inch trapdoor passage to the glassed-in tower room where it could catch overwintering houseflies. It drank from the humidity trays under my orchids in the back bedroom. All this I deduced from the droppings I found spattered everywhere when we got home. From these small white signs, I knew immediately upon our return that there was a bird in the house. But it was not just any bird. It could only be a brainy and inventive Carolina wren.

I was home for a day and a half before I glimpsed a small chestnut shadow flitting silently along the baseboard. We made eye contact, and the wren proceeded from kitchen to foyer. It paused, looking back at me, then flew down the basement stairs. I followed at a respectful distance. It flew straight to the downstairs bedroom where, upon returning from my trip, I'd found a sliding glass door left ajar and shut it, wondering what might have gained entrance while we were gone. The wren hopped over toward the door, hanging off to the side. I opened the door and stepped back. The wren flew outside. That afternoon, loud, joyous caroling told of its reunion with its mate in the scrubby woods below our house. Its deliberate navigation back to the place it had entered is typical of Carolina wrens, which pack an amazing spatial memory into their chickpea-size brains. It had survived for four days on what insects it could find in our house (the mealworm motherlode was virtually empty!). More impressive to me yet was the way it seemed to enlist my help in gaining its freedom.

The Carolina wrens I worked with for this series seemed to me more like neighbors than wild birds—chatty, a little nosy, endearing; given to barging in uninvited, but always welcome. They knew me as a source of mealworm and suet treats, rare and fabulous nesting materials, and cleverly placed boxes and buckets in which they might roost and nest. They were so bold that if I happened to leave the screen door open for a minute, say, to bring in groceries, they would flit into the house to explore and look for spiders in the corners of the bedrooms. They quickly found the mealworm stash near the fireplace and helped themselves. Discovered,

Carolina wren nest in the backyard bluebird box. June 8 2015. A finely-crafted tunnel of moss, dead leaves, pine needles, grass, twigs, petioles, hair and even a bit of snakeskin.

they never panicked or dashed themselves against the windows, but calmly continued their adventure, poking behind furniture and up and down the stone fireplace. I'd laugh and open the patio door, ask them to leave when they were finished, and they quietly complied. I felt sure they'd understand when I borrowed one of their young for a few minutes each day.

I'd never have attempted the project without first knowing how to care for nestlings, and without being able to anticipate how the parent birds would react. I thought I knew what I was going to experience, but I could never have guessed how wonderful—full of wonder—the exercise of watching a wild bird grow up would be. What better birds than Carolina wrens and eastern bluebirds to usher it all in? We were already friends.

July 20, 2002. Day 1. I've been waiting fifteen days for the Carolina wren eggs in the hanging basket by the front door to hatch. They sneaked a neat little nest of moss and grass into a madly blooming hanging basket, a haze of white and blue, and laid two eggs before I even knew it was there! I'm so accustomed to seeing the wrens poking about by the front door that I didn't even notice their nest-building activity until the female was laying eggs. Wrens are so smart, though, that they were doubtless watching me, and building only when I wasn't looking. Today is hatching day, and I peek into the nest to see a haze of gray down and dark pink skin. I tease one nestling up and into my palm and take it into the studio to paint its portrait. I'll never have a more convenient setup, twenty steps away.

Carolina wrens, about 9 hours old
July 20 2002 3:30 - 4 pm

The nestling has a peculiar way of gaping regularly, every thirty seconds or so. It's so tiny that I'm afraid I'll choke it, but I squeeze out the insides of a mealworm, and very gently

pipping egg (chalky-white)

put the semiliquid blob in its gullet. It swallows instantly, drops its head, and becomes quiet, and much easier to draw. Over the course of the next twenty minutes, I squeeze out three large mealworms for it. It's the least I can do to thank it for modeling. My little son Liam, two and a half, bends over and sniffs the tiny bird, then touches it with one finger, rolling it on its side, and sniffs it again. He's always smelled things; he reminds me of a little dog, or a curious chimpanzee. He knows what "gentle" means, and won't hurt the bird. He toddles away and lets me work.

infertile egg
Looks freshly laid

I mean to make only one painting but am so bewitched by the tiny, nine-hour-old baby that I make three studies, life size. It's so

12 tail feathers →

egg tooth

different from every angle. My middle-aged eyes are barely able to take in its details, so I take my glasses off and peer, millimeters away. The egg tooth still adheres to the tip of its fleshy bill. To my amazement, the bird has twelve infinitesimal bluish tail feathers protruding from a miniscule pope's nose off its rump. I can see the whitish zone of what might be its first fecal sac through the skin of its lower abdomen. Strands of blue-gray down crown its head, and a secondary friar's fringe goes around the base of its skull. Two long strands come off each humerus, and more off the point of the sacrum. They're meant to trap warm air around the baby, though they look ineffectual. When this baby is huddled together with the others, though, the individual strands make a bluish blanket over all of them. You can't see the babies beneath the haze of gray, until their yellow diamond mouths open up and wave.

July 21, 2002. Day 2. The female wren sits, staring me down, because it's hot and she is shading the nest. I sketch her as she sits, then decide to wait until the sun is off the nest to remove the chick. At 10:37, I work a baby up out of the nest. I try to pick the biggest of the three, all of whom are now out of the shell. I am so afraid I will injure it or drop it. I'm rarely squeamish, but the thought of my huge hard fingers on this squishy little being gives my stomach a twirl. It will be a relief when they get big enough for me to be more comfortable handling them. I notice immediately how much larger and darker the chick appears. It is transparent, its guts showing disconcertingly through the thin abdominal skin. I can see whitish urea from a forming fecal sac, greenish bile waste. The Visible Bird. Obviously, it's been fed.

The down, stuck together in a few thin strands yesterday, is now completely dry. I might be tempted to think more had grown overnight, but I know it's just a matter of the existing strands drying and fluffing out. I wonder if the female preens her babies, or if this happens on its own. The down makes a haze of Payne's gray over the baby's head and body. I note that there is no down on the rump. That makes sense, for it would doubtless get fouled by feces. I can see minute traces of yellow fat laid down over the synsacrum, which weren't there yesterday. The baby is quiet and lies still as I draw it in three poses. Its breaths are rapid and shallow. Several times,

Noticeably larger, skin duskier. Traces of fat beginning to be laid over tail.

it wiggles its tiny tail nub. It never gapes or peeps, so I don't feed it.

Melanin, a dark pigment, is gathering in the skin. Bright coral yesterday, it's now becoming dusky. The eyes, still sealed, are larger and darker gray, and the bill tip is darkening, too. I cannot grasp how such changes could have happened literally overnight. I painted this bird only eighteen hours ago, and it's noticeably bigger, darker, heavier. As I work, bluebirds are hatching out in the mid-meadow nest box. I will paint them today. I want to see how they start out so similarly, then begin to diverge into wren and thrush. I feel that I am somehow present at the revelation of a great mystery. "Here's how it's done, at last!" I wish now that I had taken a picture of my human babies every day, at the same time, lying naked as these chicks are. Instead, I have snapshots—newborn leaping to three weeks, the baby appearing as if someone had taken a bicycle pump to her, inflated her with fat and air. At least I have those. Stacks of them. It's the day-to-day, hour-to-hour changes that fascinate me in the sped-up lives of songbirds. I am consumed by curiosity. I want to draw them every hour, but for the birds' sake I must hold myself to one session a day. Birds pack so much growth and life into such a short time. It's the reason we eat full-size chickens that are just a matter of months old, the reason that Carolina wrens and bluebirds can raise three broods in a fleeting summer.

July 22, 2002. Day 3. Today when I take a baby, the female wren retreats but a yard away. Perched on a vine, she watches me take the baby, then returns to the nest without protest. In the half-hour I have the baby, it gapes several times, and I get a chance to paint its mouth color, and feed it the innards of three mealworms. It responds to my bad imitation of a Carolina wren whistle by gaping immediately. To be truthful, though, it also gapes when it's touched or blown on.

I notice that the chick's getting muscular, especially in its thighs and lower legs. The tarsometatarsus (scaly part of the leg) is longer, as are its toes. It's stronger, and is able to haul itself up on its wings in a three-point sit to gape. Its skin continues to darken and become less transparent, and its bill is a little longer, too.

The adult female wren, who's distinguishable from the male by her perpetually bent tail (a side effect of incubating), again pops out of the nest, then watches me replace the baby from her perch only a few feet away. I hold the baby out to show it to her

Down now completely dry and much fluffier. Did not gape or move.

♀ 26 hrs. old July 21 10:37–10:50 am

urea-guts are full of waste today

Day 3 July 22 2002
11:10-11:38

He's building muscle mass in legs

Toes and legs considerably better-developed

before replacing it, and she flits back into the nest, seemingly at peace with our strange arrangement. I have no doubt that she understands I am not harming her young, since she never voices a scold or complaint, and now does not bother to round the corner of the house when I appear. She's so close I could catch her in my hand. I wonder if she's noticed that my model comes back to the nest sleepy and well fed. There is little a wren does not notice.

July 23, 2002. Day 4. It's feather day! By far the most amazing change has occurred from Day 3 to Day 4. The chick is so much larger overall, darker, more defined—my task becomes more challenging each day. There's more visible detail to capture. Pterylae—the feather tracts—are now visible just under the skin on the spine, on either side of the abdomen, the legs, and the chest. They look like bluish pads, prickled with feather sheaths. Minute sheaths punch through the skin like whiskers, new feathers folded inside them. The down seems thicker, especially along these tracts. The skin is darker, more bluish and dusky. The toes, which only yesterday seemed rubbery, are beginning to bend at the joints. The chick's bones are strengthening, hardening. It's

Day 4—'Feather day' July 23

10:02-10:38

taking on angles where before there were only curves. I will see this startling change on Day 4 in indigo buntings as well, and will do the same double take, wondering what suddenly kicked in here.

Today I have seen the adult bringing spiders and once a lightning bug. I think the chicks are able to take more and coarser food now than before, and their growth is stepping up along with their intake. Two dark dots are visible on the arrow-shaped base of the tongue that weren't there yesterday. They make a nice target for a parent to feed.

I have time for only two studies between 10:10 and 10:30 before I need to put the baby back. I know I won't have time to make three studies from here on out. There's just too much detail to capture.

July 24, 2002. Day 5. For my birthday, the wren's eyes are open. It's suddenly a bird, more aware and responsive. I'm amused to see a white fecal sac waiting to emerge, visible through the skin. While I'm drawing the chick, the sac pops out, and the white bulge is gone. Fecal sacs tie up droppings in a neat membranous diaper for adults to carry away. In the forty minutes I have the chick on my drawing table, another forms. This bird illustrates input and output.

I can't believe how far the chick has come since yesterday. The feather quills that had just popped out of the skin yesterday are now over ¼ inch long. There are three ranks of them and a fourth at the top of each wing. Having so many quills must feel like wearing armor—they've got to be heavy compared with down and feathers, packed with blood as they are.

fecal sac queued up

After

12:57–1:28

Day 5 – look at the wing feathers emerging! July 24

Eye is open!

The female wren has a curious habit of feeding her young, then landing in some conspicuous place, cocking her tail, and fluttering her wings. She then hops away over the ground, fluttering. It's a distraction display, clearly directed at me. Perhaps the sight of my taking her young every day has branded me as a predator, so she half-heartedly gives a display in my honor, even when I'm watching from inside the kitchen. It's an

Day 6 July 25
1:10-1:55 pm- fed him 2
mealworms. He has stopped
gaping. Seems alert &
suspicious.

Look at those
legs!

acknowledgment, signifying that she knows she's been seen. She displays with greater vigor whenever chipmunks venture onto the front stoop. This morning I saw her lure one out into the lawn, then peck his rump all the way down the sidewalk. His tail fuzzed like a cat's and he took off lickety-split, the wren needling him the whole way. Chipmunks are omnivores, and will take eggs and chicks when they can. I'm fascinated, thinking about the various threats the wren keeps cataloged in that tiny head.

July 25, 2002. Day 6. Today I can see buffy rufous feather tips in the flank tract of feather sheaths. The wren's consciousness is emerging. It doesn't like being taken from the nest or lying exposed on my drawing table. It burrows and nuzzles into my hand and constantly turns around, looking for shelter. Its wing quills are very long now, three ranks of them, and its down is getting sparser. Its legs have lengthened greatly, the feet looking stronger. It refuses to gape now, but by stimulating the corners of its mouth I am able to tickle it into taking two mealworms.

July 26, 2002. Day 7. This nestling really acts like a bird now. Its consciousness is catching up with its physical development. It is decidedly unhappy away from its nest, and is in constant motion, turning in circles, balling up, then stretching out, propping itself on its long legs and wings, looking around. Its eyes are almost fully open, though it still has the sleepy, almond-eyed look of the young nestling. I notice that its ear openings are much more prominent today. It voids a fecal sac and eats three worms—not gaping, but grudgingly accepting them when I tickle its gape corners. It's suspicious of me, and no

12:58-1:30 Day 7 July 26
A dreadful wiggleworm, never still
for a moment. It snuggles into my hand,
turns around constantly. It's extremely
frustrating to draw—I have to hold it still!

amount of whistling or peeping can get it to gape. Drawing it or even getting its color right is increasingly challenging. My work shows it, too—quicker, less intimate and painstaking. Today's paintings look Japanese in their simplicity, even though I have the bird for forty minutes. Most of that time is taken up trying to get it to hold still. I'm cradling it in my hand and holding bits of it still so I can draw them. I much prefer painting the bluebird I'm working on at the same time. It's more phlegmatic. For the first time, I find myself looking forward to the end of the project.

July 27, 2002. Day 8. Necessity forced a solution to the wiggly nestling problem. Though I do like the quick, dashy quality of a painting done under duress, I don't enjoy the process. So I fetched a used Carolina wren nest from the garage, and installed the nestling in it to pose. It never moved a muscle. Rather, it went into hiding mode, shutting its eyes and peeking at me from time to time. As it was stock-still, I was able to relax and appreciate all that's happened since yesterday. The baby looks uncomfortable today, all prickly and laden with heavy quills. The quills are turning pale toward their tips, and tiny paintbrush ends of rufous show on the wing quills. Its head is absolutely abristle with quills, and its down is sparse, shedding off as the feathers emerge.

Tiny paintbrush tips on all the feather sheaths - it will look very different tomorrow!

I've hit on a plan to keep it still - an old C.W. nest. The chick hunkers down and closes its eyes. I can't its rapid breaths - 170 per minute!

12:10 - 12:34 Day 8 July 27

I dashed off a painting in only twenty minutes, then nudged the baby into accepting three mealworms. It's funny how it resists my efforts to open its mouth, but once I get the worm only partway in, it slurps it down with apparent relish. All in all, the used nest approach is much less stressful for both of us. If I listen closely to these birds, they tell me what they need.

July 28, 2002. Day 9. I'm away all day at an opening of a show of my paintings in Akron, and I get back around dark. As of Day 8, the female ceased brooding her young, so I have a plan to sneak my hand into the nest and get my model around 10:00 P.M., when I'm finally done painting the nestling bluebird's portrait and the house is quiet. I turn on the porch light and stick my finger in the nest and am shocked to find

all three babies striking repeatedly at me, just like little snakes. I'm taken aback and even fooled for an instant, yanking my hand back. They accompany the strikes with a wet little bill clap that sounds exactly like a striking snake opening its mouth. I've heard too many copperheads make that sound to ignore it. The whole display sends an involuntary chill down my spine before I burst into laughter. Baby chickadees and titmice will hiss like snakes when their nest cavity is invaded, and an adult female titmouse launched an incredibly convincing series of snake strikes at me as well. I'm not surprised to find such a trick up the wrens' clever sleeves. Still, with such young nestlings, I realize the behavior must be innate. Because they've never struck at me in daytime, I conclude that there must be something about an unseen threat at night that stimulates the striking behavior in nestlings.

The baby is brown today—ahead of its nestmates, as always. Paintbrush tips have blossomed into fans of feathers all over its body. Its eyes are wide open and bright. Suddenly it's adorable, a baby bird, not a leathery reptile. I paint happily until 10:15, when I put it back in the nest, feeling lucky to have had a session with it at all.

July 29, 2002. Day 10. Since I painted them late last night, I'm doing the same tonight. I've been so caught up in everything that it's getting hard to block out the time to paint, and I like to let twenty-four hours pass between sessions. So at 9:40 P.M. I put my hand in the nest, and was greeted by a salvo of snapping strikes from the babies. I was amazed at the change in the model, so much more feathery and with a longer, blacker bill. It was afraid of me, and kept its head down and tail up. Then I offered it a mealworm, and it considered it, head cocked, then shyly opened its bill. I popped the worm in, followed it by another, and the bird relaxed visibly, raising its head, looking around, tugging at the nest material, preening. What a charming little creature it is, so self-possessed and confident. I can see how intelligent it is just looking in its eyes. I offer it another mealworm, and it pecks at the wriggling larva. This is something a bluebird wouldn't do for probably another two weeks. I wonder if fledging early also means earlier self-sufficiency in feeding. Seeing this, I guess that Carolina wrens might start picking up their own food many days, even weeks, earlier than do bluebirds. I'm not too happy with my first study so I do another that helps capture the bird's perky spirit. I'm losing interest in rendering the detail of its feathers, and leaning toward looser paintings that say more about how I feel about being in the bird's presence.

July 30, 2002. Day 11. This could be fledging day for some nests. I have to tread very carefully. If the parents give the least peep of concern, I'm going to drop the baby back in the nest and bolt. At 5:10 P.M. I carefully take the eldest baby. If the parents are watching, they don't make a sound. Good. I take it in, nestled in the old wren nest. It crouches and acts very suspicious. I immediately notice that its head

July 30 2002 Day 11 – I'm walking a razor's edge – they could fledge at any minute. Head feathers are almost all out today. It holds this frightened crouch the whole time (5:10–5:40)

It started cheeping – the fledgling call – and wouldn't stop. I hurried it back into the nest.

This, very hurriedly & still don't see how we got here in 11 days.

feathers have all come out of the sheaths. It's a bird! The breast feathers, beautiful buffy ochre, are out, too, but I can't see them in the crouch the bird is holding. I offer it worms, but it politely refuses. No dice. This is clearly the last day I can paint it safely, unless I try to take it at night. As I'm finishing the second study, it cheeps, and keeps cheeping—the fledging call. *Zweek! Zweek!* Yikes. I'd wager that's the first time it's given that call, the signature call of a nestling that's making the leap to fledgling. I finish up my very loose painting and slip the bird back in with its siblings. They could fledge at any time.

July 31, 2002. Day 12. I wait all day for darkness, pretty confident that once it falls I can abduct the eldest baby, paint it, and slip it back in the nest. And it's here that I make a mistake that will inform my choices for the rest of the project. At 9:20 P.M. I reach into the nest but have trouble grabbing the baby, who evades my grasp, sidling backward and sideways. That evasive behavior should have been my first red flag. Suddenly it gives a chirp of distress and all three chicks explode, fluttering from the nest. This is exactly what I'd feared most. One drops to the ground; two are trapped under my hand. Phoebe, six, captures the grounded bird, hands it to me, then runs to find her father to help. I stand, cursing myself, holding three babies down into the nest with one hand, waiting for Bill to find a small box. Finally I tell him to go to the garage to get a small animal carrier and put a used wren nest in it. I deposit the frantic, cheeping chicks into the nest. Luckily, the adults have long since gone to roost, and if they hear this (which they doubtless do), they don't stir. I take the new fledglings inside, feeling miserable that I've disturbed them so, and do a bunch of quick studies of them as they hit the plastic sides of the animal carrier, distressed and cheeping. I do as much work as I can under the circumstances—I hate drawing upset subjects, and hate drawing when I'm upset—and turn out the lights. They fall silent. Knowing I can't risk handling them again, I leave them in the carrier in my studio for the night.

July 31 Day 12

I reach to get one at dark – it's 9:20 pm – and it shrieks, and all three explode from the nest. I hold them in it with one hand while Bill fetches a plastic box.

These sketches done until 10 pm. They're popping like corn all over the place, squirking constantly. I'll take them at at dawn and release them to their parents' care. Pride goeth before a fall – I thought I'd get away with it!

August 1, 2002. Day 13—Fledging Day. I pass a fitful night, dreaming of baby birds in peril. It's up to me to save them. In my dream, I'm putting up netting, putting baby birds in cars, thwarting cats. I awaken at 5:30, and hear the first field sparrow sing at 5:42. It's still dark, but gray light creeps under the blind. I fetch the carrier with the sleeping wren babies in their nest, and use a tomato cage to rig it up outside, right under the hanging basket where the nest is. I retreat to the kitchen window to watch the proceedings. The male wren sings at 6:18, and at 6:24 a wren appears with food. It flies to the nest, looks in, looks around, spots the carrier with its three peeping chicks, lands on the carrier, leans into the small top-opening door, and feeds a chick. On its next visit, it enters the carrier and removes a fecal sac. The pair takes turns stuffing the chicks beyond repletion. The chicks are quite calm and happy, preening and stretching, only occasionally hopping or hitting the sides of the carrier. I feel sure that they are ready to fledge and would have fledged this morning, whether I had botched things last night or not. I'm glad they spent their last night in complete safety, though, and had a huge feed this morning before leaving the nest for good. The adults keep offering mealworms and crickets, entering the carrier to try to entice them to take the food. The chicks are stuffed, and refuse most offerings. This is quite a different approach from bluebirds, which withhold food from fledging-age chicks until they're forced out of the nest by hunger. I'm amused by the way the chicks take turns being fed. They don't all gape at once. The parent birds single out each chick, and the ones not being fed seem to know that begging would be a waste of time. When two have been fed, the parents concentrate on filling up the third. There is mindfulness in everything Carolina wrens do.

The first chick pops out of the carrier around 7:00 A.M. and hops and preens on the bonsai bench. The second leaves while I'm not watching, and I take the lid off to help the third and eldest, my model, who can't figure out how to exit. It's 7:53 A.M. The wrens keep tending and feeding them in the front border. They scold when I appear, but otherwise all is peaceful. I'm so relieved! I will miss them terribly.

The wrens, my first subjects of what would eventually number seventeen, had taught me a vital lesson, one best learned right off the bat. I could not rely on the cover of darkness to take babies near fledging age and expect them to remain calm. A predator will be perceived as such, night or day, and once chicks have the slightest chance of surviving outside the nest, they will exit when threatened, whether they can fly or not. If they can hop, they'll go. I couldn't be the cause of that! Above all concerns, I placed the safety of my models. It's a dictum I would stick to for the next thirteen years, and I didn't lose a single chick to human error in that span. I'd find various ways to paint chicks on and after fledging day, but I would never risk frightening them from their nests just so I could paint their portraits. The Hippocratic oath, "First, do no harm," was in force throughout. I learned so much about Carolina wrens in this first outing that I couldn't help but daydream about my next subjects.

Skveet! A new fledgling
eyes a camel cricket.
Looks like a bit much.

How sweet! contemplating his (lack of a) navel

Day 4 July 24 1:45-2:30pm
Peepers and hungry: I fed him 2 mealworms

eyes are slit open

this toe may be dislocated

Day 5
2:20p - 2:40pm July 25
Still no feathers sprouting

1:45-1:20 Day 3 July 23.
Pterylae just visible on spine and dorsal of abdomen

Day 6 July 26 2:10-2:45pm Sketchless & reluctant to gape today. Keeps his eyes screwed shut

Lots of fat love rolls (no wings) on abdomen

A blowsy no mites.

Day 2 July 22 2003. This is the biggest of the 4, all hatched by 4:52 pm. Returned by 5:12 pm

They're getting blackberries.

Day 7 July 27 11:20-11:35
All 4 babies act very hungry today. so breathless and starts to eat mealworms, gaped lustily. Phoebe fed him 2 mealworms

pipping egg

Eastern Phoebe, newly hatched
11:57-12:15am July 21 2003
2 of the other 7 eggs are pipping

It rolls around helplessly but gapes when disturbed, like a little bird!

Day 8 July 28 9:15-9:40
She begs and I give her Nutrical hoping it'll get past the blockage.

Look at the feathers growth overnight! It's a prickly porcupine.

There's a triangular object lodged in the crop: a grain of gravel? I hope it goes down overnight. I first I'll have a vet require it. All things happen for a reason. Did I pick this clutch to paint because She urged me on her eighth day of life? I'm so upset it can hardly walk.

At 7:30 the next morning, I open the baby's mouth to find this rail particle is no longer lodged crosswise, but visible in her throat. I pull it out and can't believe she'd have swallowed it. I keep her to feed & observe. She's limping normally.

Day 9 July 29 2002
8:15 - 8:45 pm

I'm sure she looks terrific! Begged and ate well. Sibling has an airsac problem — we deflated its grossly distended neck 3x this afternoon. I have a sneaky feeling these babies aren't getting enough to eat.

July 30 2002
Day 10 4:30-5 pm
Raucous & begging. Siblings are suspicious but this one huddles forthwith. Eats in mama. It's still almost a day ahead of its sibs, despite the setback. And the airsac-swollen baby is fine once I cut open this slit. Sheath ends are getting white-bursting everywhere.

July 31 Day 11 7:40 - 8:10 pm
Feathers have really burst today, esp on head. I think this is a 8-13 hatched, she remains a day ahead developmentally. Gaped & ate 3 worms, then seemed to remember she shouldn't & hunkered down.

August 01 Day 12 5:40 - 6:20 pm. I had to admit it. This may be the last day. She's a female, and she has two sisters and a brother. How I'll miss her, and this wonderful process of coming to understand how a bird becomes.

Day 14. A female — it's a hint of blue. And white outer tail & feather ensure a consistent mark for females. Just a peek in an overcast.

Day 17. In a Gilbertson PVC box with a pine needle nest. Very risky to peek at birds this old — all eyes are on me. They could easily jump.

Day 13. This is a male, evidenced
by the extent of blue in wings
and tail. Still very tiny.
It's at the Age of Awareness
but by no means ready for the
outside world.

Day 25. July 7 2013, the day
I acquired the three orphans,
all females. They'd been hand-
raised by my friends Mil and Fran
since Day 11, June 23. I got a cell call
on a marsh in Damariscotta ME,
and they were mine to raise on my
return.

Day 32. Still begging
full time. They are beginning
to pick up the occasional worm at
their own, a behavior which started
on Day 28, but by no means call all
their calories on their own.

Day 41. They're all picking
up their own food, and
prone to stealing from
each other (or begging
from whomever has a
mealworm in her bill.)
It's almost time for
release.

Day 43. Fledging day. The tent is open, but they're still lingering inside. They're picking up all their own food now, even when I throw it in the grass. They're hyper, alert and somewhat passive.

July 25, 2013
Flank feathers are the first juvenile plumage to fall out. Soon the rusty first adult plumage will appear in their throat... patches.

July 30 2013
Elca's a shape-shifter, puffing up in the morning sun. Day 46. Susan her 2 sisters have been free for 3 days and are doing splendidly. Brick orange flank feathers and a couple of blue scapulars showing.

thinking about a sunbath

Teddy, the independent one, Day ... She stopped coming in for food at Day 56.

All three are coming in regularly for mealworms. Day 53. Aug 5 '13. Perhaps because they ... don't ... got adult plumage faster than Teddy

Day 60 August 11 '13. Two (Elsa and Joly) now coming in for food. Blue scap tail and back feathers more evident. Head will be the last to molt.

Day 66 · August 17 2013.
Ready to be on their own, but still coming down for conversation and mealworms. Head and back feathers are the last to be replaced, and they'll carry a few spangles into October. It's been quite a summer, getting these bluebirds released and on their own.

Eastern Bluebird, 2002

BLUEBIRDS HAVE PLAYED a pivotal role in my life since I moved to Connecticut in 1982. It was there that my friend Robert Braunfield built the first bluebird nest boxes I would tend; there that I began a lifelong journey of inquiry into the natural history and breeding biology of this wondrous bird. That there is a thrush, rich rust and spectral blue, which will nest in a simple wooden box, coming as if on command to inhabit the humblest housing, remains an amazement to me. What other thrush will do that? I resolved to be the bluebird hostess with the mostest, devising management protocols that might be called cutting edge but are probably closer to fringe.

I've been monitoring my own trails of eastern bluebird nest boxes since then, handling many hundreds of nestlings in the course of managing them. When parasites (bluebird blowfly, *Protocalliphora sialia*, and chicken mite, *Dermanyssus gallinae*) overrun them, I remove the nests and make new ones with fresh material, replacing the babies in a clean if somewhat clumsy nest. Sometimes a baby bird swallows something it shouldn't, like a grass stem, and needs intervention. Some are orphaned or injured by marauding house sparrows or tree swallows and require urgent care. Some, having lost their parents, may be cross-fostered: integrated into another box with a same-age brood, to be raised with their own kind.

Each spring, after freak spring snowstorms and cold snaps, when their parents can't find enough insects to feed them, I go from box to box, snatching nestlings back from death's door. I gather them from the nest and warm them under my coat against my own bare-belly brood patch until they come out of torpor and are able to eat. I give them the homemade bug omelet I've brought, scrambled eggs laced with dried flies. When cooking, it smells as nauseating as it sounds, but it's manna to a starving birdlet. I replace the warm, full-bellied babies in the nest. I leave food for the adults to give them, and come back three more times each day to warm and feed them until the cold snap passes. Letting nature take its course has never been my style. What I do is more fairly described as intensive bird ranching. Each life is precious to me, well worth working to save. The reward is that bluebirds in the vicinity of my twenty-six-box trail are now a common sight. Fall finds flocks of up to fourteen adorning the power lines over rolling hay meadows. In a good year, my boxes will fledge close to 100 young bluebirds, as well as a dozen or more Carolina chickadees and tree swallows: one potent way to make the world a more beautiful place.

April 30 2011
Looking down
into a nestbox
at a bluebird nest.
She's found ruffed grouse
feathers to line it. I haven't
seen a grouse on our land for 5 years.

Over the decades, I've watched the small, layered miracle of bluebird development unfold before me over and over. I've kept careful notes so I'd know when each clutch of eggs was laid and when it was due to hatch. It wasn't long before I internalized the flow of data I was recording and knew almost to the minute when the eggs in a given clutch would be pipping. The fourteen-day incubation period clocks away in my head. Without even checking my notes, I can walk up to a bluebird box and catch a hatchling still wearing an eggshell helmet on its tiny pink head. Peeking in a box, I can age the young birds with one glance. And I know when they have grown so old and well feathered that even a quick look into the nest box carries the risk of having the brood explode, fledging in my face like so much feathered shrapnel. It is good to know these things, good to be attuned to bluebirds. They showed me the way.

July 21, 2002. Day 1. The bluebirds in the mid-meadow box are hatching. How can it be almost two weeks since I surprised the female as she was laying the third egg? It was still wet and glistening as she scooted out of the box. That was my fault, for going out on my nest box rounds before the sun came up. I should have known I would surprise a female laying her egg. I resolved never to check boxes so early again. But I check my notes and find that was July 8, thirteen days ago, and here, probably thanks to the high ambient temperatures, is the first hatchling. This is likely the first-laid egg hatching now. Two of the three remaining eggs are beginning to hatch, showing whitish pips and fractures around the large end. It's been recently discovered that hearing the peeps of more advanced embryos speeds the development of embryos in later-laid eggs, so they can all hatch synchronously.

Ooh, boy, this bird is tiny. My fingers feel like huge sausages, so I use my pinky to tease the first-hatched chick out of the nest and head for the house. I'm struck by its yellowish coral tinge. Its wings and legs are a pure, translucent yellow. It's huge in the abdomen and it rolls around helplessly, heavy head hanging between its legs. As I draw, I notice that it gapes every thirty seconds or so, as if on autopilot, hoping, I'd imagine, that someone will stuff its mouth with caterpillars. It rests in between gaping bouts. As its eyes are sealed shut, I don't know if it's sleeping or not. Just for fun, I give a low, two-part bluebird whistle, and the nestling snaps to, gaping wide, as close to standing up as it can get. This feeble little thing hatched less than six hours ago, and it already knows it is a bluebird. I squeeze out the innards of a couple of mealworms and reward it for its performance.

tipping egg

The egg I've painted is pipping. Tiny fractures appear on the large end as the chick picks a hole in the shell from the inside. To do this it uses a special muscle on the back of its neck, which soon regresses once its work is done. You can see that muscle in the top chick, a thickness of neck at the base of its skull. Once a bluebird egg starts pipping, it usually hatches within six hours. The adults carry away the shells.

Eastern Bluebird, newly hatched
11:57–12:15 pm July 21 2002
2 of the other 3 eggs are pipping

The nestling doesn't seem to have much control of

lots of fat laid down over rump + in abdomen.

· It already has mites.

Day 2 July 22 2002. This is the biggest of the 4, all hatched by 4:52 pm. Returned by 5:12 pm

its position in space. I see how badly it needs the nest walls and its siblings to support it and wedge it into place. I shore it up with tissues and paint two quick portraits before hurrying it back to the nest. I have it drawn, painted, and back in the nest within twenty-three minutes. The parents are watching, calling. They will have to put up with my daily intrusion. I wish I could explain why I've taken their baby, but I'm afraid if I bring the painting out to show them, they'll drop something on it.

July 22, 2002. Day 2. All four bluebirds have hatched. I pick the largest one, probably the first-hatched, and head for the house. It's 4:52 P.M. I have it back by 5:12. I paint two poses. There's an artery clearly visible in the bird's neck, which pulses with blood. It's laid on a lot of fat overnight, and its rump and abdomen are laced with yellow. It's still in poor control of its heavy head, and I can already see that its development is proceeding more slowly than that of the Carolina wrens. But it gapes and begs and swallows lustily, responding again to my bluebird whistle. At this stage, hatchlings just look like a bag of guts. The feather follicles on the bluebird are only barely visible as stippling along the flipperlike wings; the wrens have had blue pterylae, or feather tracts, since hatching. It's a rare and compelling exercise to paint two disparate species of almost the same age on the same day.

July 23, 2002. Day 3. The bluebird chick looks like a bigger, slightly more robust version of itself. Its color hasn't changed substantially. I can just discern the pterylae beginning to show under its skin. Birds aren't evenly feathered all over their bodies; anyone who's plucked a chicken or even looked at the small holes in its skin can tell you that. Feathers emerge and grow from pterylae, which are distinct lines of follicles. These usually run down the center of the breast, up the sides of the neck, down the spine, along the sides of the legs. The feathers grow out and flop over to cover the parts of the skin that don't have pterylae.

1:15-1:38 Day 3 July 23. Pterylae just visible on spine and sides of abdomen

The baby's abdomen is quite transparent and I can see the loops of its intestine. It's laying on quite a bit of fat, too. All four babies peeped and gaped when I opened the box

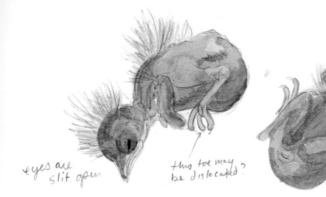

eyes are
slit open

this toe may
be dislocated?

at 1:15. I had the chick back by 1:38
P.M. It did not gape until I whistled,
then I fed it twice while drawing it, so
it wouldn't suffer for being away. It's overcast
and thundering today. I hope it rains. It's been
brutally hot and humid for a long time and all
Creation could use a break. (We wound up getting an inch. Lovely!)

July 24, 2002. Day 4. I pick the largest baby, sure it's the one that hatched first,
and head for the house. It looks almost a day ahead of its siblings in development. It's
active and its eye is just beginning to slit open. It responds to the tap of a pencil or my
voice by gaping and peeping, so I feed it two headless mealworms. It swallows lustily.
The pterylae are visible under the skin today, looking like smooth bluish streaks along
the scapulae, flanks, spine, chest, and wings. No feather sheaths are poking through
the skin yet. The bird is still waxy and surprisingly yellow. I know that soon it will turn
dusky blue, but for now I'm enjoying this remarkable color.

I'm just about to carry it back to the nest when it tucks its head under its chest
and goes to sleep. It's such a sweet, vulnerable position that I have to draw it. I think
what a wonderful netsuke carving this tiny bird would make. The best I can liken this
to is figure drawing, but in miniature. I'm glad I'm doing this now, while my eyes are
still good enough to see the detail that's growing ever more complex. I have it out
of the nest for forty-five minutes, from 1:45 to 2:30 P.M. I don't mean to, but it's so
beautiful, and I reason that if I feed it twice, it ought to fare well. All its siblings peep
when I put it back in the warm, humid box. My old friend Lois
Darling, a skilled scientific and popular illustrator, once said
that to draw something is to fall in love with it, for that
time when you're absorbed in really looking at it. I can look
at her drawings and see that it's true. It's true for me, too. I
am smitten.

How sweet!
contemplating
his (lack of a)
navel

July 25, 2002. Day 5. This bird is such a contrast to the
faster-changing Carolina wren. It's still naked, without any
feathers sprouting. It looks like the same baby as yesterday, just inflated. It's pleasantly
phlegmatic and still gapes lustily when I whistle, so I feed it four mealworms. The
pterylae are increasingly visible under the skin as blue zones, but no feathers break
the outline. Its wings are paddlelike, in sharp contrast to the Carolina wren's, which

had ¼-inch-long quills by Day 5. Open-cup nesters must hurry it up and develop more rapidly, trying to stay ahead of the myriad predators of all stripes that are looking to eat them. Being cavity nesters, eastern bluebirds have the luxury of developing at a more leisurely pace in the safe, warm confines of a woodpecker hole or nest box.

July 26, 2002. Day 6. Still waiting for feathers to sprout on the bluebird. Though the pterylae are more and more obvious, lending the bird a bluish cast, the only sign of feathers is a slightly serrated edge to the flipperlike wings. It's beginning to be more restless, but is still a lamb compared with the frenetic little Carolina wren nestling. Though its eyes have opened, it keeps them screwed shut. Its consciousness is emerging. It is beginning to distinguish between normal, expected events and strange ones. Today, it refuses to gape, and I know that it knows it's out of its nest, and doesn't like it. Whistling like a bluebird no longer elicits gaping, so I tickle it into accepting three mealworms. I wonder if I have the same chick, because the chick I take on Day 7 gapes as usual. This bird may not be my usual model.

It's eerie how I never see any sign of the parents, other than the continued growth of their four healthy chicks. I'm sure they see me coming and make themselves scarce.

July 27, 2002. Day 7. The chick is bigger all over, with visibly longer legs, but still featherless. When will the change happen? To my surprise, the chick's very hungry, and gapes, peeping, the whole time I have it out of the nest. So do its three nestmates. As there's a mite problem, I take out their nest, scrape out the box, and replace it with fresh grass. I'll keep this nest, microwave it to kill the mites, and use it to contain the baby while I paint it. I pop the nest in the microwave and am amused to see a peppering of dead mites on the paper towel afterward. When the nest is cool, I pop the baby into it. This works like a charm, calming the restless nestling into sleep. I paint one study, then accidentally hit a paintbrush on the side of

Day 5
2:20 pm – 2:40 pm July 25
Still no feathers sprouting

Day 6 July 26   2:10–2:45 pm · She's restless
& reluctant to gape today. keeps his eyes
Screwed shut

they're getting blackberries!

Day 7 July 27 1:30–1:53
All 4 babies act very hungry today.
80 breaths/second She ate 8 mealworms,
gaped lustily. Phoebe fed him & PoPo watched

the palette, triggering an instant bout of gaping and peeping. I let Phoebe, six, feed the chick as many mealworms as it will take while her brother Liam, two and a half, watches. Midway through its feeding of eight mealworms, the baby voids a large fecal sac, and I can see by its pinkish tinge that the parents have been exploiting the large crop of blackberries in the field. I have not seen this tinge before today. Day 7 seems to be a day when the babies can accept fruit and tougher insects. I have noticed that bluebirds don't take mealworms to their young before Day 6. That's why I feed them only the insides, or the freshly shed white worms. And I take off the larva's head, just to be sure it doesn't chew the chick's esophagus on the way down.

July 28, 2002. Day 8. A huge change in the nestling—the sheaths have burst the skin, perhaps two-thirds of an inch long on the wings, and the feather tips of the pectoral tract are fluffing out of the sheaths—creamy white. Yesterday it was smooth, with bluish pterylae; today it's a little porcupine. I was away all day at a show opening, and raced home at dusk. I had my fingers crossed that Day 8 would be the day, as it has been in my past experience, that the chicks' thermoregulation kicks in, allowing the female bluebird to quit brooding them at night. I visited the box with just enough light left so the female could find her way back should I spook her off the nest, and found the chicks alone. Hooray! It was easy to find the chick I've been working with—it's a quarter larger than its nestmates.

But it seems to have swallowed some huge, hard object that has lodged in its esophagus. The obstruction protrudes out to its right, under its ear, and appears to have set up quite a bit of irritation, as there's swelling and fluid in the crop. This doesn't keep the baby from begging, though, so I feed it a white mealworm—probably an ill-advised thing. It swallows it, but I'm not sure the food can pass the obstruction. So I give the bird a shot of a pastelike veterinary supplement called Nutri-Cal, which will liquefy and work its way down to the baby's stomach in time. I decide to keep it in the studio overnight so I can check on it first thing in the morning. If the obstruction is still there, I'm going to get the bird seen by a veterinarian. If no local veterinarian will help me—and that is a distinct possibility around here—I will remove the object myself, if I have to make an incision in the crop. I'm so upset I can hardly draw the chick. If I didn't believe things happen for a reason before, I surely believe it now. That baby was going to need me, and that's why I chose to paint it.

July 29, 2002. Day 9. I get up around 7:00 to check on the baby. The swelling is down and at first I think the mass has digested and passed down. Instead it has centered in the bird's throat (it had been lodged crosswise in the crop), and to my delight when I open its mouth I can see the end of the object, black and very hard. I pull it out with tweezers and cannot believe that it keeps coming, and coming—2⅛ inches of an ash leaf stem, doubtless from the nesting material. I'm sure I'm not half as relieved as the bird must be to have it out. The ash petiole is as hard as any toothpick, pure inflexible wood. I cannot imagine how or why the chick chose to swallow it. In my routine box checks I've learned to check nestlings for inappropriate items in their mouths and throats. If they're going to eat something they shouldn't, it's nesting material. Anything poking into the gullet will stimulate a swallowing reflex. It's quite common for nestlings to start swallowing a long piece of grass or straw and just keep going. But this flint-hard petiole was a very bad choice, if one were to choose a foreign object to swallow, and I'm delighted I was there to remove it. It's nearly as long as the chick, and I hope it hasn't pierced its intestine. The baby looks dehydrated and weak. It voided three normal fecal sacs overnight, so I know food was getting by the obstruction, but some internal damage may remain. I keep it for observation and feeding with Nutri-Cal, water, and tender mealworms until 9:00 A.M. The chick has turned the mental corner where it no longer trusts me. It would have at this stage in its development anyway, but the intervention and force feeding haven't helped, I'm sure. It keeps its eyes screwed

Day 8 July 28 9:15-9:40

look at the feathers growth overnight! He's a prickly porcupine.

She begs and I give her Nutrical, hoping it'll get past the blockage.

there's a huge hard object lodged in the crop— a grasshopper leg?

I hope it goes down overnight—if not I'll have a vet remove it. All things happen for a reason—did I pick this chick to paint because she'd rigged me on her eighth day of life? I'm so upset I can hardly work.

At 7:30 the next morning, I open the baby's mouth to find this ash petiole is no longer lodged crosswise, but visible in her throat. I pull it out and can't believe she'd have swallowed it. I keep her to feed & observe. She's eliminating normally.

by the dried-out white tips of the feather sheaths. The keratin coating is now flaky and dead, and the sheaths have served their purpose of protecting the soft, blood-filled feather quills while they're emerging.

July 31, 2002. Day 11. The baby I operated on for its ruptured air sac shows not a sign of trauma and is growing well. All the babies are right on schedule, feathers bursting the sheaths. I can't quite sex my model but think she's a female. She begs when I whistle, but then seems to remember that she shouldn't and hunkers down again. I'm bemused by the growing consciousness of this bird, which I've been feeding since the day she hatched. An eleven-day-old bluebird, which had never seen a human, would refuse to gape for me unless it was in imminent danger of starving. In fact, while checking my boxes, the first sign of a severe food shortage, as in inclement weather, is opening a box and being met by wide-eyed older nestlings gaping hungrily. Normally, once the eyes open, young bluebirds play dead on seeing a human, hunkering down in the nest cup and keeping their eyes tightly shut. I always marvel at the thought process that would cause a starving young bluebird to try begging from a big, scary human. So young, and yet determined to overcome its fear and save itself if it can.

I find that bird consciousness creeps in, hand in hand with improving vision. This bluebird has acclimated to me; has learned to associate me with food and begs freely, until she seems to catch herself and remember that she shouldn't. What she has learned—that I am harmless and a source of extra food—is at war with what instinct hisses into her ear. That voice is getting louder every day, preparing her to fledge.

August 1, 2002. Day 12. With feathers emerged sufficiently for me to see the quality and amount of blue they have, I know the model chick is a female. She has two sisters and one brother. Females have a dusty turquoise cast to their wing and tail feathers. Males show a clearer cobalt blue color, and more of it. I bring her into the house in the late afternoon, and find that feathers have all but covered her body. I paint her portrait slowly, with a sense of regret, because I would so love to keep going, to show her as she gets lovelier and sleeker every day. But I can't compromise the safety of the entire brood, and I know they could boot out of the nest as early as Day 13, so I say goodbye. When I return to the box, one of the chicks has its bill up by the entrance hole, and it hurriedly falls back when it hears me. They're old and wise, and not a safe bet for handling anymore. I marvel at the chance that led me to save this chick from a probable death from swallowing the ashwood petiole. If I'd been concentrating on another chick, I might not have picked up on her problem. And I was able to help her sister with her air sac problem. Now they're all fine, though I can venture no more than a quick peek—I dare not touch them anymore.

August 01 Day 12 5:40 - 6:20 pm Much as I hate to admit it, this may be the last day. She's a female, and she has two sisters and a brother. How I'll miss her, and this wonderful process of coming to understand how a bird becomes.

Day 13. This is a male, evidenced by the extent of blue in wings and tail. Still very tiny. It's at the Age of Awareness but by no means ready for the outside world.

I hated to stop painting bluebirds on Day 12. There was so much more change to come. It would be eleven years before I had an opportunity to follow up on what seemed, even back in 2002, like a study interrupted. Though I couldn't handle them for fear of triggering premature fledging, I'd snapped some photos that I could work from, of older nestlings in boxes. Most bluebirds fledge around Day 18, and in the decades I've been observing them, I regard the post-fledging period from Days 18 to 25 as one when bluebird fledglings disappear. In reality, they are hiding quietly in dense cover, being fed by their parents until they are strong enough for sustained flight. Though they may be nearby, we rarely see them in this stage of their development.

In late June 2013, I was leading a large group of National Audubon Society's "Joy of Birding" campers through a seaside meadow near Hog Island on the Maine coast. The grasses were alive with singing bobolinks when my cell phone rang over their musical din. The West Virginia caller said that bluebirds had been nesting in his plastic newspaper box, and had eleven-day-old young when the female bluebird was hit by a

Day 14. A female - for a hint of blue. And white outer tail feather edges - a consistent mark for females. Just a peek in an occupied box.

Day 17- in a Gilbertson PVC box, with a pine needle nest. Very risky to peek at birds this old all eyes are on me. They could easily jump.

car. The weather was cold and rainy, and the male was not able to both brood and feed the young, which were fading fast. Would I take them? Well, not right this second. . . . I gave Mil and his wife, Fran, detailed instructions on how and what to feed the birds, arranged to be on call for advice, and agreed to take the birds and finish raising them upon my return from Maine. They would be far too old by then to cross-foster into another box for adoption.

The three orphans were all females, and Mil and Fran and their Boston terrier, Hobo, had done a wonderful job of raising them. Lacking proper caging, the couple had given over one of their bathrooms to become an aviary. The young were flying well by the time I got them on Day 25. As it happens, this is around the day in their natural development when they would start following their parents over longer distances. I installed them in a spacious nylon flight tent. In its gentle confines, they could strengthen their wings and learn to pick up their own food.

When they dropped off the birds, Mil and Fran brought their Boston terrier along. All three birds perched nonchalantly on Hobo's head and back. Yet when my Boston terrier, Chet Baker, asked to be let inside the fledging tent, the birds panicked. I was bemused to see that their acceptance of Boston terriers extended only to the one they knew. I have seen this pattern repeated in several wild birds that I've raised for release. They quickly acclimate to Chet Baker's presence, showing no fear of him, but a strange dog in the yard incites panic. I was glad to have corroboration that birds can distinguish and discriminate between individuals of the same breed.

Having raised and released two orphaned bluebirds in the mid-1980s, I remembered that the process of gaining independence was lengthy. These young bluebirds, however, drew it out beyond my expectations. Too, some individuals are quicker to learn to feed themselves. I named the three Ida, Elsa, and Toddy, in honor of my mother; my mother-in-law, who started *Bird Watcher's Digest*; and our friend, the longtime editor of *Bird Observer*. I ordered mealworms, 10,000 at a time, from my supplier, and fed the larvae unmedicated chick starter and carrots for extra nutritional value. I left open dishes of water and mealworms in the fledging tent. They bathed enthusiastically and often, but the birds continued to beg insistently for food.

Day 25, July 7 2013, the day I acquired the three orphans, all females. They'd been hand-raised by my friends Mil and Fran since Day 11, June 23. I got a cell call on a marsh in Damariscotta ME, and they were mine to raise on my return.

Day 32. Still begging
full time. They are beginning
to pick up the occasional worm at
their own, a behavior which started
on Day 28. But they still in call all
day, dawn to dusk.

Though the three started picking up the occasional mealworm around Day 28, they were still being fed on the hour, dawn to dusk, on Day 32. I could see the neural pathways forming as one by one their muscles made the painfully slow connection to their brains. If I seem impatient, try to imagine having to be home from dawn to dusk to feed three birds every hour, on the hour. I tried to help by presenting a mealworm on tweezers, which elicited gaping. I'd then lay the mealworm at the bird's feet. Their first reaction was to continue gaping toward the food, giving begging trills. One by one, they'd surrender to the impulse to pick up the food. They would juggle the larva with a contemplative look, being used to having food pushed right into the gape. A look of

Day 41. They're all picking up their own food, and prone to stealing from each other (or begging from whomever has a mealworm in her bill.) It's almost time for release.

mild surprise would cross their faces when they'd finally manipulate the worm to the back of the bill and swallow it. That is, if the other two didn't snatch it away first. I loved watching the other two crowd over and beg from Toddy, the first to pick up her own mealworms. They took to grabbing worms from her bill as she picked them up, having found a transition between being fed and picking up their own. For her part, Toddy learned to swallow faster.

By Day 41, the three were all picking up their own food. I wanted them to be entirely self-feeding before opening the tent, which occurred on Day 43. For those last two days, I moved the tent from the shelter of our garage to the yard, and began tossing mealworms into the grass. When they were able to still-hunt by dropping into the grass to ferret out their food, I knew they were ready for release.

Day 43. Fledging day. The tent is open, but they're still lingering inside. They're picking up all their own food now, even when I throw it in the grass. They're hyper alert and somewhat pensive.

July 25, 2013
Flank feathers are the first juvenal plumage to fall out. Soon the rusty first adult plumage will appear in those threadbare patches.

July 30 2013
Elsa's a shape-
shifter, puffing up
in the morning sun.
Day 46. She and her
2 sisters have been
free for 3 days and
are doing splendidly.
Brick-orange flank
feathers and a
couple of blue
scapulars showing.

Captive bluebirds raised by wild-caught parents in a Michigan aviary were observed to start self-feeding around Day 25, and to begin dropping to the ground to seize prey between Days 28 and 34 (Pinkowski 1975). Parent bluebirds normally fed their young until about Days 35 to 40 in Pinkowski's study. My birds were clearly coddled, but did self-feed on schedule.

If I had to generalize about the process of "soft release" as described here, I'd say, "If you do soft release right, it takes forever." Leaving the nest at Day 17, for a bluebird, is just the beginning of a wild apprenticeship that continues for months.

Ida, Elsa, and Toddy may have been ready to find their own food, but they were by no means independent on Day 43. Toddy, who was the innovator of the three,

thinking about
a sunbath

Toddy, the independent one, Day 48. She stopped
coming in for food on Day 56.

stopped taking handouts and left the area on Day 56. Young female bluebirds tend
to disperse from their natal area. Elsa and Ida never got the memo, and continued to
come in for occasional mealworm feedings through Day 66. This site fidelity likely
has more to do with the eastern bluebird's tendency to exploit an easy handout than
any deficiency on their part. There I was, offering, and they were happy to accept the
subsidy. I enjoyed watching them molt their white-spangled gray body feathers, and
slowly replace the rusty chevrons on their breasts and flanks with fresh, smooth feathers
of fawn red. They were beginning to look like adults, and I was privy to the progress of
their molt, a rare opportunity I documented in photos and paintings.

All three.
are coming in
regularly for
Mealworms.
Day 53. Aug. 5 '13.
Perhaps because they
eat better, Elsa and
Ida got adult
plumage faster than
Toddy

After Day 66, Elsa and Ida spent more and more time afield, and eventually stopped coming in altogether. I am accustomed to the annual disappearance of our nesting bluebirds in late August and September as they flock up for fall foraging, so I took their departure as nothing unusual. December 28, 2013, was a golden morning, and Chet Baker and I were setting out for a run when I noticed a dozen bluebirds sitting on a power line on the county road less than a mile from our house. I watched them for a few minutes, then slowly advanced toward them. As I approached the power line, the flock became visibly nervous. Ten bluebirds lifted off, circled, and flew, calling, toward a wooded border. Two immature females stayed put, and allowed Chet and me to walk directly under the wire. "Elsa! Ida! So good to see you!" They cocked their heads and fixed bright eyes on me but showed no fear.

I don't band the birds I release, so such magic moments of inference are all I have to tell me when a release has been successful. I told the two how happy I was to see them in a wild flock and wished them luck with the rest of the winter. There they were, at Day 199, consorting with wild birds, but unconcerned at our approach. It's so rare to get a message back from my fledglings, raised so tenderly and released with such apprehension and hope. They never call, they never write. . . . For a foster bluebird mother, it doesn't get any better than that. I continued on my way with a big smile, a full heart, and a deep understanding of what it takes to become a bluebird or to launch three: the best gift of all.

Day 60 · August 11 '13
Two (Elsa and Ida)
now coming in for food.
Blue scapulars and back
feathers more evident.
Head will be the last to
molt.

Day 66 - August 17 2013
Ready to be on their own, but still coming
down for conversation and mealworms.
Head and back feathers are the last to be
replaced, and they'll carry a few spangles into
October. It's been quite a summer, getting these
bluebirds released and on their own.

Day 5 May 31 '03. Rainy, pouring. I'm sure they're not getting much food – so I feed the babies 2 worms each. This one eats 6 in a half-hour. So it's much better off for being a model.

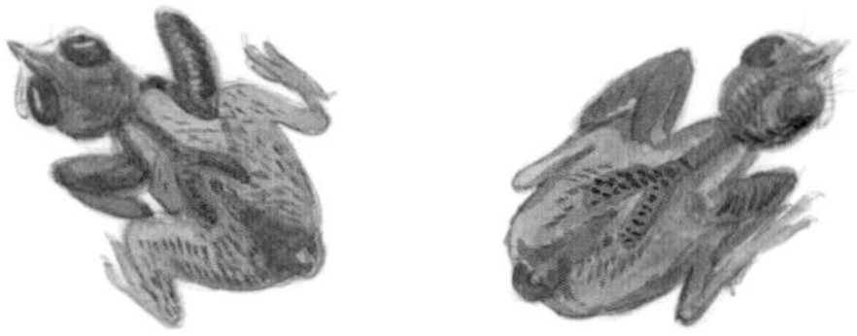

Day 4 May 30 '03 Today I'm really hard-pressed to tell my model from the other 2. Prickly little thing. It gapes willingly and eats 2 worms, in halves.

Day 3 7pm – 7:25pm Wow – it's growing so fast! Look at the pterylae and feathers sprouted since yesterday. It's starting to look wing-heavy – a swallow hallmark. Ate 2 white worms May 29 03

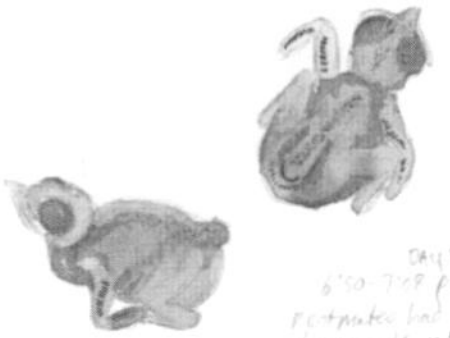

Day 2
6:50 – 7:09 pm May 28 2003 [illegible] and its two nestmates had a good day – [illegible] thunderheads and [illegible] how it's filled out! It ate a whole [illegible] swallows and gapes much better. [illegible] seems to be in a hurry developmentally, to [illegible] feathers. I'm amazed to [illegible] feather [illegible] under its transparent skin. [illegible] Ate 1 worm

Day 1
7:40 – 8 pm May 27 2003 I believe these baby tree swallows hatched this morning. There are 3, and we tossed out a rotten egg. It gaped and ate 3/4 of a white mealworm, diced up into 4 portions. Down is whitish. Very feeble and roly-poly. Ate 1 worm

8-8:25 AM Day 6 June 1 '03. Clear above but v. cool. Babies look great. Feathers are bursting sheaths! Fed it 4 worms

7:50-8:25 pm Day 7 June 2 '03. What a change! At first I'm a bit worried as I hear some crepitation (swallowing or breathing. I can't discern). But it eats 5 worms, then preens under its wing 3 times. This is the youngest bird I've ever seen preening, but then it's the youngest bird I've seen get feathers. Warm & lovely today. No wonder it's grown so much. Its eyes are probably open, but it's keeping them shut.

11pm – 4:45 pm Day 8
June 03 '03. It's barely grown at all today, the only change being in its feathers. I've fed the brood twice, at 1:30 and 4. It's been pouring nonstop since midnight. Note rubbery pads formed by the erupting feather tracts.

It relaxes in the warmth of the lamplight, and stretches a wing and preens. Today the [illegible] are quite vocal – I'm sure it's hunger.

Betwixt and between – not quite a lizard, not quite a bird. Day 9 June 4 '03
It didn't rain today, and it grew some, mostly catching up from yesterday's starvation, and popping feathers all over. It's very sensitive to noises and jumps at the slightest sound. I expect it to be much more appealing tomorrow.

Day 10 June 5 '03. It's so sweet today venturing a peek around when it thinks I'm not looking. It's so fluffy – what I'm seeing is the underdown. And I realize with a start that the only pink I can see is its leg!

Day 11– June 6 03   Today was the most beautiful of the year– and the chick grew like mad. 10 mealworms! and still room for more. It seems less frightened today, as if it knows better what to expect. This is when it gets fun!

Day 12 June 7 03 3:35–4pm. The chick is nearing its heaviest weight of its life (usually on day 14). It must lose weight in order to fledge. It clings firmly with its toes and chirps when handled– it's feeling fledgy! I really want to keep going, but we'll see what tomorrow brings.

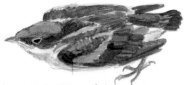

Day 13 June 8 03 4–4:35 pm. Quite a change in behavior. It creeps away, looking for cover, and burrows beneath my hand. If this is sketchy, that's why.

Day 15, snuggled in the nest

Day 17, just a quick peek and then withdrew. They can go anytime now.

Day 14– June 9 03 – our last together. Consciousness has dawned in these now-sparkling eyes, and though it's far from airworthy, it may try to fledge. I can see it trying to figure out a way out of this mess and I know that painting it any more is a bad risk. Farewell! There's still so much to know but your welfare comes first. Thank you.

It takes a while to learn to catch dragonflies!

Day 20. The young enjoy flight and subsidy that will travel along with them into late summer. I feel as if I'm seeing their real selves, as distinct from the cowed, frozen beings in the nest box.

Tree Swallow, 2003

"IF YOU DON'T write it down, it never happened." Roger Tory Peterson stood, scribbling on a small pad, as the dying day painted the sky red behind him. I was pleasantly surprised to see him at the small boat landing where I'd learned to come on September evenings in Old Lyme, Connecticut. A gravel parking area looked out over the Great Island salt marsh, where hundreds of thousands of tree swallows, barn swallows, and purple martins came on early autumn evenings to roost in the *Phragmites* reeds that had invaded its edges.

I knew Dr. Peterson, but as a twenty-something artist and aspiring writer, I'd never worked up the courage to call him Roger. I loved running into him around town, and I tried to keep my cool when happy accident or the occasional reception brought us together. Sometimes I mailed him sketches and descriptions of bird behaviors I'd witnessed, and he'd always send back a letter of appreciation. But this encounter was one I'll remember forever, here in the dusk beneath swirling swallow birdnadoes that circled and chittered, then funneled with an unearthly jet-roar whoosh into the reeds to sleep. This little-known autumnal ritual of roosting swallow flocks remains among the most impressive ornithological spectacles I've ever witnessed. To share it with one of the fathers of field ornithology in his local patch, and have him give me what turned out to be a major life directive, was transformative. I didn't know then how transformative it would be, but epiphanies often go unrecognized until they're conjured later, to be savored.

This little axiom that Dr. Peterson shared reinforced my resolve to record the things I observed for the modest posterity of my own life. As I pulled out a 2003 document called "Swallow Nesting Log," I said a silent prayer of thanks that I'd taken the great man's advice, even when I was young and could still recall the details of everything I'd seen or done. My brain is full now, and I haven't found any backup hard drives to contain the overflow of a mind that seems to be set on Low Boil. Write it down I must, and write it down I have. Reading twelve-year-old notes summons up an experience long forgotten, of painting my third nestling bird series from tree swallows living in a nest box in our meadow. Because these notes are fully realized, instead of the quick jots I made in later years, I'll transcribe them verbatim.

May 27, 2003. Day 1. Hallelujah! I've started the swallow's pictorial journey, and am so looking forward to watching it grow. I chose the smallest chick to paint, on purpose. It's a tough spring for tree swallows; in fact for all birds. The only good thing about a cold, wet spring for birds is that it keeps the ratsnakes in their winter homes. Rain and cold make finding insects, particularly flying ones, really tough. The swallows often have to commute to water, sometimes as far as the Ohio River eighteen miles away, to find any food to bring back. They store big wads of flying insects in their gular region, coming back looking full-throated, if they can find that much.

In choosing the smallest baby to paint, I hope to give it a survival edge as I did my wren and bluebird subjects in 2002. They grew faster and more consistently than their nestmates, thanks to the three or four extra feedings they got in the half-hour I was working with them. So I figure I'll enhance this baby's chances of surviving at all by painting it, and in so doing thank it for working with me. As if it had any choice!

It's small and incredibly delicate, its legs and feet so tiny. It rolls around helplessly. I'm amazed to see blue pterylae already visible in the translucent wings; they look just like the stained bones in the embryos we used to examine in bio lab. It's a delicate shell pink all over, brighter coral over the lungs, and a livid purple-red on its round abdomen; that's the liver shining through. Its gape corners are white; its bill faintly yellowish. Its skin is practically transparent. At one point, I jog the Tupperware container and am surprised to see it gape. I dice up a tender white mealworm into quarters and the bird accepts it greedily. Enhancement program has begun.

The female swallow has been most steadfast throughout the incubation, and I had to pick her up off the nest this evening to choose a chick. When I returned the chick thirty minutes later, she was on them, of course, and I simply reached in and deposited it by her side. How odd, I thought, to have a human reach in and nudge your missing baby back under your wing, while you were thinking it must have been taken off to be eaten!

May 28, 2003. Day 2. I looked in the nest and said, "Wow! You guys had a good day!" They were so much fatter and more rounded out. The smallest of the three is still the smallest, but not by as much. It's much stronger today, and it gapes and swallows better. I fed it a diced mealworm. Today was beautiful, moist and warm with big piles of thunderheads that, thankfully, never let down on us. The swallows were able to forage and feed the young all day, and it was warm enough, at last, for the female to contribute instead of hunkering down on the nest. I wonder how much weight she has lost incubating and brooding the young in this cold, wet spring.

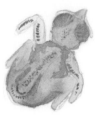

DAY 2
6:50–7:08 pm May 28 2003. The chick and its two nestmates had a good day – It was sunny, with big flaurry thunderheads and soft, moist air. Wow – how it's filled out! It ate a whole mealworm in progress. It swallows and gapes much better. It seems to be in a hurry, developmentally, to grow feathers; I'm amazed to count twelve minute tail feathers and individual wing feathers taking shape under its transparent skin. I'm in love!
Ate 1 worm

The nest is thickly lined with white feathers. A study conducted in Michigan found a direct positive correlation between the number of feathers lining a tree swallow nest and the number of young that live to leave it. More feathers translate to more fledglings. So much of what tree swallows do and are is shaped by their need to nest in cavities (historically, old woodpecker nest holes, and now artificial nest boxes as well). This puts them into stiff competition with cavity-nesting bluebirds, chickadees, titmice, and wrens. Competition is a major driver in their early spring occupation of nesting territory, as they attempt to arrive and get started nesting before other species. The cold temperatures at the onset of nesting have also shaped a rather elegant adaptation other cavity nesters do not share: lining the nest with feathers. The swallows must travel far and wide to obtain the feathers they need, and they have the wings to do it.

Tree swallows prefer feathers with a lot of down at the base; body feathers from goose and turkey are favorites. The downy, well-insulated nest allows a female tree swallow to leave her young uncovered for longer periods of foraging. Swallow babies are born naked, with a puzzling lack of down; they transition directly to feathers, the way woodpeckers do. It behooves their parents to provide a downy nest if their chicks have none. One of our favorite spring rituals is to buy packs of white goose feathers at a craft store, climb our bird-watching tower, and stand, feathers in our outstretched fingers, until tree swallows gather the courage to hover close, snatch them, and bear them off to their nest. Watching the swallows release the feather and then swoop to catch it by its shaft, then carry it to insert it, shaft tip first, into their woven straw and grass nests, is one of the many joys of April. It's that familiarity, their trusting nature, that I so love about tree swallows.

Tree Swallow,
just hatched—
a surprise
wild turkey
feather in
the nest.

I'm determined that, no matter what turn the weather takes, these chicks will make it through. They're easy to feed and I have the worms and the will to save them. I'm not going anywhere for a couple of weeks anyway. Swallows are so prone to abandoning their nests when the weather turns nasty—they have to in order to get enough food for themselves. I'm sure I could carry the young through if I had to.

I notice already the major difference in this swallow versus the wrens and bluebirds: this bird is in a big hurry to make feathers. The blue pterylae on the wings were visible on hatch day! And on Day 2 I can make out individual feathers in the wing tracts, visible through the transparent skin. And I can count twelve tiny feather points coming out of the tail. This bird is so minute it really taxes my old eyes, and I have to take my glasses off just to see the detail well enough to draw it. I remember this from last summer. It gets easier as the bird grows, but then there's so much more detail that it takes longer.

As much as Phoebe [then six years old] loves to watch me paint, I do a lot better when she's not hanging over my shoulder asking questions and talking to me, so this afternoon I sneak out while the kids are eating, get the chick, and sneak back to the studio to do my work. It feels like a betrayal, and it is. I let Phoebe carry it back to the box as consolation. She's so sweet, so gentle with the tiny nestlings. Liam [then three and a half] looked at the chick and said, "Oh! A bluebird!" I corrected him, and he said, "Oh yeah. It's a swallow."

Painting baby birds is so addictive that I have a hard time reining myself in. I found a robin's nest at chest level in a blue spruce as I was mowing today. It has only two eggs, but she's already incubating and highly aggressive. She almost scalped me two days ago as I innocently walked by the spruce. I thought at the time that her strafing my head was a coincidence. Now I know she was trying to scare me off. What a gal! How I would *love* to paint a robin chick. I'd give anything just to try to match that deep, deep luscious teal blue with my paints—these are the loveliest robins' eggs I've ever seen.

I'm trying to figure out how I could protect the robin's nest from predators, even though I'd be laying a scent trail to it with my visits. I know I can't protect it, so I mustn't try to draw the chicks. The same goes for a cardinal nest with two eggs that I'm watching along the driveway. It can't be a yard off the ground, clearly visible in a honeysuckle tangle. So tempting! But I would be a cad to betray their location to predators just for the joy of painting their young. When I came inside, I asked Liam if he'd like to see the robin's nest, and he came running across the lawn, all white hair and pumping elbows, saying, "I'd LOVE to!" These kids are in tall corn.

May 29, 2003. Day 3. When I open the box, the smallest chick is sprawled atop its siblings, wings embracing them. I have to lift it and check to make sure I've got the same one I painted last night. The supplemental feeding is beginning to tell. But its feather development is a bit behind, so I'm sure it's the same one.

The baby is beginning to get the wing-heavy look of a swallow. The wings seem to be growing at a faster rate than those of the bluebird or wren. This makes sense to me. They've got much longer to grow so they have to get started sooner. Swallows are constant creatures of the air, and their wings are proportionately longer and stronger

than those of the more earthbound wrens and thrushes. By the same token, swallow legs are short and weak. No striking development to report there. The legs are pink, rubbery, almost flaccid.

Day 3 7pm - 7:25pm Wow- it's growing so fast! Look at the pterylae and feathers sprouted since yesterday. It's starting to look wing-heavy- a swallow hallmark. Ate 2 white worms. May 29 '03

I'm amazed to see the feathers developing all over the body and poking out. It looks like it was badly shaved, with stubble. I feed it two mealworms today; though it doesn't seem much interested in food, I tease the corners of its waxy white mouth until it opens up. It seems to lack the "autopilot" gaping behavior I've noted in the very young bluebird and wren: raising the head every few moments whether there's stimulus or not. I wonder why. Swallows take long flights, often commuting to open water to gather boluses of small flying insects. Given this, perhaps swallow visits are fewer and much farther between, so it might just be a waste of energy to keep opening up every twenty seconds or so.

I put the chick back in the box, where its mother has returned and is already brooding the other two. The May sunshine is bright, and it's dark in the box. Goose feathers arch over her back, hiding everything from sight. The only hint that she's in there is the velvety feel of her back, and a quick double snap of her bill as I deposit her chick by her side. Such a steadfast sitter she is!

May 30, 2003. Day 4. I guess this birdlet is going to bypass down and just go straight to feathers, like a woodpecker. It's only four days old and covered with a tiny blue stubble of feathers. It's bigger and much rounder, its bluish cast stronger. I notice that its wings are thicker and heavier, as if they're swelling from within with the growing feather sheaths. It's even harder to tell from its siblings today. By tomorrow there may be no difference at all. Those extra feedings are telling on it, I guess. I feed it two white mealworms, cut in halves this time. The gape is yellow with a red center, and the flanges remain creamy white. Curiously, it doesn't respond at all to my swallow whistle imitations, to movement, jiggling, or blowing, like most nestlings do. I have to nudge the corners of its mouth, and its bill flies open. It gapes briefly and I stuff the mealworm in.

Day 4 May 30 '03 Today I'm really hard-pressed to tell my model from the other 2 prickly little thing, it gapes willingly and eats 2 worms, in halves.

I'm sitting after dinner relaxing a bit (we have a family of four as houseguests this weekend), when suddenly it hits me that I've got to paint the nestling, and I leap up and trot out to the box as the light is beginning to fade. That was close. If I miss a day, I miss so much.

May 31, 2003, 3:30–4:30 P.M. Day 5. Such a nasty day, pouring hard but warm, then turning cool (50s) with a building northwest gale and fine soaking rain. Terrible weather for nesting birds! I pick a slot when it's not pouring and run out to feed all three babies two white mealworms apiece. They seem pleasantly surprised. The largest of the three has one eye open, like Popeye.

I head for the house with the smallest cradled under my shirt, against my chest. It has grown considerably despite the cold and lack of food. I feed it six mealworms in the half-hour I'm drawing it. The nest, never substantial, is beginning to disintegrate under my attentions (I take it out of the box when I fetch the baby each day) and I plan to build a new, sturdier one and line it with the same feathers they're in now—but the weather is too bad and the female is sitting when I return, so I'll do that tomorrow. I'll have to be sure to include the great blue heron and turkey feathers they incorporated when they built it. I put a crock of mealworms out for the bluebirds, who have large, very hungry babies in the side-yard nest box. They've been begging from me all afternoon, sitting on the deck railing, looking purposefully into the windows, seeking me out. I haven't fed them this spring. Bluebirds shouldn't get unlimited mealworms in spring or they'll go into hyperproduction, lay too many eggs, and try to raise too many young. But today is too much.

Day 5 May 31 '03- Rainy, pouring. I'm sure they're not getting much food - so I feed the babies 2 worms each. This one eats 6 in a half-hour. So it's much better off for being a model.

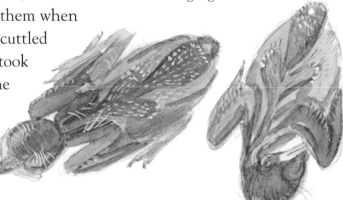

8·8:25 PM Day 6 June 1 '03. Clear all day but v. cool.
Babies look great. Feathers are bursting sheaths! Fed it 4 worms

June 1, 2003, 8:00–8:25 P.M. Day 6. A beautiful day today, but very cool and windy toward nightfall. The three chicks look good. Feathers are beginning to burst from the sheaths. Tiny white tips appear at the sheath ends. I feed the chick four whole mealworms. It's funny how it refuses to gape, but surreptitiously opens its bill when I nudge the corner, and engulfs the worm almost without acknowledgment. Then it rewards me with a fecal sac. It makes a stain on the paper, so I paint a picture of the fecal sac over the stain. I find the fecal sacs interesting; it's all data. I have time for only one view of the chick tonight, and it's getting so feather-studded that I'll probably have to stick to one from now on. There's just too much detail to capture any more. I reconstruct the nest with a thick cup of dry grass and reline it with feathers from the old nest cup. I'm sure they'll be warmer for it. The swallows' original nest was incredibly flimsy, the chicks practically lying on the bare wood floor of the box. The female swallow is getting wise to the process, and she now exits the box as I approach. Birds are so smart. There's a great blue heron feather in the nest, along with a bunch of turkey feathers. It's amazing how warm that feather-lined nest cup is. Good thing, because we'll have a light freeze tonight—June first!

June 2, 2003, 7:50–8:25 P.M. Day 7. There's a great big change today. It was sunny and warm all day, and doubtless good aerial foraging. The babies are big and blue with feather sheaths, and white stars of emerging feathers dot them. The female was on them when I came to the box and she scuttled down to the bottom when I took the nest out, then fled out the hole while I was looking at the chicks. I brought the chick in and was a little alarmed to hear some kind of crepitation, a crackling sound, in its breathing, which seemed

7:50-8:25 pm Day 7 June 2 '03. What a change! At first I'm a bit worried as I hear some crepitation (swallowing or breathing I can't discern). But it eats 5 worms, then preens under its wing 3 times. This is the youngest bird I've ever seen preening, but then it's the youngest bird I've seen get feathers. Warm & lovely today. No wonder it's grown so much. Its eyes are probably open, but it's keeping them shut.

labored. I fed it five worms without much difficulty, though, and afterward it relaxed and preened under its tiny wing. I've never seen such a young bird preen. I think it's probably fine if it eats and preens. Preening is always an indicator of well-being. A sick bird doesn't maintain its plumage. The gape is yellow instead of pink today, but I can't get it to open its mouth so I can paint it. Its eyes have probably opened, but it's keeping them shut.

June 3, 2003, 4:00–4:45 P.M. Day 8. Oh, what a day—it has been pouring since before midnight, with only two brief pauses. The nestlings were starving by 1:30 P.M. when I fed them for the first time. They stood up and cheeped when I opened the box, even though their mother was atop them! Clearly, they associate me with food! She stayed in the box while I took them out, one by one, in the pouring rain, huddled over them, and fed them seven worms apiece. When I came out at 4:00 P.M. to get the model, I fed them again. This time, both parents were out foraging despite the rain—forced into it. I hoped that by having me here subsidizing the young, the adults will be able to find something to eat themselves.

Not much change in the baby today—just a little more feather emergence, fluffing out along the flanks. There's a curious effect of the emerging tracts—a rubbery bluish pad is rising along the pterylae as though many small eruptions were pushing the skin up. I imagine that when the sheaths burst the baby will go from rubbery to feathery in a matter of hours, and I hope to be there. It relaxes in the lamp's heat, and stretches its neck and wings, and even preens a bit. How nice to be warm, dry, and have a full belly on a day like this. Lucky bird.

11pm–4:45pm Day 8
June 03 03. It's barely grown at all today, the only change being in its feathers. I've fed the brood twice, at 1:30 and 4. It's been pouring nonstop since midnight. Note rubbery pads formed by the erupting feather tracts.

It relaxes in the warmth of the lamplight, and stretches a wing and preens. Today the chicks are quite vocal—I'm sure its hunger.

Most people have no idea how close to the line birds live during nesting season, especially aerial insectivores like swallows. My friends at the Purple Martin Conservation Association in Pennsylvania are feeding their martin colony mealworms and scrambled eggs to get them and their young through this cold, rainy spring. Even the bluebirds suffer terrible mortality, and they take their food from the ground. I put out two bowls of mealworms for the bluebirds, which had the bad judgment to fledge from their dampish box today. When I went to put the second batch out, the female bluebird was bobbing in an inch of water for a dead mealworm at the bottom of the bowl—the only one remaining. The cries of the fledgling bluebirds coming from the pussy willow were much louder and stronger than they had been at noon. I felt a glow of relief and happiness that they had found and accepted my offering.

I feed the baby twice in the hour I work with it, and when I take it back to the box, I feed its siblings yet again. I know they will make it through today, and I hope that the scattered showers they're calling for tomorrow don't turn out to be a constant deluge like today.

June 4, 2003, 7:25–7:50 P.M. Day 9. Betwixt and between—the chick is not quite a lizard, not quite a bird. It didn't rain today, at least, though it stayed very gray and warm. The birds mostly caught up from yesterday's starvation. Their feathers unfurled but there wasn't much growth. I notice that today the bird is much more sensitive, recoiling and huddling down at the slightest noise. It keeps its eyes screwed shut. I made the mistake of having a couple of glasses of wine before dinner and found it much more difficult to draw! I ought to have my license revoked.

Betwixt and between - not quite a lizard, not quite a bird. Day 9 June 4 '03 It didn't rain today, and it grew some, mostly catching up from yesterday's starvation, and popping feathers all over. It's very sensitive to noises and jumps at the slightest sand. I expect it to be much more appealing tomorrow.

Day 10 June 5 '03. It's so sweet today, venturing a peek around when it thinks I'm not looking. It's so fluffy — what I'm seeing is the underdown. And I realize with a start that the only pink I can see is its leg!

June 5, 2003, 7:10–7:35 P.M. Day 10. The chick is all feathered today, much more appealing and birdlike. It's suddenly fluffy. I'm seeing the underdown emerging along with the feathers, giving it an overall charcoal cast. As I'm mixing my watercolors, I realize with a start that the only pink on the bird now is its legs and toes! Yesterday I did an underpainting of pink all over its body. It's so sweet, the way it keeps its head down and its eyes shut, but it ventures a quick peek around when it thinks my attention is elsewhere. It seems unable to believe it's out of its box, and it wants to see the outside. It faces around and takes a few glances outside at the bird feeders before hiding again. I'm wondering how long I will be able to continue drawing it. It's acting a bit fledgy. Though I thought swallows would be slower to develop, it seems quite precocious compared to the bluebird — almost more like the Carolina wren in its developing consciousness.

June 6, 2003, 7:25–8:00 P.M. Day 11. Today was probably the most beautiful day of the year thus far, warm, low humidity, light breeze, clear as a bell. The swallows swirled low over the meadow and high in the air all day, feeding like mad. Not surprisingly, the babies were big warm feathered hulks this evening. As always, I picked the one with the least-developed feathers, though it can hardly be called a runt. It's probably only a half-day behind the others now, and it's plenty big and strong. It seems less frightened tonight, and it eats ten mealworms eagerly though with that cool, tree swallow offhandedness. "If you're going to stick a worm in my bill I'll swallow it, but I won't gape for you."

There's a thick layer of smoke-gray down, with charcoal feathers rapidly overlaying it. The wing feathers are lengthening and paintbrush-tipped. The gape flanges are shrinking noticeably, and the gape, which started out whitish pink and stayed thus for four days, is now bright yellow-orange.

Day 11 - June 6 '03 Today was the most beautiful of the year - and the chick grew like mad. 10 mealworms! and still rooting for more. It seems less frightened today, as if it knows better what to expect. This is when it gets fun!

The family crowds around when I bring the chick inside each evening. We're all conscious of the miracle unfolding.

After putting the chick back in the box, I walked out to the orchard to check a couple of empty bluebird boxes. I couldn't count how many wood thrushes were singing at once along the north-facing sugar maple slope. It was better than I could imagine heaven could be, the sky darkening, the air heavy with honeysuckle scent and fresh-mown hay, and wood thrushes, singing a requiem for the day. My Catholic friend Steve says, "It's sacrilegious, but I'm afraid Julie and Bill will be disappointed when they see heaven." That's a very real possibility. It doesn't get any better than this, southeast Ohio in early June, in the evening, with wood thrushes singing, six at least. Maybe as many as eight.

June 7, 2003, 3:35–4:00 P.M. Day 12. A good day for tree swallows. It didn't rain all day, after another inch overnight. The chick now clings firmly with its toes and

Day 12 June 7 '03 3:35-4pm The chick is nearing its heaviest weight of its life (usually ca day 14). It must lose weight in order to fledge. It clings firmly with its toes and chirps when handled - It's feeling fledgy! I really want to keep going, but we'll see what tomorrow brings.

Day 13 June 8 03 4–4:35 pm. Quite a change in behavior. it creeps away, looking for cover, and burrows beneath my hand. If this is sketchy, that's why.

chirps irritably when handled. It's alert and peeks around but keeps its eyes mostly shut. My painting looks very slapdash to me, but my model was in constant motion. A minor drawback of working from live models.

June 8, 2003, 4:00–4:35 P.M. Day 13. I note quite a change in behavior today. The chick creeps along when I put it on the drawing board, looking for a place to hide. It burrows beneath my hand and keeps itself all scrunched up so it's hard to judge its size. This is the first time I've seen it walk or use its legs for locomotion. Fledging is near! And I can't do this much longer. I'd hate to think this is the last painting I'll make. I'm going to try it again tomorrow, Day 14, when it should be at its heaviest weight. It will weigh more tomorrow than it ever will in its life, and will actually have to lose weight in order to fledge! Chimney swifts do this, as well—fatten up then slim back down so they can fly. They may be fortifying for the last push of growth in their flight feathers, then finding themselves needing to lose weight to be flightworthy. Both aerial insectivores I've studied do this.

June 9, 2003, 4:15–5:20 P.M. Day 14. I know this is the last painting, so I do two. There's a consciousness in the now-sparkling eyes that wasn't there even yesterday. It's no longer producing fecal sacs, and the nest will start to get messy from now on. It's at its heaviest, at up to twenty-four grams, and it will lose weight from now on, as its feathers continue to grow and its parents begin to lose the race to keep up with its metabolism. All that is preparation for flight, though, and as it should be. It will fledge at a weight of around twenty grams—the equivalent of my losing twenty-five pounds in one week! Wouldn't it be nice . . .

Day 14 – June 9 '03 – at last together. Consciousness has dawned in these now-sparkling eyes, and though it's far from airworthy, it may try to fledge. I can see it trying to figure out a way out of this mess and know that painting it any more is a bad risk. Farewell! There's still so much to know but your welfare comes first. Thank you.

It hides in the curve of my hand, and at one point it puts its head down between its legs in an attempt to disappear. It's so sweet and frightened, but it knows the drill come feeding time—the mealworms disappear down its gullet, ten of them, like happy spaghetti. I know that this brood of swallows has fared far better than it would have had I not been checking and feeding them all through the rain and cold. I think the chicks probably would have died on their eighth day, and what a loss that would have been. Next season, I want to work with chickadees, and if this season is typical, it looks like I'll be in for some intensive feeding and tending—but it will be worth it! It feels good to know that my project has helped its subjects thrive and grow.

I paint a few more studies of older nestlings from quick snapshots taken in other nest boxes. The fourteen-day-old swallows' disheveled feathers smooth out; tails lengthen; eyes grow brighter still. Tree swallows, having very little leg, need to fly competently on their maiden launch. No hopping about on the ground or clambering in shrubbery for them; they may leave the box and disappear over the horizon on their first flight. I have seen adult tree swallows from our nest box park their fledglings on a power line near a small pond and return to feed them over the course of a morning, but here is where my knowledge of their post-fledging life leaves off. I'm in good company; tree

Day 15, snuggled in the nest

swallows, thanks to their propensity to nest in boxes, are one of North America's best-studied birds, but no one seems to know how long their parents feed them after fledging. Some accounts state that the young are on their own as soon as they leave the nest; others assert that young are fed for "a few days."

Fledging begins a journey that leads young tree swallows to flock with other swallows. They're drawn to water, to riverbanks, and shores, where insects abound in late summer. Seeing mixed swallow flocks massing on power lines is a signal of autumn here in southeast Ohio. I never see them, lined up like musical notes on a score, without thinking back to that evening in perhaps 1986 in Old Lyme, when fate and a spectacular autumnal gathering of swallows brought me and Roger Peterson together. Though I was starstruck in his presence, I'd always tried hard not to be intrusive when we'd meet. I hoped he knew what he meant to me, how living near this giant of ornithology had inspired me, how his simple adage about

Day 17, just a quick peek and then withdrew. They can go anytime now.

writing everything down had helped drive my life's work. Ten years later, he was gone. I never got a chance to say goodbye, never knew if *he* knew all that he had given me. His boyhood friend Bob Sundell came up to me at the 2008 opening of a show of my paintings at the Roger Tory Peterson Institute in Jamestown, New York. "I wanted to tell you what Roger said to me years ago, before I'd ever heard of you. He said, 'Zickefoose. Remember that name. She's one to watch.'"

Day 20. The young enjoy flight and subsidy that will travel along with them into late summer. I feel as if I'm seeing their real selves, as distinct from the cowed, frozen beings in the nest box.

It takes while to learn to catch dragonflies!

Day 6 July 09 '08. The ♀ spends her day on a bare branch equidistant between feeder area and the very sensitive to their close-fitting cradle. She visits only about every 10 minutes to fill their crops, then disappears again. Giant baby hummingbirds have long waits between feedings.

July 10 '08
Day 7 Hard to see inside nest. Dark! Fluttered out. Nest is beginning to stretch! Eyes are still green.

July 8 Day 5. ♀ feeding young. She drives her bill deep into the baby's gullet. I've drawn an X-ray view. The fluid is pumped directly into the baby's crop. Young boy with a rapid pumping motion, everything the mother's bill.

Black-waved Flannel caterpillar with intensely irritating setae.
Megalopyge crispata

Day 4 July 7, '08. I'm frustrated at an inability to see salient details, but not in such murky light from their nest is an unacceptable risk. Aside from their crop, the long black stamen down that makes but for the long black stamen & down still their backs, they look more like hairy caterpillars than birds. I'm surprised that these caterpillars would have unclearer will have remained for the nest size-homing triangular increase. Be. To not non-homing. They are most peculiar looking, and unappetizing.

With their yellow stringy down, they look like flannel moth caterpillars — very poisonous with yellow hairs that cause a terrible rash. Is that the point?

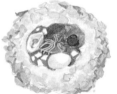

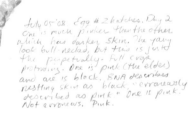

Contents of crop gray-tan as fresh body. May be aphids or tiny gnats

July 06 08 Day 3 A tiny thing! I'm drawing so fast, If I wasn't about jays, crows, and... It goes within the 2 feet. She finds a large black rat snake in the grass 3 minutes & that evening. The ♀ is back on the nest.

July 05 '08 Egg # 2 hatches. Day 2 One is much pinker than the other which has darker skin. The young look bull-necked, but this is just the perpetually-full crop protruding. One is pink (the elder) and one is black. BNA describes nestling skin as black, "erroneously described as pink." One is pink. Not erroneous. Pink.

Day 1 July 4 '08 Egg 1 hatches. The nestling very pink, with golden fuzz still pasted down. Eggshell in fragments on nest floor, luminous into birth & hatchling. It takes...

June 25 '08 nest first discovered. Female still incubating.

Ruby-throated Hummingbird
2003, 2008

July 11 '08
Day 8 Pinfeathers erupt on spinal tract. Eyes slit open; they're beginning to see something. Gape bright yellow-orange. Here's the view a mother hummingbird gets.

Day 18? Primaries still in sheath at base — generally all sheaths are gone before flight

Day 9 July 12 '08 The heads have darkened but remain stubbornly bare; only the flossy spinal tracks of down cover the birds. A weird reptilian corrugation appears on their heads as feathers begin to push up from beneath. Eyes are slitted, almost certainly open but perhaps not wide. Bill is darkening and lengthening notably.

Day 16 — she props herself woodpecker-like and stretches mightily to feed young almost as big as she is. Heads pump like sewing machine needles. Gape still bright orange.

Day 10, July 13, '08.
Their heads are sprouting feathertips. I'm frustrated by how much is hidden beneath the descending nest rim, but that's what keeps them warm while she's away, which is always! The buff-white tips of contour feathers are emerging. Note how left-hand chick leans its side from Day 9 on. Wonder if it was always its sibling?

"Noah" who came in on Day 15 and was raised by Sharon Wallace & raised by me summer 2007

Day 11, July 14 '08 Eyes wide open! Really filling the nest cup now, and their bills stick visibly up above the rim. Warblers would be fledged and flying by now — the difference in their developmental arcs is striking. These babies and their kind — they remind me of swifts, taking their own sweet time. Rufous feather tips bursting. The only way to tell which head belongs to which body is by feather direction. Top head goes with left body.

Day 14 Emerging wing feathers are looking streaky. The sides are pinfeathers; the white streaks drying in preparation to unwind.

Day 12 July 15 08. Feathers are emerging — russet paintbrush tips. Down persists on one, but not the other.

Day 13. Eyes wide — a kindle of pinfeathers. This, July 16, 2008, would be their last on Day 14. A gray & blue jays came into our yard saving every thing and branch and the hummingbirds were taken.

Rufus watches
a storm coming

Rufus sits
quietly high
in the branches
all day. Joe and
Bella bully him
relentlessly at the
feeder, so he's still dependent
on me 7/27. (Day 33)

Day 33   7/27/07   Joe
All are feeding
themselves
at last
today. Even
Rufus & Baby

July 18: Preening like big
fella. I spotted these
doves today and thereya
much flutter too

watching an distant
flour moth

Bella scratching

Ruby-throated Hummingbird, 2003, 2008

I FOUND MY first and to date only ruby-throated hummingbird nest on May 14, 1993, the kind of day that's drenched in golden sun. I spotted a female hummingbird gathering the inner bark fuzz from dead goldenrod stalks near our mailbox. Guessing that she would return, I dropped what I was doing and sat down at some distance. Since I rarely leave the house without binoculars, I was ready for whatever transpired.

The hummingbird zipped up and down, picking at the goldenrod stems, accumulated a wad of buff-colored fuzz, and disappeared stage left, into the deep emerald deciduous woodland of our east forty. She returned a few minutes later for another elfin load of fuzz. I tracked the direction of her lightning departure, and as soon as she was out of sight, I scuttled into the woods on the same trajectory and sat down at the spot where I'd lost sight of her. I grinned as I settled into the leaves to disappear. Sure enough, she whizzed by me on her way back out to the goldenrod stand. When she came back, I followed her as far as I could with my eyes, and repositioned myself farther along her trajectory into the forest. It took two more sightings and repositionings before I caught sight of her hovering at an oddly angled branch, 15 feet up in a red maple laced through with grapevine. At this point I was quite deep in the woods on a southeast-facing slope.

She sits tight through windstorms and seemingly endless rain.

The bird seemed to be incubating while constructing her nest, as she'd settle down and sit for long periods after working on it. She'd reach over the edge of the nest and tremble her bill rapidly as she shaped the outside. It was already well plastered with pale green lichens. Once a broad-winged hawk took off only 30 feet away, startling us both. The hummingbird shot off the nest. When she returned, she looped beneath it, hovered briefly directly overhead, then plopped into it bottom-first, like a soft-boiled egg into a cup. But she settled down so purposefully and deeply into the nest that I felt sure she already had eggs, even as she was completing nest construction. After the two-week incubation period, I visited whenever I thought of it, and stuck around long enough each time to see a nest visit and ascertain that its contents had not been raided by a snake or jay. I remember the hot, humid afternoon that I saw two small bills pointing skyward from the nest cup. The nest began to look stretched out and sloppy, the bills got longer; I could see the young birds' white feathered throats, and not long after that it was empty. I felt blessed to have witnessed the entire nest cycle, or what little of it I could through binoculars from 30 feet beneath it. I burned to know what was inside that nest.

Fifteen years later, Nina Harfmann, a dear friend, photographer, and writer, would find a female ruby-throat attending a nest not far from her front door on the other (Cincinnati) side of Ohio. It was June 25, 2008. By July 4, the

June 25 '08 Nest, first discovered while under incubation.

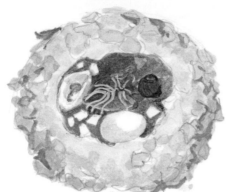

Day 1 July 4 '08 Egg # 1 hatches. The
nestling; very pink, with golden floss
still pasted down. Eggshell is in
fragments on nest floor. Membrane
is to left of hatchling. I later find
it in the lawn.

incubating hummingbird had weathered a violent thunderstorm, sitting tight throughout the swaying and tossing of the sugar maple branch to which she'd anchored her walnut-size nest, to successfully hatch both of her pea-size white eggs. Nina found the eggshell membrane on the lawn and knew a chick had hatched. There began an incredible journey for Nina, and for me. These paintings were made from Nina's photographs, a priceless record of early hummingbird development.

July 5, 2008. Day 2. The second egg hatches. The nestling's skin is black, while the first-hatched bird is bright pink. It's a difference that will last until their sixth day of life. I'm amused to find the Birds of North America account stating that the skin of all ruby-throat nestlings is black, "erroneously described as pink." This turns out to be variable, as does so much in nature.

Contents of crop quite dark on
pink baby. May be aphids
or tiny gnats.

July 05 '08. Egg # 2 hatches. Day 2
One is much pinker than the other,
which has darker skin. They
look bull-necked, but this is just
the perpetually-full crop
protruding. One is pink (the elder)
and one is black. BNA describes
nestling skin as black, "erroneously
described as pink." One is pink.
Not erroneous. Pink.

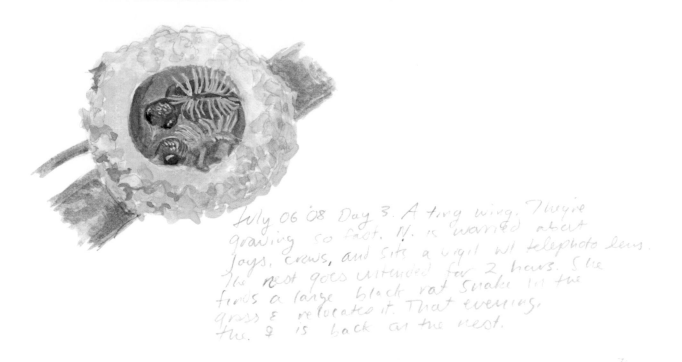

July 06 08 Day 3. A tiny wing. They're
growing so fast. N. is worried about
jays, crows, and sits a vigil w/ telephoto lens.
The nest goes untended for 2 hours. She
finds a large black rat snake in the
grass & relocates it. That evening,
the. ♀ is back at the nest.

July 6, 2008. Day 3. Nina is torn about photographing the nest, worried that she'll lead predators to the nest by visiting it, and writes me to ask how best to document the chicks' development. We decide together that she should wait until the female hummingbird has left, make sure no jays or crows are in the vicinity, then limit her visits and photos to one per day, and to be careful not to touch anything near the nest.

On July 6, Nina decides to sit at a distance well beyond the hummingbird's comfort zone and watch the nest with binoculars and telephoto lens. The chicks go unattended for the entire two-hour period. When Nina gets up to leave for work, she finds a large black ratsnake stretched nearby and relocates it. Its presence may have prevented the bird from approaching her nest. The female hummingbird is back on the nest at nightfall, as it begins to rain again. Watching wild bird nests is not for the faint of heart.

July 7, 2008. Day 4. Painting from the photographs, I'm frustrated by my inability to see salient details such as wings and feet, but taking these minute scraps of life from the nest would constitute an unacceptable risk. You might crush them just trying to handle them, even if you could justify the risk of leading predators to the nest. Nina's quick photo each day seems a good compromise, and I just have to be satisfied with what I can see in the photos, which isn't much!

The chicks are naked but for long yellow strands of down on their backs. They are very peculiar looking. They remind me of something I've seen, but I can't dredge it up. Suddenly it hits me that they look like caterpillars! More specifically, the nasty caterpillar of the black-waved flannel moth, *Megalopyge crispata.* Most people don't know that there's a caterpillar right here in Ohio (and like the ruby-throat, widely

Black-waved Flannel caterpillar with intensely irritating setae. *Megalopyge crispata*

With their yellow stringy down, They look like flannel moth caterpillars - very poisonous with yellow hairs that cause a terrible rash. Is that the point?

Day 4 July 07, '08. I'm frustrated by my inability to see salient details but taking such minute birds from their nest is an unacceptable risk. Still naked but for the long blonde strands of down on their backs, they look more like hairy caterpillars than birds. I'm surprised that their bills have remained yellow and stubbornly triangular throughout, but they're lengthening. They are most peculiar looking, and unappetizing.

distributed east of the Mississippi) that's toxic enough to be dangerous. The luxuriant setae—detachable hairs—of the flannel moth caterpillar are so toxic that just brushing against them can create an excruciating rash on exposed skin. Marked swelling and pustules may develop, along with nausea, which can persist for twelve or more hours. Sensitive individuals have been sent to the hospital by a chance encounter with a flannel moth caterpillar. Unrelenting pain from the venom in flannel moth setae is said to radiate immediately outward to the chest and lymph nodes. The more I think about it, the more sense it makes that something as helpless as a baby hummingbird should possess some kind of defensive mechanism, even if it's just looking like something dangerous. This could be Batesian mimicry in a bird! Named for English naturalist Henry Walter Bates, Batesian mimicry describes a situation in which a harmless organism evolves to look like one that's dangerous. A well-known Batesian mimic is the edible viceroy butterfly, whose bold orange and black color pattern matches that of the poisonous monarch. Thus disguised, tasty viceroys are largely safe from bird attacks. I'm theorizing that helpless hummingbird chicks might look enough like toxic flannel moth caterpillars to repel most predators. I'm so pleased by this synchronicity that I paint a flannel moth caterpillar alongside the chicks.

In the world of happy chances, the one that caused my friend John Wheatley to send me an interesting link just a few weeks later was electrifying. I'd said nothing to anyone about my just-conceived Batesian mimicry theory; Wheats just sends me interesting links from time to time. There, I viewed a 2012 video by University of California, Riverside researcher Gustavo Londoño. A drab gray-brown tropical bird called the cinereous mourner has a single chick that sports conspicuous bright orange natal plumage spangled with silver. An orange crest tops its head, and long strange filaments of down wave gently above it all. Why should any nestling be so bizarre and conspicuously colored, when every selective pressure should point toward cryptic coloration? The first investigators surmised that the chick might be poisonous to eat, but that guess was based on museum specimens only and couldn't be corroborated. Video of a live chick sitting alone in the nest, though, revealed a sinuous, continuous motion of its neck and head that was strongly reminiscent of a crawling caterpillar. As it happens, a huge and as yet undescribed flannel moth caterpillar is found in the same Peruvian forests as the cinereous mourner. I hate to think what an encounter with a 5-inch tropical flannel moth caterpillar might feel like, and there's a real chance I might not live to report back. A 3-inch-long Amazonian species called "el raton" (the rat) is said to have killed people. The undescribed Peruvian caterpillar is the same size and the same shade of orange, spangled with gray and black, as the cinereous mourner chick. Nature can be as wonderful as it is terrible, and I was hugely pleased to have corroboration that Batesian mimicry is now known in birds—and perhaps even

July 8. Day 5. ♀ feeding young. She drives her bill deep into the baby's gullet. I've drawn an X-ray view. The fluid is pumped directly into the baby's crop. Young beg with a rapid pumping motion, engulfing the mother's bill.

Day 6 July 09 '08. The ♀ spends her day on a bare branch equidistant between feeder and nest, the young snoozed in their close-fitting cradle. She visits only about every 90 minutes to fill their crops, then disappears. You'd think baby hummingbirds would need more frequent feedings!

in the ruby-throated hummingbird. Like the ruby-throat, the mourner spends twenty days lying in its nest—a long, vulnerable time for a small bird.

July 8, 2008. Day 5. I decide to draw a side view of a chick being fed. The act looks alarmingly violent; the chick stretches its neck upward, and the female plunges her bill deep down into its crop. She brings up nectar and insects from her crop as the chick makes a rapid pumping motion with its head, entirely engulfing its mother's ¾-inch-long bill.

July 9, 2008. Day 6. Nina's observation of the hummingbirds' feeding schedule bolsters my theory of protective camouflage for nestling hummingbirds, for the chicks were left alone for surprisingly long periods. Nina observed the chicks "tucked securely into their inch and a half-wide nest, a stretchy spider web structure lined with plant down . . . snug and warm as a fine woolen cap." The female sat all day long on a bare branch 40 feet away, visiting Nina's feeders every ten to fifteen minutes, while keeping watch on her nest. She visited the nest only every ninety minutes or so, "standing at the rim just long enough to feed her young from her crop, before disappearing again across the yard."

"Perhaps she trusts the warmth of the woolly nest she has given them to snuggle them when she cannot. And, as inactive as they still are, knows they need less nourishment than she. Or perhaps, being the sole parent, time is best spent being vigilant, rather than resting with them beneath the low, leafy branches."

July 10, 2008. Day 7. The chicks' down is beginning to fluff out, and they're losing that caterpillar look as they grow. The eyes are slit open.

July 10 '08 Day 7 Hard to see inside nest. Down is fluffing out. Nest is beginning to stretch! Eyes are slit open.

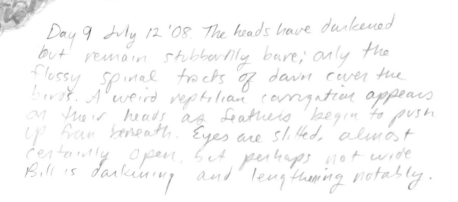

July 11 '08
Day 8 Pinfeathers erupt
on spinal tract. Eyes
slit open. They're beginning
to see something. Gape
bright yellow-orange.
Here's the view a mother
hummingbird gets.

July 11, 2008. Day 8. Eyes are open, and pinfeathers are erupting on the spinal tract. Gape is brilliant orange, but revealed only when the mother is there to see it.

July 12, 2008. Day 9. The chicks' heads have turned darker but remain bare. They're weird, reptilian, corrugated as the feathers begin to push through from beneath the skin. Only the flossy spinal tracts of down cover the birds. Bills are darkening from yellowish and lengthening noticeably.

Day 9 July 12 '08. The heads have darkened
but remain stubbornly bare; only the
flossy spinal tracts of down cover the
birds. A weird reptilian corrugation appears
on their heads as feathers begin to push
up from beneath. Eyes are slitted, almost
certainly open, but perhaps not wide.
Bill is darkening and lengthening notably.

July 13, 2008. Day 10. I'm frustrated by how much of the chicks' bodies is hidden beneath the overcurling nest rim, but that's what keeps them warm while their mother forages, preens, and watches over them from her post. By now the nest is noticeably stretched, and it's that organic evolution of the nest with its occupants that makes me decide to paint it each time I paint the young. I love the fact that it's constructed with stretchy but strong material. Plant down and cobwebs are Nature's spandex. And so it grows with the chicks, its rim rolling over to keep them warm. There's enough room in it so one chick lies habitually on its side, a detail I find endearing.

July 14, 2008. Day 11. Eyes are wide open. The nestlings really fill up the nest cup, and their bills poke above the rim. I stop to reflect that a warbler or Carolina wren chick would be feathered out and flying by now. These babies aren't even close. They remind me of chimney swifts, taking their own sweet developmental time, hiding for as long as possible in caterpillar disguises. Rufous feather tips are bursting through the sheaths. I struggle to decipher what's going on in the photos, as the nestlings resemble one bird with a head at each end. The only way to discern which feathers belong to which bird is to note the direction they're growing.

Day 12 July 15 08. Feathers are emerging - russet paintbrush tips. Down persists on one, but not the other

July 15, 2008. Day 12. One bird still retains the stringy yellow down; the other has shed it as paintbrush tips of rufous push out of the sheaths. I'm still agog at how long it takes hummingbirds to begin to feather out.

July 16, 2008. Day 13. Their eyes are wide; they're bundles of pinfeathers. Today would be their last to change and grow. These two were not among the lucky ones. Nina writes: "The yard is full of jays. I could hear them outside on this hot, steamy morning, coming closer and closer—even through closed windows, as the air conditioner drones noisily behind the house. They're everywhere, swooping down into the highest branches and searching along each one. Even the maple tree. Where is Mama? They've come too close. And I cannot scare them away. The nest is empty."

In her poignant words, Nina captured the swift finality of nest predation. Nothing she did over the course of her study could have contributed to this event. Jays will be jays, and young hummingbirds, however we may wish otherwise, are on their menu. I never witness such predation events without marveling that any nestling makes it to adulthood, so abundant, diverse, and avid are the predators waiting to take them. Jays, crows, ratsnakes, raccoons, housecats, opossums, squirrels, mice—even white-tailed deer, purportedly seeking the calcium in their bones—are voracious predators of low-nesting birds. Time in the nest is the most vulnerable period of any bird's life, and ruby-throats clock three weeks there before they are ready to fly, far longer than any other small open-cup nester. It is likely that a hummingbird, being an aerialist with weight restrictions, lays the largest egg it can energetically afford to. But this egg is still tiny, and from it hatches a chick that will take a very long time to develop and mature.

Day 13. Eyes wide, a bundle of pinfeathers. This, July 16, 2008, would be their last. On Day 14, a group of blue jays came into N's yard, scouring every twig and branch. And the hummingbirds were taken.

Day 14 (guessing) Wing feathers are bursting sheaths. The babies are porcupines, the white sheaths drying out preparatory to bursting.

Chimney swifts, also aerial foragers, may be bound by the same restrictions to lay relatively small eggs, which produce slow-growing chicks.

The elaborate camouflage of a hummingbird nest, which resembles a lichen-encrusted knot on a branch, as well as the possible Batesian mimicry of the bizarre-looking chicks, all play into this lengthy but essential vulnerability. It takes a very long time to make a flying hummingbird, as I had discovered in the summer of 2003.

On July 9 of that year, a violent straight-line wind brought down two hummingbird nests, both of which found their way, occupants still inside, to my kitchen table. I had seen nestling hummingbirds from 15 feet below, but I'd never fed one, much less raised it to flying age. The sudden responsibility of being a mother to four young hummingbirds was overwhelming, but I couldn't let them die.

The head pumps rapidly as the baby tries to swallow the eyedropper. The crop is a translucent pouch — it's easy to tell when he's full.

The far hummingbirds rode their lichen-covered cradles to the ground when the boughs broke.

Because I'd taken care of an injured adult the summer before, I have on hand a jar of powdered hummingbird maintenance diet for use in zoos and aviaries. I mix it up and administer it with a dropper. The birds gape willingly when I make a rapid thin peeping sound through my teeth, and their heads pump up and down like sewing-machine needles as they gulp the brownish solution.

"Magic," who came in on Day 15 and was raised by Sherri Killen, released by me summer 2007.

I examine the hummingbird food label and find that it's made with soy protein. I wonder when a hummingbird ever saw a soybean. I have seen hummingbirds catching gnats in midair, robbing spider webs of small insects, even gleaning aphids from birch leaves. I know female hummingbirds must supply quantities of insect protein to their young. Going solely on instinct, I decide to supplement the chicks' diet with mealworm innards, squeezed out of the hard, chitin-armored larvae like toothpaste, and administered on the end of a round-tipped toothpick. The animal protein seems to agree with them, and they are noticeably brighter by nightfall. I will learn later that some hummingbird rehabilitators order vast quantities of live fruit flies from biological supply companies, purée them, and feed them to their charges. Gut maternal instinct produces thriving hummingbirds.

From the state of their pinfeathered heads, I guess the four to be around Day 15 when they come in. I'm so overwhelmed by work of caring for them that I don't find the wherewithal to paint them until they reach Day 18. To span the development between Nina's thirteen-day-old chicks and mine, I patch in with a painting of another orphaned hummingbird I cared for. I smile to see the paintings I've done from my orphans—loose and a little sloppy, but so full of life.

Day 16–she props herself woodpecker-like and stretches mightily to feed young almost as big as she is. Heads pump like sewing machine needles. Gape still bright orange.

Once the chicks appear to be thriving, I relax into the routine of feeding them every half-hour, as much as one can relax when jumping up every thirty minutes to wash utensils and feed four baby hummingbirds. I keep my eyedroppers and the babies scrupulously clean, for I know that bacteria will be my greatest enemy in raising healthy chicks.

Day 18? Primaries still in sheath at base—generally all sheaths are gone before flight

July 12, 2003.

Day 18. All the pinfeather sheaths have burst. They really look like birds. I'm thankful they've stopped their sewing-machine begging. Now they quietly open their gapes and allow me to drop nectar into their gullets. I had been forced to wash them with wet cotton swabs after every meal when they were bobbing up and down, throwing nectar everywhere. On the hygiene front, hummingbirds don't make fecal sacs, but shoot liquid droppings over the nest rim, so I keep them in an easily washed plastic "critter keeper." I've ordered a huge shipment of mealworms so I can always find enough

Baby and Bella Day 17-18? Sweetgum nest—a bit younger by 3 days. They lost their head pinfeather sheaths this morning. This is Day 4 that I've been caring for them

Saturday July 12 2003

Rufus and Joe Day 18? This nest 3 days older. The crop shows on the front bird's neck. A little russet down on lower back

The tongue extends at least the bill's length beyond its tip. In the hour or 2 after eating, the bird extends it, bringing nectar up out of the crop.

They explore their surroundings by licking and tasting.

freshly molted white larvae that I can tear into bits and administer. I try to give each of the four birds one larva per feeding.

Young hummingbirds explore their environs with the only tactile organ they possess—their tongue. They run their rice-noodle tongue over everything. If I get close enough, they even run it up my nose—a test of steel nerves if ever there were one.

I've decided that adult hummingbirds get their cranky and territorial demeanor from being crammed into a small nest with a sibling as youngsters. When they try to preen, half the time they wind up preening their sibling. When they exercise their wings, they beat each other over the head, taking turns until both are thoroughly irritable, voicing tiny hummingbird growls.

When one flaps, the other hunkers down and emits an insect-like, buzzing, annoyed growl throughout. It's being buffeted about the head.

July 14, 2003. Day 20. We're out of people food, and because I must feed the nestlings every hour, I bring the hummingbirds along on the half-hour ride to the grocery store. They're in their plastic carrier with the two nests, still on their branches, taped to its walls. I put the carrier in the shopping cart, because it's too hot to leave them in the car. As I place a pineapple carefully beside the box, two of the babies leap from their nest and buzz around inside it. I look up to the rafters of the warehouse food store and thank the stars the birds are well contained. There'd be no getting them down from there!

They often wind up preening their twin—whether by accident or design.

July 15, 2003. Day 21. It's time to move Charlie the macaw out of her glassed-in 8 × 10 foot room and move the hummingbirds in. This is much easier said than done. It takes me all day to relocate Charlie's cage and clean and prepare the room for hummingbird occupation. This includes taping newspaper over all vertical and horizontal surfaces and outfitting the aviary with fine-twigged birch branches for perching. At noon I open their plastic carrier for a feeding and one baby lifts vertically from its nest and lands on my arm—its first real flight. Even in the maelstrom of preparing their quarters, I take a moment to blink back tears and feel thankful that their unlikely mama has somehow gotten them this far.

Overwing scratching—not blindingly fast but dinosaur-slow and delicate.

When I move the tank into the aviary and open it, two babies in one nest buzz straight up into the fine branches near the ceiling. The other two will stay in their nest for another day before one of them flies. Their nests are infested with tiny mites, so when all the young have flown I microwave the nests to kill the parasites. The fallout looks like fine pepper. There's nothing I can do about the mites already on the birds. I get the sense that fleeing mites is part of the impetus to fledge, at least in this instance.

watching an Indian
flour moth

Bella scratching

Rufus 7/25
Day 31

July 17, 2003. Day 23. The last hummingbird fledged today. They're all perching, preening, and exercising, but not flying very much. Now that the birds have fledged, I'm privy to some behavior that I've witnessed only once in the wild. When they're hungry, they give a piercing peep that carries quite a distance. This is how their mother finds them. I know I must keep them in the aviary until they can feed themselves and fly strongly, but I don't know how long that will be.

July 18, 2003. Day 24. I hang a small hummingbird feeder from one of the birch branches, and spend most of the day watching the birds. I want to see what they'll do when I wet them with a fine spray from my plant mister. They preen and fluff and look immeasurably better after their bath. On this evening, I let two hours go by without feeding them and rush to the aviary to find them all peeping loudly. I'm feeding them with a dropper, apologizing and fussing over them, when I feel the slight wind of wings on my back. I turn to find Adventure Joe hovering at the feeder I've hung for just such an occasion. My face splits in a proud grin. They're on their way! I can taste the sweet nectar of independence. I have been lashed to the mizzen feeding these sprites once or twice an hour, dawn to dusk, for the past nine days. It feels like forever. No matter what I'm doing to care for my human home and family, I must keep these babies in the front of my mind. A hummingbird's stomach can't wait.

July 19, 2003. Day 25. The last bird to fledge is being harassed by its older sibling, and in the afternoon I find it lying on the aviary floor. I surmise that it's been driven into the glass in an altercation. There's a long, sad story of convalescence, but no redemption. I name this doomed hummingbird Buzz, because that's all he can do with a broken wrist. Over the months I kept him, unable to bring myself to euthanize this hand-raised bird, Buzz taught me that a hummingbird robbed of flight can never be a hummingbird. I have

Buzz—the last to fledge
Its nestmate, who fledged today
(July 17) around 1 pm—2 days
after the first and a day after
its uppity nestmate. It keeps its
baby pose, bill up

learned to euthanize those brought to me with broken wings before I have a chance to fall in love with them.

July 22, 2003. Day 28. Bela refuses all but three feedings today, because he's using the feeder! By 5:00 P.M., Adventure Joe is following suit. Both are intensely curious about the feeders I bring in. When I see one rubbing his chest on the water-beaded surface of a feeder, I hit on the idea of spraying down hosta leaves with water. To my delight, the birds roll around on their bellies and sides like tiny seals until they're soaked to the skin.

July 26, 2003. Day 32. As much as I'd wished the birds would feed themselves, they're still peeping and gaping. I fed Bela and then copycat Joe in flight today. Their flying skills are advanced enough to allow them to hover in one place while being fed from a dropper. I'm concerned that they are tussling and fighting over the feeder in the 8 × 10 foot aviary. I don't want another collision or injury. I'm up against the wall, not wanting to release the birds before they're self-feeding, but worried sick that they'll hurt themselves in this space, the only one I've got that's remotely suitable for them. I had yet to discover nylon-screen tents for housing birds.

Bella July 25 03. She's self-
sufficient now—I've fed her
perhaps twice all day. She
probes my pencil and eraser
as I try to draw.

July 18- Preening like big
folks. I sprayed them
down today and they're
much fluffier for it.

July 28, 2003. Day 34. Bela is a male, that's for sure. He's chasing Joe and Rufus all over the aviary. By day's end, enough testosterone has kicked in that he's doing shuttle display flights to a birch leaf, even trying to copulate with it. He won't let the other two use the feeders, so I have to feed them with a dropper. Push has come to shove. My dream of the perfect release, with all the birds self-feeding, is dashed by the need to protect them from injury. It's time to release them, however imperfectly, to the real world beyond the cruel glass.

July 29, 2003. Day 35. I find both Bela and Joe doing shuttle displays and mounting leaves. Males, both. Rufus is spatting with both of them, finally asserting himself at the feeder. I remove the screen from the aviary window. Bela darts immediately out into the clear air, flies back inside, then back out and is gone. Adventure Joe picks at a cobweb on the open window, then rises straight up past the chimney and darts left. Rufus heads out toward the orchard. The aviary is perfectly silent. It's over, and they didn't even look back to say goodbye.

The next chapter in our story begins around 4:00 that same afternoon. I'm hanging out one of countless loads of laundry that have piled up while I've been playing hummingbird mother when I hear a familiar peeping. "Find that bird, Phoebe!" She points to Adventure Joe, sitting on the line, no bigger than one of my clothespins. Needing no urging, she skitters to the kitchen to prepare a vial of food while I keep him there, talking. She hands me the dropper and I fill his crop. From the top of a birch comes a peep from Bela, but he won't come down to be fed. I head to the garden to pick beans, and Rufus flies to the fence, begging. I have to keep a vial of nectar on me at all times. I'm staggered to think that these birds have had the sense to stay around and seek me out in this strange, limitless new world. All my other fledglings do, but for reasons I can't explain I'd underestimated these birds. They're like Tom Thumb: tiny but perfectly capable, and 100 percent bird.

Over the next three days, Bela demonstrates that he prefers the nectar

Adventure Joe comes back.
July 29, 2003

in my abundant flower gardens. Rufus and Joe continue to follow me and seek me out all day long. Fed, they retire to distinct quarters of the yard, where they sit and wait for me to pop out of the house again. For my part, I pick up their nearly ultrasonic peeps at an amazing distance, and as I write twelve years later, I still react to ruby-throat fledgling calls as if poked by a cattle prod. My natural maternal instincts have proven to be as fluid and adaptable as the hummingbirds themselves.

July 30, 2003. Day 36. Bela eats at a small feeder on the patio. I keep it stocked with protein solution. Wild hummingbirds don't care for the brownish stuff, which is a very good thing, considering that there may be as many as 150 using the yard and gardens. Rufus and Joe continue to peep for me to come feed them. I'm working in the studio when I hear it, startlingly close. Rufus is perched on the chain of a hanging basket on the front porch, staring into the house and yelling through the screen door. Had the door been open, I feel sure he'd have come in and found me in the studio.

Rufus watches a storm coming

August 2, 2003. Day 39. This is the first full day I haven't hand-fed them. Well, I give them a little top-off at evening. Forty days is a long time to be dependent, but they're finally making their way. I've hidden little formula feeders around the yard where they can find them. I haven't mown the yard since releasing them, because I'm afraid I'll scare them away. Finally, I start up the rider mower. To my amazement, Joe and Bela fly right overhead, buzzing me, and perch unruffled at eye level as I roar by. They are all bird, bold and adaptable, resilient and resourceful. They form bonds to their caretaker. If these birds are anything to judge by, I believe the reference *Birds of North America* underestimates when it asserts that ruby-throats are fed only until Days 22 to 25. I will find out years later that avian rehabilitators who work with ruby-throats recommend release after Day 40. I feel a twinge of satisfaction at having pulled mine through that delicate post-fledging period outside, at large. Had I known about nylon fledging tents in 2003, I'd have had it much easier! But what fun I'd have missed.

August 6, 2003. Day 43. They're becoming wild birds. Rufus and Joe have turned skittish. But they're still attracted, still want to make some contact. We ate dinner outside, and Bela came down and prodded the bright orange Sungold tomatoes in my salad, a disarming thing if ever there were one.

Rufus sits quietly, high in the branches all day. Joe and Bella bully him relentlessly at the feeder, so he's still dependent on me as of 7/27. (Day 33)

August 8, 2003. Day 45. I was standing by the big humming-bird feeder on the front porch when Joe and Rufus flew up. Taking advantage of my presence, which frightened all the wild birds away, Joe chose a port inches from my face, and Rufus joined him. I smiled to see the two brothers treating me as a big harmless bodyguard, feeding in peace while I held back the crowd of competitors.

Bela takes
a rain bath,
inches from
my face.

Ruby-throated Hummingbird, 2003, 2008 〰 91

April 17, 2004 — I've never seen two adult male ruby-throats sit touching shoulders. Could it be Rufus and Joe? Same twig, same feeder... perfectly tame... 7 months and an ocean crossing later, they've come home.

August 13, 2003. Day 50. I see ruby gorget feathers coming in on the streaked throats of all three fledglings. Even Buzz, stuck in his tank, has them. All four are males. No wonder I had so much trouble with fighting in the aviary!

This was my last journal entry for my hummingbird summer. I will never forget how these minuscule birds turned my life upside down, and in doing so, taught me so much about how a hummingbird grows, learns, and thinks. With the remove of a dozen years, I know that I will likely never again experience such a thing: to be rewired and transformed into a mama hummingbird. They came to me at the right time, when I had two children, three and a half and seven, at home and needing my care as well. Being tied down to feeding the birds every half-hour wasn't as big a stretch as it would be now. I'd apologize to Phoebe and Liam for being distracted and drawn away, but having watched them tenderly caring for the feathered sprites, I think the tradeoff was a fair one. The birds were a gift, and a privilege to attend. I'd say that our bond ended that September when they vanished, pulled south on migration to Central America, but it didn't.

On April 17, 2004, Bill stepped out, coffee mug in hand, to listen to the morning chorus and take the sun. A male ruby-throat zoomed up, hovered briefly in front of his face, then poked his beak in between each of Bill's fingers. It was a hummingbird handshake, without doubt. Later that week, a second adult male ruby-throat appeared, and he shared a perch with the unnaturally tame male who'd approached Bill. I'd never seen two adult male ruby-throats share a perch in peace. Joe? Bela? Is that you? Wanting to test my hunch, I filled a small feeder with the brown maintenance solution the three had been raised on. Three male ruby-throats wove loops in and out of my arms as I hung it up, fighting to be the first to feed.

As I compiled the paintings for this book in 2015, I found many holes in the continuum, the biggest one in my hummingbird record. My painted journal of the hand-raised birds' development, done in 2003, started at Day 18. The chances of my finding a nest I could look into were practically nil. I knew I had to depict Days 1 to 17, but how? I took to the Web, and as fate would have it, the only photos of hummingbird development from that time had been made by one of my dearest friends. Yes, Nina's experience ended at Day 13 in tragedy, but my life studies picked up almost right where hers left off. Opportunities present themselves, and the wise naturalist grabs her chance, for such perfect circumstances for study may never align again. Serendipity is our muse and guiding force. Some part of Nina, I'm sure, still mourns that pair of hummingbirds, taken so young by jays; grieves over her journey of inquiry, cut short. Painting the hatchling birds from Nina's images seemed like a way to honor their brief lives, and bring some solace to my friend. Nina's work, worry, and heartbreak had not been for naught.

In this unrepeatable sequence of events, separated by years but all weaving together neatly at the end, I have to believe there was something more than chance at work. There was the curiosity of two like souls, the chance windstorm that brought me four homeless babies at once; the hand of fate, cruel and benevolent at once. There was instinct, goading me to keep my tiny charges thriving, to do whatever it took to launch them. There was instinct working, and luck too, that got three of them from Ohio to Central America and back to my front porch the next spring. There is wonder in all birds, but in hummingbirds there is magic.

Ruby-throat
in the Nepal
rose

Diderfore

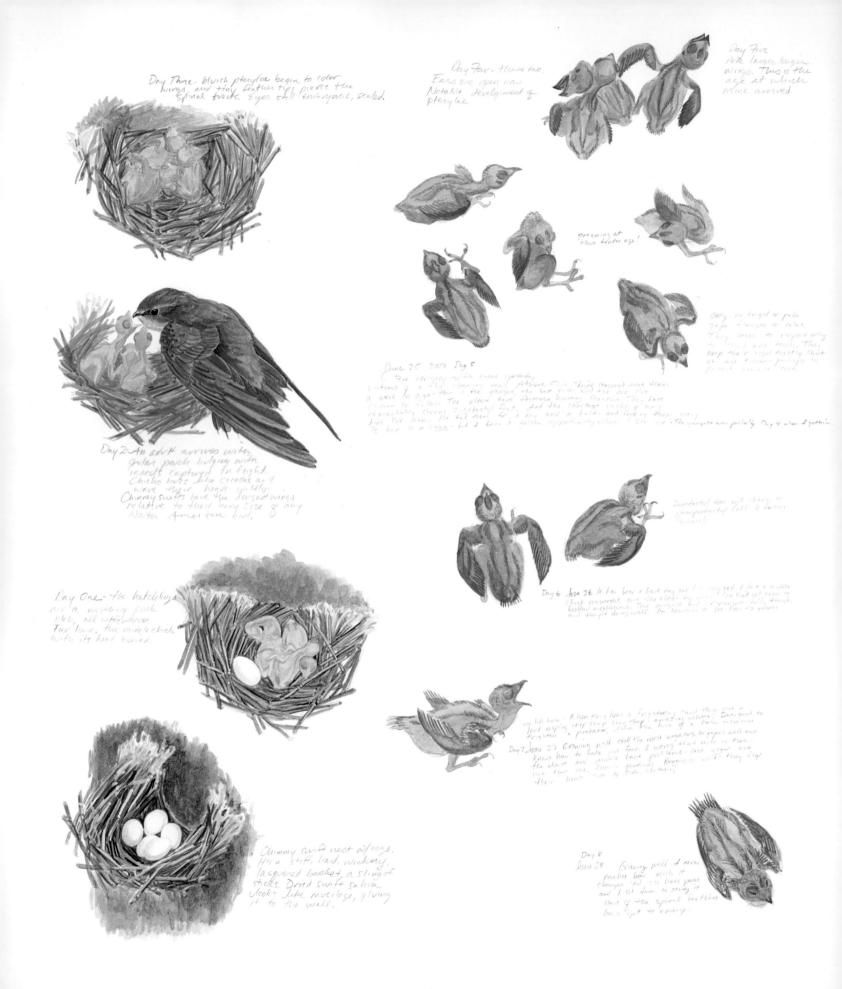

Day 2: An adult arrives with
gular pouch bulging with
insects captured in flight.
Chicks buzz like cicadas and
wave their heads wildly.
Chimney swifts have the largest wings
relative to their body size of any
North American bird.

The two chicks that survived clung to life, grew, and eventually thrived. Their eyes were sealed shut, and would be until Day 14. They responded only to sound and touch. I'd nudge them or blow on them, making a fluttering sound with my tongue, and their bills would fly open. Making a sizzling sound like a sewing machine, they'd drop their heads down and wave their open bills back and forth. I was forced to grasp each chick's head, turn it right-side up, and stuff it full of formula or insects. It was difficult, to say the least. I'd never seen a chick beg downward, much less had to feed one. As always, thinking hard about a bird's natural history held the answer.

A chimney swift's nest is a tiny basket of twigs, glued with saliva to the vertical chimney wall, and cantilevered outward. The chicks sit in it, their heads hanging down over the rim. When the adult enters the chimney, it dives in, doing a sort of controlled free fall, then it brakes and swoops upward to cling to the nest rim. This puts the adult bird below its young as it feeds them, hence the odd downward searching motion of the chicks' heads as they beg. This weird head motion persisted until they were old enough to cling vertically and climb, at which point I could pop a cricket into their upturned gapes with ease.

I was intrigued by the lack of pale gape flanges on the nestlings' bills. There seemed to be no visual cues in their appearance whatsoever, save a reddish gape lining. I reminded myself that chimneys are very dark places, and swifts likely locate their young by sound and touch rather than sight. Chimneys are also dirty, with a continual fallout of gritty soot. Why should a young chimney swift open its eyes before it's two weeks old? There's nothing much to see. It all made sense when I thought about it. The other thing that impressed me were the chicks' feet, which were incredibly strong from Day 5. If one latched onto my finger, it took both hands working in concert to peel the toes back one by one. Clinging well is the chicks' most basic adaptation, for falling equals death in a big chimney. Like bats, which I would begin working with years later, swifts cling as if their lives depend on it.

Day Three- bluish pterylae begin to color wings, and tiny feather tips pierce the spinal tracts. Eyes still embryonic, sealed.

Day Four - these two.
Ears are open now.
Notable development of
pterylae

Day Five
Note larger, longer
wings. This is the
age at which
mine arrived.

The swifts are completely naked, innocent of down. Like woodpeckers, it seems they will go directly from bare skin to pinfeathers to feathers. From time to time, even at Day 5, they preen at their flanks and wings, rearranging nonexistent feathers. I keep them as clean as I can given that they don't produce fecal sacs, instead just squirting poop randomly behind them, and often all over each other. I'm constantly swabbing them with cotton swabs, and I change their tissues every time they get soiled. I feed them every forty minutes, and it feels like all I do is feed them and clean up after them.

Theodore Roosevelt said that to truly know a man, you must share a tent with him. I find myself smiling wryly as I wipe swift bottoms, but this homely act leads to some more thought about why it might be that swifts don't produce fecal sacs. Most songbirds feed a chick, then wait for it to turn around and produce a bundle of feces, neatly contained in a membranous sac. The parent bears this off and drops it some distance away, keeping the nest clean and relatively odor-free. Swift droppings are something else again. Baby swifts hearing nature's call wiggle their rump, back up, cling tightly to the nest rim, and shoot liquid droppings as far out into space as they can, like young raptors. This makes them a special joy to care for, but it makes perfect sense in a chimney, where climbing predators are not an issue. Chimney swifts forage constantly in flight, and energetically, it's very expensive to make more trips to and from the nest than necessary. The parents visit the nest infrequently as a result, and fecal sac cleanup would be an unnecessary burden.

I think about how difficult it must be for an aerial creature like a swift to gather nesting material and construct a nest. Chimney swifts build tiny twig hammocks only

3¼ inches across and 1¼ inches deep. It takes them two to three weeks to complete a single nest, but it's understandable when you consider how they work. I've seen them fluttering among dead branches protruding from the leafy canopy of an oak, breaking off a twig with their feet, then transferring the twig from foot to bill in flight. Each twig is carried into the chimney in a single flight. The birds stack them from shortest to longest from the inside of the nest outward. Twigs averaging ½ inch in length are used for the inside base, then longer and stouter twigs up to 2 inches long are used for the outside wall. The birds glue these together with gooey saliva, which gives the

preening at this tender age!

Oddly, no bright or pale gape flanges or colors. They seem to respond only to sound and touch. They keep their eyes tightly shut at all times - perhaps to protect against soot.

June 25, 2004. Day 5
Five chimney swifts came yesterday, victims of a flue cleaning near Athens, Ohio. They're staggered more than a week in age - this is the youngest, the best eater, and the one I've chosen to follow. The elders have feathers bursting sheaths. They have remarkably strong zygodactyl feet. And the shortest necks of any bird I've seen. I've had them for a day and a half. and feeding them every ½ hour is a chore - but I know a golden opportunity when I see one. The youngest was probably Day 4 when I got him.

Zygodactyl toes will change to pamprodactyl (all 4 facing forward).

Day 6 June 26 It has been a hard day and I'm very sad. I lost a middle chick overnight, and the eldest by noon. I can't get them to swallow mealworms. This youngest and 2d youngest will, though, and they're doing well. I'm heartened to see this is young!!

completed nest a high, lacquerlike finish. As the chicks sit in the tiny basket, it's easy for them to shoot feces out over the rim, and any that land in the nest simply roll off this shiny surface. Holding a nest in my hand, I realize that everything about its small size, cantilevered design, and hard-surfaced material has to do with keeping the chicks clean and free of their own excrement. Raising them artificially, I use stacks of tissues and swabs to keep them as clean as they would stay in the wild.

Efficiency in their energy-intensive foraging is another swift hallmark. Swifts have a distensible throat area—the gular pouch—which they cram with small flying insects, making a large food bolus. They have a strong tongue that I've seen them use to clean out the corners of their mouth. The adults doubtless use their tongue to divide the food bolus among as many as seven babies in a single visit. If the swifts had to fly down the chimney for each and every insect they caught, they'd wear themselves out quickly.

crop full here - When they hear a frightening sound they give a loud rasping shep shep shep shep - amazing volume! Designed to frighten a predator, like the hiss of a baby titmouse.

Day 7 June 27 Growing well. Still the most vigorous. He gapes well and knows how to take his food. I worry about each in turn - not this one, frank goodness. The eldest and middle have problems - lack vigor. But begging is wild - they flap their heads side to side, chittering.

Day 8
June 28 Growing well — I never
realize how much It
changes 'til 24 hours pass
and I sit down to study it.
Most of the spinal feathers
have yet to emerge.

Just by being a foster mother, I'm figuring out a lot about swift biology, but I still worry that I'm not keeping up with this brood's needs. Feeling the stress of having lost three of the five, I wonder if all my effort will go to naught, and I become depressed. My journal entry from this day reads as follows:

I go to sleep thinking about them after the last feeding at 10:30 P.M., and wake up at 5:30 A.M. thinking about them. I can't go anywhere or do anything else. It reminds me most of having a newborn to care for. Who would think that raising baby swifts could be so stressful? The house looks like a tornado hit it and I can't summon the energy to pick up a toy. There are ten gazillion crunching underfoot. Bill asked his family over to dinner and I fell apart. We had to ask them to bring steaks and corn. There was no food in the house, because I hadn't been able to get to the grocery store, so I picked the snap beans and peas twice, then went out into the meadow and picked daylily buds and milkweed buds for a found-food stir fry. Otherwise we'd never have had enough food.

Transcribing my notes eleven years later, I laugh in disbelief, but it wasn't funny to me then. These are things I'm glad I've done, but I can't say I yearn to do them again.

Day 9. He stopped gaping
this morning — dehydrated. I've
been using electrolyte, which has too
much sugar. Back to water, better by
the afternoon. He's touch and go.
June 29 04

Day 10. A spurt of growth. He's doing really well. Primaries continue to emerge, and upper tail coverts are coming out.

June 30
Day 14-sibling. He has beautiful eyelids today, and he peeks out, then shuts his eyes.

I decide to jettison the lamp and keep the swifts instead in a small cooler with a jar of hot water for warmth. I give them pediatric electrolyte after each feeding. They perk up, and their droppings take on a better consistency in the warm, dark, humid environment. It's much closer to natural conditions than baking under a brilliant light bulb.

There appears to be a four-day span between the two remaining chicks. The bigger one is at Day 12 on June 28, and its tail feathers have emerged. The vane ends in a strong, needlelike spine that helps the bird prop itself vertically in chimneys. Unlike *Apus apus*, the common swift, which has pamprodactyl feet (all four digits facing forward),

This is the elder sibling (Day 12?) Couldn't resist. Tail is so stiff and spiny. Today both are able to take 4-5 mealworms at a single gulp - and have figured out how to grab them, making my life infinitely easier. I feed them every hour on the hour, and still keep them in a small cooler w/a jar of warm water, ca 80°. Eyes should open @ 14 days. First flight 20-30 days. Fed for 1 wk after first flight as @ chimney.

July 1. Day 11 and 15. I've added live Enclats to the diet and am keeping them well hydrated. The elder is flapping his wings a lot today. The younger opened one eye, briefly, when I washed his face.

chimney swift feet are anisodactyl, with three toes facing forward and one back. The hind toe can swing forward at will. When I change the tissues in their strawberry basket nest, I have to tease each toe out of the soiled tissues, toe by toe and foot by foot. Then I simply hang the birds on the front of my shirt, where they climb up and tickle my neck. They'd make a great conversation piece at luncheons and parties if it weren't for the splashy droppings that roll down my midriff.

Elder - Day 13. Lots of preening. His eyes opened on the evening of this day.

overwing scratcher

A 14-day-old chimney swift, last to leave the nest. Its eyes have just opened. Now it will crawl, climb and exercise its wings for another 14 days, until it's ready to leave the chimney for good.

The little hammock of a nest is shiny, lacquered with the adults' saliva—all that holds it together.

Painting these hand-raised birds is quite a different experience from taking wild nestlings out of the nest every twenty-four hours. Painting wild birds is like periodically seeing someone else's kids, and being immediately able to perceive how they've changed since you saw them last. It's a fresh surprise every day. But I can't perceive the change in these hand-raised birds until I compare yesterday's painting with today's—I'm with them constantly and the continual changes slip by me. I'm thrilled to see how they're growing, as evidenced by the paintings. The pure joy of painting them is definitely compromised by the worry and work of raising them. I have taken the deaths of the other three very hard. I think I got a little cocky, raising those four hummingbirds so well, if not easily. To have apparently healthy birds just up and stop eating is so upsetting. Not to mention losing my little models for such a once-in-a-lifetime opportunity . . . Oh, I hope these make it.

June 29, 2004. Days 9, 13. What a scary day. The little one stopped begging yesterday afternoon, while the big one just got more vigorous. About noon I called expert avian rehabilitator Astrid MacLeod to ask what to do. She said the first sign of dehydration is loss of appetite. It turns out that the pediatric electrolyte I'd been using to rehydrate them was actually robbing them of water because it's so high in sugar! She suggested giving them plain water (as I have no lactated Ringer's solution lying around) and said the ailing chick would probably perk up in a couple of hours. Just like clockwork he started gaping again. Now at nightfall the big one has fallen silent—still eating but not chittering or climbing around. It's a struggle to keep them hydrated. Astrid is into nutrition on the cellular level. It's scary how much she knows. I feel like such a bird rehabilitation piker when she speaks to me. It's very humbling. I don't have a gram scale or a microscope or any knowledge of chemistry or nutrition; I'm more a witch doctor. I'm glad there are Astrid MacLeods out there, worrying about elemental calcium and ion transport. Just tell me what to feed the things. I'll do my best.

The painting went well. Both were preening, so they can't be that badly off. The big one is all feathered except for its head, which has a thorny crown of pinfeathers. The little one is still plug-ugly at Day 9. The elder's eyes opened tonight at 10:30 P.M., on Day 13. Its eyelids are beautiful. It peeks out, then quickly shuts them again. It seemed surprised to see the tweezerful of mealworms coming at its mouth. It's only felt them before now. Imagine!

July 2, 2004. Days 12, 16. They've made a complete turnaround today. With the aggressive hydration, they're begging and the elder chick is chittering again. Thank

July 2 Day 12 and 16.

goodness. I'm amazed at how much water they need. I can gauge if they're getting enough if they are producing enough droppings, and I can look at the droppings to see if they're dehydrated. I want several droppings per hour, and I keep changing the paper toweling so I can keep track.

The younger had both eyes open and flapped its wings for the first time today, on Day 12. It's about as homely as it gets, while its fully feathered Day 16 sibling is suddenly lovely. They're twin apices of ugliness and beauty in one berry basket. I've moved them from the cooler to a basket as they no longer seem to need supplemental heat. I can watch them as I work. I was amazed to see the younger try to pick up a dropped

Day 13 July 3

Day 17 July 3
First grown-up chitter. His eyes are open except when asleep.

Day 14

July 4 Day 18
They're lethargic today—but better
by afternoon. They definitely
do better on an all insect
diet.

mealworm, something no twelve-day-old bird I've ever seen would do. This must be a presage of its aerial foraging, I think, which demands that it recognize food items and snap them out of the air immediately upon fledging.

I'm so enjoying painting them, because I can take my time. I spend an hour with them every afternoon. I feel no rush or compunction to return them to their nest. This *is* their nest. I can't help but think what a valuable scientific record this will be for anyone who studies the species. I believe so strongly in this project, and know now that it will be the work of a lifetime—as long as I'm messing with baby birds, I'm going to be painting them, too. I don't know what species fate will bring me, but I feel compelled to paint as many as I can.

Soon enough, I'll have to put up their screened enclosure, meant for keeping mosquitoes off picnic tables, but ideal for fledgling birds. It measures 15 × 17 feet, twice the minimum recommended area for a flight cage for chimney swifts. And it still won't be big enough, but it's the best I can do. It'll be the best $99.00 I've ever spent. I never could have built a bird-safe flight cage for that. It's soft nylon screening, so it

Day 15—This one joined
its sister by 8 pm, hanging
happily and exercising.

July 5 Day 19
This is Amelia.
Her name was clear
as she beat her wings.

Sasha - Day 16 - July 6
Eating better and flapping a lot -
Stimulated by the arrival of FIVE MORE
older chicks! I'm pretty stressed out!

can't hurt their feathers, and I can take it down and roll it up when it's not needed. I'll let the swifts fly around in it all day, and at night when they return to their artificial chimney (which I'll ask Bill to construct out of barn board), I'll bring them inside. I must, for the raccoons are just awful this year, getting into everything.

July 6, 2004. I got an influx of five more chimney swifts, a bit older (twenty-one days?) than my two, at noon. They'd fallen down a high and inaccessible flue on Saturday, and the homeowners had kept them alive for three days with small balls of raw hamburger, fed five times a day. Amazing. They looked great, having been parent-raised, but were underweight and a bit dehydrated when they came. The young girl who fed them had found that only two would gape readily; she made the others open their mouths by roaring at them! Chimney swifts have an instinctive reaction to loud noises that includes making an incredibly loud rasping noise, with wide-open gapes. *Reeaaaah! Reeeaaahh!* they shriek. I think of it as a predator defense; it's certainly unexpected and scary. When the birds rasped in fear with bills wide, she stuffed hamburger in their mouths. I have to hand it to her for her ingenuity. They were understandably very fearful when they came but have settled beautifully into a straw wastebasket with the two I've been raising, now called Sasha and Amelia.

For their part, my two hand-raised babies seem thrilled to be with other swifts, and they all huddle in a soft charcoal cluster. On July 6, I started feeding all seven chicks a bug omelet as their staple. They like it fine. I scramble up an egg, finely crush an eggshell and add it back in, and put 2 tablespoons of dried daphnia, bloodworms, or other insects into it. Then I fry it up—it smells nauseating and looks worse, a gray mess with stray insect legs sticking out of it. But the swifts eat it with gusto, and it's no

July 7
Amelia - Day 21 -
She fluttered from her "chimney" and clung to the outside. Nothing gets past her now - her eyes constantly search the sky.

Sasha Day 17 - finally looking like a bird. Energized by the new 5 swifts - both are eating well and alert. They are tame, and the new ones are settling down beautifully. They're very tactile creatures and must be in contact to be at ease.

trick at all to feed a nickel-size gob to each one and be done with it for the next hour.

At Bill's suggestion I color-coded each of the new birds with a dab of acrylic paint on its forehead. Because I now have seven to keep track of, and a babel of ear-splitting rasping and head waving ensues when I take the towel off the strawberry basket, it's essential to mark them to be sure each gets fed. I wind up calling them Pink, Green, Red, Blue, and White.

July 8
Sasha - Day 18 - It's hard to believe this is the same bird in the first paintings. Amelia would not sit for her portrait today. She flew to my chest and clung there - very endearing. Sasha is watching me draw his picture here, head moving with each movement of the pencil.

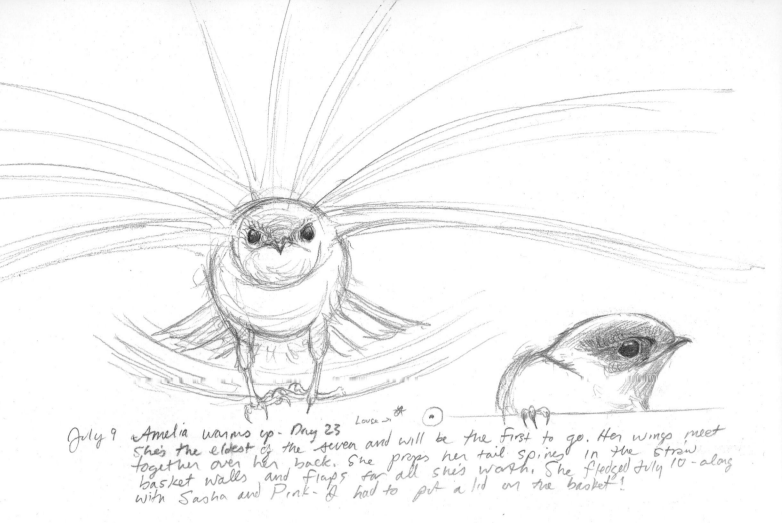

July 9 Amelia warms up - Day 23 Louse → ☿ ⊙ She's the eldest of the seven and will be the first to go. Her wings meet together over her back. She props her tail spines in the straw basket walls and flaps for all she's worth. She fledged July 10 - along with Sasha and Pink - & had to put a lid on the basket!

July 8, 2004. It's fledging day (Day 22) for Amelia. Well, it's hard to say exactly when she fledged. Chimney swifts leave the nest, barely feathered, around Day 14 and clamber/flutter on chimney walls for another week. For several days Amelia's been climbing to the top of the basket and fluttering her wings madly. Now she's impossible to contain in the basket and refuses to sit for her portrait, fluttering to my chest and clinging there. Once she flutters down and manages to land and cling to my smooth calf, so sharp are her nails and strong are her toes. Ouch! So I paint one more portrait of Sasha, who's eighteen days old and finally free of sheaths on his head and body. He's beautiful. He watches every stroke of the pencil, with minute turns of his snakelike head. But for the shape of his eyes I'd never know it was Sasha. These are the two babies I've hand-raised since Day 5. The bug omelet seems to agree with them well. I've been feeding lots of live mealworms today, too. It's great to have all seven clamor for food and gobble it down. That's how it ought to be.

July 10, 2004. Sasha, the younger of the two hand-raised babies, fledged today, around Day 20. I knew it only because when I went to feed them there were only six open mouths. Liam, playing in the living room, calls out. "Mommy! There's a bird in the chimney!" Brought into our home naked and blind at perhaps five days of age, Sasha knows a chimney when he sees one. He's attracted to the stone fireplace, and knows enough to fly up into the flue. I'm glad I keep the damper closed as, marveling at the power of instinct, I reach up to peel Sasha off the sooty stone.

July 11, 2004. Day 21 (Sasha), Day 25 (Amelia). It's Phoebe's eighth birthday. In between baking a pink cake and wrapping presents, we put up the nylon fledging tent and Bill constructed a "chimney" of rough boards, about 4 feet high, which we stood up in the middle of the tent. It was a joyful moment when we released these birds into the comparative freedom of the big tent. They stayed in their basket, then started making little flights in the evening. By dark they had forsaken the straw basket for the artificial chimney. I peeked inside and was met with seven pairs of eyes sparkling at me from a mass of sooty brown feathers.

July 14, 2004. Days 24, 28. The swifts flew wildly last night, careening around their soft net tent and obviously enjoying themselves. And they flew again this morning—it was such a show! They land atop one another and squabble and chase each other. Who would think swifts would be so playful? We enter the tent by unzipping it as we edge our bodies inside, and immediately zip the flap securely when we're in. Amelia is a little stinker—she'll land on my thigh as I zip myself inside, trying her best to get out. She reminds me of some housecats I've seen. They've become such strong fliers I'm sure we'd never see them again if they got out. As soon as we're inside, the swifts land on

Looking down on
three swifts sleeping
Red and Willa have each
thrown a wing
over yellow.

our shirtfronts, shoulders, and heads, stopping for a little chuck under the chin and a kiss and are off again. It's really something to be festooned in clinging swifts. Of course Phoebe adores this, and so do I. We're looking forward to this evening's flight. When they tire, they all drop into the big wooden chimney Bill hammered together for them and sleep. Only then will they eat—they can't be bothered with crickets when there's flying to do.

They're eating probably less than half what they did before they started flying. The Birds of North America species account says they lose as much as 3 grams just before fledging, and since they're all now refusing food I am trying not to be too worried. Sooner or later they eat. Amelia, who flew first, went through the anorexia first, worrying me almost to death. She's at Day 28 now and is eating better. I feel strongly that they want to catch their own food, but I must wait to release them until their flight feathers are completely out of sheath and they are flying with ultimate control and strength.

July 19, 2004. Days 29, 33. There was something in the birds' eyes this afternoon that made me realize that they *had* to go today. By the Birds of North America account, they're supposed to leave between Days 28 and 30. The account further states that adults stop feeding the young after that first flight. It seemed so abrupt, so draconian to me. Since I couldn't sprout wings and feed them in flight, I caught all seven and brought them into the house to stuff them with calcium-dusted crickets once more. I fed them again in the car before carrying their little straw wastebasket out on the Harmar Village trestle in Marietta, Ohio. Bill, Phoebe, and Liam came along, Phoebe already weeping quietly at the prospect of releasing her funny, frenetic companions.

We had to take the birds into town to release them, because swifts need old stacks and chimneys for nesting and roosting. Marietta is swift heaven, sitting as it does on the confluence of the Ohio and Muskingum Rivers, full of old buildings with uncapped chimneys. The sky turned from cerulean to peach, and chimney swifts were swirling in great numbers high overhead. It was a perfect night for release, as there had been a caddis fly hatch that day. The evening sky high above was seething insect soup. I asked Phoebe to uncover the basket. Pink leapt without hesitation into space, flying like a fluttery bullet high out over the Muskingum. Red, Blue, Green, and White followed.

I smiled to see Sasha and even Amelia, once my boldest adventurer, crouched in the bottom of the basket, their flat heads making rapid arcs as they traced birds flying high overhead. As each baby fledged, a squadron of wild swifts broke rank and swept it up into the flock. My mouth fell open as I watched our hand-raised swifts dive, circle, swoop, and cut side to side, reveling in their new freedom. They even set their wings and tried gliding, like children on new birthday bicycles. Finally Amelia and then Sasha could resist the call of the sky no longer. By then we could hardly make them out for tears.

No one spoke on the ride home. It was dark by then, and the streetlights along the Muskingum made lit balls of swirling caddis flies. I sighed happily, knowing I'd done everything a person could to launch seven healthy swifts into life. I thought about the work, the worry, their recurring anorexia, the fake chimney we'd had to construct, the tens of thousands of mealworms and crickets, and the sloppy formula setting up like cement on the countertops. And I thought about my kids, in on the whole adventure, living what it meant to be a mother to seven swifts. Phoebe was still sniffling quietly. She was happy and sad at the same time. She'd always known we were raising them for release, but she would miss feeding them; it was she who'd come up with the innovation of turning the cricket forceps upside down, to better fit the angle of their mouths. A small voice came from the back seat. "Will those birds be okay in the night?" asked four-year-old Liam. Certainly, they had both learned much about compassion and caring for smaller beings.

I told Liam and Phoebe that the same flock that swooped down to take our babies in had certainly shown them to some huge stack for the night, where they could sleep amidst hundreds of new friends. They'd all make the flight to South America together, too. We had had a rare peek into the lives of some of the world's most fascinating birds, and without us none of them would have even lived. They were launched now, and they'd be fine with the Marietta flock to show them around. That seemed to satisfy him, and we drove the rest of the way home in companionable silence. Phoebe and Liam didn't know it, but in their compassion and caring for the seven swifts, they'd impressed me deeply. On the railroad bridge this evening, I had decided it was time to get them a puppy, a creature they could love without apprehension or reservation, and never have to let go.

Day 6 June 30
10:55 AM – 11:20 am Get a load of this pose,
hanging onto its own right wing. I can't believe
its eyes are opening at Day 6. Lots of fat deposits.
A few mites and a louse-fly looking thing, tiny and
black, thats two bugs and crawls all ※
over it. The sparrow added a green macaw feather
to the nest today. I love this continuing decoratiness.

9:50 – 10:15 AM Day 7 July 1 2006. About a broken! The size discrepancy
in the brood is becoming more marked each day. Two
of the 4 have primordia ½" long on the wings, and are
big, and blue with blood feathers. They are about Day 5.
This chick won't settle until I cup my hand around it.
It has a lot of mites and a louse, which runs all over
its body.

June 29
Day 5 12:05 pm – 12:20 pm Nice growth today – and fat deposits all
around the tail forming. I find it interesting how little
primordia the right primary – not big blueberries sticking
out, but almost flush w/ the skull. skull is closed, and
w/the neck, surging forward. Light infestation of mites today

From Day 1 these birds
have voided in a long tubular fecal form – no sacs!
What's with that? Peculiar to Ploceidae?

10:30 – 10:45am June 28 Day 4. The 5th
egg has been removed, probably having been
judged infertile. This birds photo reminds
me a bit of EARwigs – translucent
bag of guts, just getting bigger every day.
It's a strong little thing.

12:30 – 1:20pm Day 8 July 2 06. A leaky bag of guts it defecates constantly.
clambers and crawls all over my palm, inconsolable away from its
broodmates. Only at last it settles down I draw these. Entering the sensory-
overload stage, when there's too much to take in. There's definitely someone
there today behind those flat black eyes.

12:20 pm – 12:38 pm June 27 Day 3. It
clambers aggressively up my fingers,
trying to be into the pile. 4 have hatched
now. There's still an egg, it'll be interesting to
see if it still hatches, 3 or 4 days gone the 1st.
It smells dry, like hay and carbon paper. No down at all.

12:45 pm – 1:05 pm June 26 Day 2. Such a
transparent bag of guts! I can see red
liver, yellow fat deposits, blue stomach.
It eats two syt white mealworms.
It gets cold very easily and I must keep
it pressed against my cheek, breathing
on it, or it gets pallid and still. The first
hint of purplish on wings + spine. 3 hatched, 2 eggs

2:38 – 3:20 pm Day 9 July 3 06. The fear response has set in,
making this baby crouch quietly, eyes shut, hoping not
to be noticed. It certainly makes for a better model,
although I miss its lively clambering pose. All pins
are bursting sheaths today. Crawling with mites. Bird says
avg fledging age is 14 days but may boot if disturbed at 10!

5:08 – 5:40 pm June 25 2006 Hatching Day
House Sparrow Passer domesticus
so naked, so blind. This is going
to be interesting.

House Sparrow, 2006

Mites and a
blowfly larva

12:43 – 1:20 Day 10 July 4 '06
The birdlet holds stock still the entire time. It shrilled in protest when I
picked it out, though – a sign of fledging readiness. It knows what it doesn't
like. I like these paintings. Tomorrow it will be a different bird.

Day 11 July 5
1:15 pm – 1:55 pm. The big change
is occurring. I can see his crown
and back stripes. Wingbars too.
Today, it finally voids something
resembling a fecal sac. Mites
are crawling EVERYWHERE
Tomorrow may be our last day.
The adult gave an alarm
call for the first time today
which could cause them to
leave. Is fledging truly occurs
at Day 14. Day 12 will be
pushing it.

pink-red grape

Such a riot of color,
texture and life is
crammed into the house
sparrow's little wooden
box. Signature seed heads
and yellow straw curve
up the back, arching
over a nest cup lined
with plant down.
Feathers of cardinal,
flicker, downy wood-
pecker, broad-winged
hawk and chestnut-
fronted macaw (Charlie)
punctuate the jumble.
Mourning dove, too.
And a bit of blue
yarn. And so much
more. The
adults add to
it every day.

Day 12 July 6
The last day. He chirped
and was pretty nervous, then sat
stock-still for an hour while these
were done. I'll miss these birds but
not their myriad parasites!

Day 13 July 7 2006. I'm amazed how much sleeker and
more self-possessed this bird is today. It reacts with fear to
every stimulus. Now it's really farewell. I'll miss you!

House Sparrow, 2006

"THE CHILD IS the father of the man." Three times during the thirteen years of work on this project, a child's clear logic has trumped my prejudice, making me aware of an opportunity right in front of my face. Having tended nest boxes for eastern bluebirds, tree swallows, and chickadees since 1982, I'd developed a kind of tunnel vision. The only birds worth hosting in my boxes, I believed, were the ones for which they'd been built. When house wrens and house sparrows attempted to claim a box, I'd quickly clean out their nesting materials to discourage these competitors and make room for more desirable tenants. House wrens are native songbirds, but they can be incredibly destructive, piercing eggs and throwing out other birds' young. More than that, males will stuff all available boxes full of twigs, rendering them uninhabitable. It was these "dummy nests" that I removed. House sparrows are even more destructive, able to overpower and kill eastern bluebirds, tree swallows, and chickadees in their quest to take over nest boxes. They're persistent and sneaky, and nearly impossible to shoot, for they seem to have an instinctive fear of firearms, however well concealed.

House sparrows need little introduction for anyone who's ever filled a bird feeder or tried to establish a bluebird nest box trail. These tough little brown birds, imported from England to New York City in 1852, purportedly to control wireworms, found nourishment in the form of undigested grains in the droppings of horses, then the primary mode of transport in America. And wherever there are animals being fed or fast food being dropped, house sparrows flourish to this day, widely distributed through both urban and agricultural areas worldwide. They invaded Iceland and Rishiri Island, Japan, in 1990, and are still spreading: the world's most widely distributed wild bird.

This stocky, solid little Old World sparrow is, with the Eurasian tree sparrow, the only *Passer* species to have become established in the New World. There's almost nothing house sparrows won't eat; sputzies flying with huge pieces of white bread in their bills were a common sight in my suburban Richmond, Virginia, neighborhood when I was growing up. They take a variety of insects; I recall seeing one in flying pursuit of a frantic Chinese mantis, almost as big as the sparrow. And I've seen them in parking lots from Arizona to Pennsylvania, hopping methodically along the fronts of cars and trucks, scavenging freshly killed insects from their grilles. Plucky and inventive, house

Adult
feeds a recently
fledged (ca
Day 20) House
Sparrow in the
Rose of Sharon
"Satin Blue"

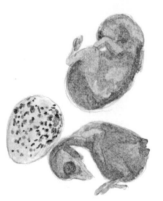

5:38 - 5:50 pm June 25 2006 Hatching Day
House Sparrow Passer domesticus.
So naked, so blunt-billed. This is going
to be interesting.

sparrows dog human heels wherever they occur, scavenging spilled grain at elevators and chicken yards; sorting through the litter at fast-food establishments, a habit that has earned them the derisive label "Burger Kinglet."

I might be forgiven, then, for neglecting the house sparrow in my quest to document the development of native birds in my nest boxes. I threw their trashy nest materials out as soon as they appeared in my nest boxes. But spring being what it is, with both songbirds and me migrating to far-flung places, one house sparrow nest got away from me. Two greenish, brown-speckled eggs had already been laid on June 12, 2006, when I discovered the nest in a little-used box on my clothesline support pole. The nest was a multitextured work of art, with mourning dove, cardinal, broad-winged hawk, and a host of other feathers woven into the straw, rootlet, and grass cascade running up the inside back of the box.

I expressed my regret at having to throw it out to my daughter, Phoebe, then a wise nine-year-old. "Why don't you let them hatch, then paint the babies?" she asked. I stood, mouth agape, unable to come up with a counterargument. I mulled it over, muttering to myself, then came to Phoebe that afternoon to thank her for her insight, and the opportunity to paint a new species, right under my nose. I mentioned in the Introduction that this child asked me the same question two other times, urging me to paint the starlings that took over our martin gourds, and the house wrens that pierced the pipping bluebird eggs in one of my nest boxes. As that wise child helped me see, birds are birds, and they are all fascinating, exotic and invasive or native.

I pull a blind, pink, nearly transparent hatchling and one unhatched egg from the riotous mass of feathers and straw and begin my journey. I fall at once in an artist's infatuation with its roly-poly, stub-limbed form, and know I'm in for a good ride in painting it.

When I go on Day 2 to retrieve a chick, the male house sparrow is brooding the young. I'd always known the male as the head-pecking invader, primary executioner of incubating female bluebirds, so seeing him hunkered down warming his young is disarming. He flies out of the box, and I borrow a nestling. Today I can see its red liver, yellow fat deposits, and bluish stomach through its skin. I feed it two soft white mealworms. It gets cold and inactive very quickly, even going pale, so I keep it cupped in my left hand and pressed to my cheek while I'm painting with my right. It quickly pinks back up.

Phoebe keeps asking me why I don't like house sparrows. She is obviously already smitten with this little pink blob, looking forward to tracking its development. I explain again that house sparrows kill bluebirds, tree swallows, and their chicks in the most brutal ways, and once we're done with this project, we'll go back to our zero tolerance policy. There are mobs of house sparrows at the feeders: two males and eight females and associated young. They take over quickly when you let them nest. They're said to spread at a rate of up to 140 miles per year when introduced to a new area. I don't doubt that for a moment. They're very, very good at breeding and dispersing.

June 27, 2006. Day 3. I'm amazed to find the eggs hatching sequentially, with the fourth of five eggs hatching two days later than the first. This doesn't happen in other passerine nests with which I'm familiar. I work with the first-hatched chick, and at only three days of age, it's clambering around constantly, even climbing atop my finger, using its stubby bladelike wing buds and legs. Such a strong little thing! It's got such a strange head, its blunt bill giving it a reptilian look. It's staying resolutely naked, too, unrelieved by any down at all. It's a delight to paint. I can see its whole structure.

12:45 pm - 1:05 pm June 26 Day 2. Such a transparent bag of guts! I can see its red liver, yellow fat deposits, blue stomach. It eats two soft white mealworms. It gets cold very easily and I must keep it pressed against my cheek, breathing on it, or it gets pallid and still. The first hint of pterylae on wings & spine. 3 hatched; 2 eggs.

12:20 pm - 12:38 pm June 27 Day 3. It clambers aggressively up my fingers, trying to be atop the pile. 4 have hatched now. There's still one egg. It'll be interesting to see if it still hatches, 3 or 4 days after the 1st. It smells dry, like hay and carbon paper. No down at all.

June 28, 2006. Day 4. The development of this bird reminds me of the eastern bluebird: a translucent bag of guts that seems simply to get larger each day, without notable changes in feather development in the first week. Feathers, in fact, are taking their time coming in, which helps explain why the male house sparrow is sitting on his babies every time I open the box, whatever the weather. I'm impressed at his commitment. I always knew house sparrows were interesting birds, and I'm enjoying learning a bit about their home life. I worry that going forward I won't be able to kick them out of my boxes, having witnessed such dedication in the male. I discard the thought, remembering that the first bluebird I find pecked to death on her eggs will harden my heart.

June 29, 2006. Day 5. The chick has grown considerably, and the first fat deposits are forming around its tail. The baby's eyes are curiously recessed in its head—not the great bulging blueberries I see on most songbird nestlings. It reminds me of a starling—all yellow gape flanges, the low-profile eyes still sealed shut. It's very active, leading with surging movements of its neck, scooting around its blanket of tissues. From Day 1, these sparrows have voided feces in a long, tubular dropping; there are no neat round fecal sacs. I wonder at a reference in the literature to fecal sacs. Has anyone actually looked at the nestlings' droppings? They are not sacs. They're a mess.

10:30 - 10:45 am June 28 Day 4. The 5th egg has been removed, probably having been judged infertile. This bird's path reminds me a bit of EABluebirds.— translucent bag of guts, just getting bigger every day. It's a strong little thing.

June 29
Day 5 12:05 pm – 12:20 pm Nice growth today — and fat deposits all
around the tail forming. I find it interesting how little
prominence the eyes assume — not big blueberries sticking
out, but almost flush w/ the skull. Still climbs, leading
w/ the neck, surging forward. Light infestation of mites today

June 30, 2006. Day 6. Today when I opened the nest box, I saw that the sparrows had added a green feather from my macaw, Charlie, which gave me a broad grin; they may be the only sparrows in the county with a Peruvian parrot's feather in their nest. They must have found it near where I burn Charlie's cage papers. My nestling's eyes are open! More fat deposits, more mites, up from the smattering yesterday, and a strange fast-crawling insect that looks like a wingless fly. It crawls all over the nestling as if it's looking for something. Blue feather quills are finally breaking through the skin and poking out of the small tail nub known as the pygostyle. I thought it would never start feathering out. The baby is fidgety and nervous, and it grabs its own wing with its foot and hangs on tight. I'm charmed, but I manage a quick sketch of it, and paint it in that awkward pose. It says something I can't put in words about this bird's tenacity. If there's nothing to climb on, I'll climb myself.

Day 6 June 30
10:55 AM – 11:20 am. Get a load of this pose,
hanging onto its own right wing. I can't believe
its eyes are opening at Day 6. Lots of fat deposits.
A few mites and a "louse-fly" looking thing, tiny and
black, thats this big(•) and crawls all
over it. The sparrow added a green macaw feather
to the nest today. I love the continuing decoratress.

Such a riot of color,
texture and life is
crammed into the house
sparrow's little wooden
box. Signature seed heads
and yellow straw curve
up the back, arching
over a nest cup soft
with plant dawn.
Feathers of cardinal,
flicker, downy wood-
pecker, broad-winged
hawk and chestnut-
fronted macaw (Charlie)
punctuate the jumble.
Mourning dove, too.
And a bit of blue
yarn. And doubtless
much more. The
adults add to
it every day.

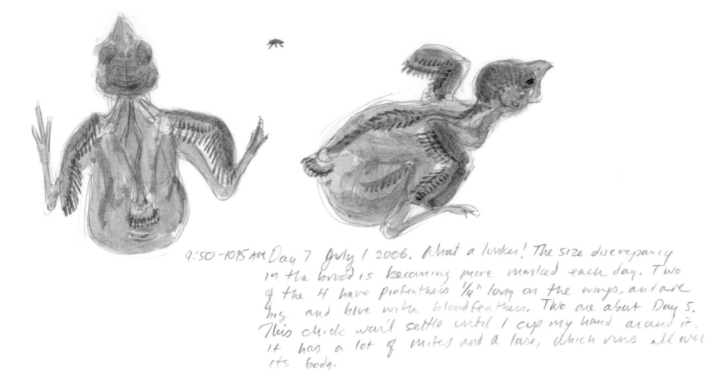

9:50-1:05 AM Day 7 July 1 2006. What a lunker! The size discrepancy in the brood is becoming more marked each day. Two of the 4 have pinfeathers 1/4" long on the wings, and are big and blue with blood feathers. Two are about Day 5. This chick won't settle until I cup my hand around it. It has a lot of mites and a lose, which runs all over its body.

July 1, 2006. Day 7. What a lunker! This is the day the size discrepancy in the rapidly growing chicks hits me hard. The two smaller birds are at Day 5 developmentally, while the two larger have ¼-inch-long pinfeathers on the wings, and are finally sprouting blood feathers all down their back and flanks. My subject won't settle down until I cup my hand around it: the most restless chicks I've dealt with (that is, until I meet house wrens).

12:30-1:20 pm Day 8 July 2 06 A leaky bag of guts. It defecates constantly, clambers and crawls all over my palm, inconsolable away from its broodmates. When at last it settles down I draw these. Entering the sensory-overload stage, when there's too much to take in. There's definitely someone there today behind those flat black eyes.

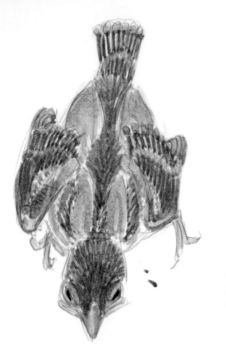

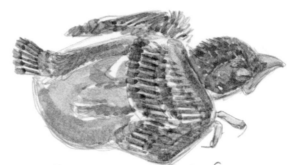

2:38 - 3:20 pm Day 9 July 3 '06. The fear response has set in, making this baby crouch quietly, eyes shut, hoping not to be noticed. It certainly makes for a better model, although I miss the lively clambering poses. All pins are bursting sheaths today. Crawling with mites. BNA says avg fledging age is 14 days but may boot if disturbed at 10!

July 2, 2006. Day 8. I get the feeling that the chick is almost done growing from a weight and size standpoint. I don't see how much bigger and fatter it can get and still be a house sparrow. It will not settle down today, and defecating constantly, it clambers and crawls all over my left hand as I struggle to sketch it with my right. It's a leaky bag of guts, inconsolable away from its nestmates. When it finally settles down I draw two studies. There's so much going on all over its body. Greatly lengthened wing feather sheaths are popping open to show brown paintbrush tips of the feathers to be. I am at sensory overload, struggling to record every detail, even as the birdlet festoons me with feces. There's definitely someone there today behind those flat black eyes.

July 3, 2006. Day 9. The fear response has finally set in, and the baby crouches quietly, its eyes screwed shut, in hopes of escaping my notice. It peeks at me and raises its head for the first time; backs away when I move my hand toward it; cowers lower when I peer at it. It's thinking: the first step in the fledging process. It's reacting appropriately to stimuli, obviously making a connection between what I do and what it should do in response. Finally it sits perfectly still for its portrait. It makes a much better model this way, although I miss the lively clambering poses it struck yesterday, before its dire situation became clear in its mind. It's crawling with mites, but healthy and still strong, so I won't intervene. The reference *Birds of North America* warns that house sparrows fledge around Day 14 but may leave prematurely if disturbed on Day 10.

July 4, 2006. Day 10. The baby shrilled in protest when I carefully picked it out of the jumble of warm skin and pinfeathers—a warning sign of premature fledging. Eek! Everyone stayed put despite its call to action, so I quietly withdrew with my model and

Mites and a
blowfly larva

12:43 – 1:20 Day 10 July 4 '06. It shrilled in protest when I
The birdlet holds stock still the entire time. It shrilled in protest when I
picked it at, though – a sign of fledging readiness. It knows what it doesn't
like. I like these paintings. Tomorrow it will be a different bird.

bore it to the studio. Mites and a blowfly larva drop off the bird as it sits stock-still on my drawing board. This little thing is infested. I haven't seen many nests that had both mites and blowflies. The mites probably come in on the feathers, sourced from myriad locations, with which house sparrows adorn their nests. Blowflies likely track the adult birds' movements and home in on the nest by smell and sight. The capital (head) and spinal tracts are bursting the sheaths, and the bird looks slightly less reptilian today. Tomorrow it will be unrecognizable, but nicely so.

July 5, 2006. Day 11. For the first time, an adult sparrow gives its low, urgent *jiv jiv* alarm call when I go to the box. I'm delighted to see the birdlet almost entirely clothed in feathers today. Cream-colored wingbars and back stripes and a rusty crown stripe have emerged—it got its field marks today! For the first time, it voids something resembling a fecal sac. I still can't figure out why these birds don't make proper fecal sacs. Is it something lacking in the *Passer* genetic

Day 11 July 5
1:15 pm – 1:55 pm. The big change
is occurring. I can see his crown
and back stripes. Wingbars too.
Today, it finally voids something
resembling a fecal sac. Mites
are crawling EVERYWHERE.
Tomorrow may be an last day.
The adult gave an alarm
call for the first time today
which calls cause them to
leave. If fledging truly occurs
@ Day 14. Day 12 will be
pushing it.

pink-red gape

makeup? I've no other members of this Old World genus to compare it with, so it will remain a mystery for now. Mites are crawling everywhere—up my wrists and arms, headed right for my eyebrows. I don't know why they end up there, but it's very annoying. I can't imagine having to sit in a nest seething with them.

July 6, 2006. Day 12. The nestling cheeped when I took it out of the box, then sat stock-still for an hour while I painted. It's crawling with even more mites and blowflies, but I feel lucky to have this audience so close to its natural fledge day. Yellow gape flanges are still obvious, signaling its youth, but otherwise the bird looks quite mature, with a lengthening tail and snappy wingbars and back stripes.

July 7, 2006. Day 13. When the time came around to paint, I couldn't resist at least peeking in the box, though I knew I was risking causing an explosion of babies. The next thing I knew, I was taking a chick, which struggled and flapped a little, then settled down nicely for the session. I got away with it, and am so glad I did! I can't get over the change from the ruffled little nestling of yesterday to the sleek almost-fledgling of today. It tracks every move I make with its eyes and slight turns of its head. It's hyperaware of where I am at all times. Today, it's truly time to say goodbye, and I slip the chick back into its nest and creep away.

Day 12 July 6
The last day. He cheeped and was pretty nervous, then sat stock-still for an hour while these were done. I'll miss these birds but not their myriad parasites!

I have to smile at myself, being ever so careful not to disturb the nesting of a pair of pestiferous house sparrows. I have to confess that I gained a whole new respect for the species in the process of painting it. I remind myself that birders in Britain, where the house sparrow is both native and on the "red list" of drastically declining species, are deeply concerned about a 66 percent decline in its numbers between 1994 and 2001, one mirrored from Dublin to Moscow. Causes are not clear; loss of insect prey base; changes in insect, grain, and weed seed availability due to intensive agriculture; even electromagnetic waves from cell-phone towers have been suggested as impairing the hatch rate of sparrow eggs. The lesson? To take no bird for granted, no matter how abundant.

Working with them, I got a palpable sense of intelligence from the chicks, with their scrappy, proactive, lemme-outta-here behavior. Clean, they're not; I'm impressed at the volume and variety of parasites that inhabit their nest. But they are survivors, and I find that out in the coming months as, encouraged by their nesting success, the house sparrows bring friends to my yard until there are a few dozen of them haunting the feeders and forsythia and squirting out of the blue spruces and Russian prune hedge when I walk by. From here on out, I'll be hauling out nesting material as soon as it appears in my nest boxes, but it will take a couple of years before the infestation is contained. Give them an inch, and they'll take a mile, in best house sparrow style.

Day 13 July 7 2006. I'm amazed how much sleeker and more self-possessed this bird is today. It reacts with fear to every stimulus. Now it's really farewell. I'll miss you!

12:35 pm - 1:15 pm   Day 7 June 2 2006
At my first time stage lookup like phoebes to me...

4:25 pm - 4:45 pm Day 9 June 4 2006
Eyes are open! There's so much going on here...

12:30 - 1 pm Day 3 or 4
May 30 2006 What a funny little thing! This bird probably hatched May 27...

Day 10 2:30-3pm June 5 '06
Finally feathering out - though I'm struck by how far behind a same-age CAWR it is! It finally warmed up today. Its breast is yellow and silky feathered out...

Day 3 It's impossible to discern individuals in this bare & gray fuzz that covers the chicks...
Just an egg.

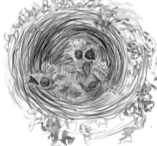

Day 2 Larger stronger still pillow. This is just a hint of the nest cup & its size.

2:05 - 2:50 pm Day 11 June 6 '06...

A let 8 mites...
I got them off...
A haze of gray down!

7 AM - 7:35 AM June 27 2005 Day 1 or 2 Eastern Phoebe.
There is one other sibling and an unhatched egg.
These eggs (a clutch of 5) were laid the week of June 6. They'd be second brood for the phoebes, who fledged 5 young on the...
It's unexpectedly yellow! and its tiny day-old eyes are straining to take in the details. Amazingly long bill.
A strong cheep, just like its parents. This chick was found the next day.
Massive infestation of chicken mites...

Eastern Phoebe, 2006

Eastern Phoebe, 2006

I<small>T WAS AN</small> eastern phoebe that told us, back in the summer of 1992, that we should buy this southeast Ohio house where I sit, twenty-three years later, looking out at now-mature plantings, at swarms of finches around the feeders. Looking back up at us through deck flooring on the day we first saw the house, a female phoebe stolidly sat on her eggs. I wanted to make our nest here, too. I wanted to buy this place. I straightened up from my crouch, smiled at Bill, and said, "If that's not a sign, I don't know what is." For phoebes had always been among

my favorite birds, and a nesting phoebe seemed like an extravagant blessing, a green light from the Universe to make the biggest purchase of our lives. Four years later, we would settle on Phoebe as the perfect name for our first child, a red-headed elf, now grown into a kind, lovely young woman who, like her namesake, is a gift.

Since I'd started this project in 2002 with eastern bluebird and Carolina wren as my first subjects, I had wanted to paint young phoebes. Aside from its iconic status in my life, I knew that eastern phoebe was one of only two possible choices of flycatcher for me. Great crested flycatchers are rare nesters around here, and though they will use nest boxes, which would make them accessible to me, none had yet shown interest in ours. If I could somehow make sure a phoebe's nest was safe from climbing ratsnakes, I could easily skitter up a stepladder under the deck, collect a chick, and paint it each day. I was overjoyed to find a pair starting a late nest under the deck in June 2005. Incubation went well despite rainy weather, and when I saw the adults flying back and forth with food, I knew my work could begin. I climbed the stepladder and teased a new hatchling out of the nest. I'd never seen a yellow hatchling, nor one with such a long bill. Perhaps the oddest thing about it, though, was its voice—a sweet *chip* that sounded exactly like an adult phoebe's call.

I was used to songbird nestlings that sounded like nestlings, with thin peeps. I'd never heard anything like this strong *chip* note coming from a tiny yellow blob of protoplasm, only hours out of the egg. Reading Donald Kroodsma's groundbreaking book *The Singing Life of Birds*, I learned that New World tyrant flycatchers like the eastern phoebe hatch with the species' characteristic song already encoded in their brains. Raised in isolation, with no opportunity to hear another phoebe sing, an eastern phoebe will still sing its species-specific songs, in a characteristic sequence, flawlessly. Apparently, call notes are included in that innate code.

The tiny yellow bird rolled around on its tissue, chipping, as I painted. I saw tiny red specks moving about on it, clustered in its ears. Chicken mites! This debilitating parasite comes in on the feathers with which phoebes like to line their nests. Such an infestation can quickly kill nestlings. I cleaned the chick as best I could with a toothpick and cotton swab and returned it to its nest. Because I felt I had already disturbed the phoebes enough for one day, I hatched a plan for tomorrow. I'd remove the babies and place them in a tissue-lined container, and remove the mud and moss nest with a spatula for a flash heating session in the microwave. I'd station my aptly named human Phoebe, eight, on the ladder to keep the parent birds from returning and finding their nest and chicks suddenly gone. While she stood guard and kept the chicks warm, I'd heat the nest through, killing all the mites, put it in the freezer to cool it back down, then replace the chicks and nest on the shelf. I should be able to do the entire maneuver in less than ten minutes. I was sure I could rid the nest of mites without using harmful pesticides or causing desertion by the adults.

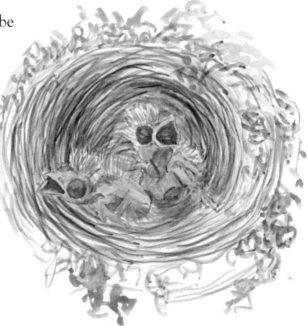

A lot of mites
in its ears.
I got them out
but fear for it.
A haze of grey down!

7AM–7:25AM June 27 2005 Day 1 or 2 Eastern Phoebe.
There is one other sibling and an unhatched egg.
These eggs (a clutch of 5) were laid the week
of June 6. They're the second brood of the gutter
phoebes, who fledged 5 young on the
It's unexpectedly yellow! and so tiny my poor old eyes
are straining to take in its details. Amazingly long bill.
A strong cheep, just like its parents! This chick was dead the next day.
Massive infestation of chicken mites. Bummer.

I gathered Phoebe and all the necessary gear, climbed the ladder, and reached into the nest to find the chicks cold to the touch, dead in only one day. Mites swarmed up my hand and arm. It was a disappointing end to a wonderful notion. The big sheet of watercolor paper went back into the flat file, with two tiny yellow chicks in the lower left corner.

Spring 2006 was cold and rainy. A pair of phoebes showed up in April and fussed around, examining all the platforms, shelves, nooks, and ledges around our house. In the end, they settled on a little plastic relay box, just as the first pair had. I returned from a festival in West Virginia on May 30, 2006, to find their eggs had hatched, and the chicks were already four days old. I hoped the mites were gone. I rolled a chick out of the nest and examined it—clean as a whistle. Whew!

I'd have to fill in by guessing at the age of chicks in photos scrounged online for Days 2 and 3.

This is tricky, especially when chicks in a phoebe nest are almost completely obscured by a halo of soft gray down that sprouts from their heads and backs. I did my best, making informed guesses. Day 2 chicks were still a startling coral yellow, but by Day 3 a pinkish gray hue had crept in.

Day 2 Larger, stronger,
still yellow. This is just
a detail of the nest cup,
life-size.

Day 3. It's impossible to discern individuals in the haze of grey down that covers the chicks — & that's needed by such ugly nestlings. There are 5, but I'll paint 1 from here on out.

I decided to paint a nest of five, if only to show what an interwoven mass of flesh and fuzz I was faced with. Until I tease a chick out of the tangle, I have no idea which parts belong to which individuals. I wound up drawing what I suspected was there under all that down, then painting down over the top of it, obscuring everything.

What funny little birds. Now on Day 4, they were covered with long grayish yellow down, long-billed and strange looking. The down was amazingly thick, but phoebes are open-cup nesters and early nesters to boot. More than that, they often nest under dank, cold rock ledges, bridges, and even caves, so their chicks had better be coated with down. Down tracts lined even the abdomen, something I'd not seen before. This would likely be the only flycatcher I'd ever have my hands on, and I was enjoying it thoroughly. I marveled at their weak legs and feet, so different from the strong grasping appendages of chickadees and titmice.

12:30 – 1 pm Day 3 or 4 May 30 2006. What a funny little thing! This bird probably hatched May 27. Amazing amount of down but its an open-cup nester, fond of caves and dank bridges. Bill quite wide at base. Legs and feet small and weak, esp. compared to a chickadee. I'm not used to seeing abdominal tracts of down. No mites!

Day 5 saw darker skin and even thicker down, with dark pterylae beginning to show along the spine and wings where feathers would soon emerge. The first pinfeathers were beginning to emerge along the thigh. Today, an adult phoebe dove twice, almost striking my hand as I selected a chick. I'm glad to see them so invested in their young.

June 1, 2006. Day 6. The bird's skin continues to darken, and wing feathers are emerging as pointed sheaths. It's become apparent that the phoebe's development will trace an arc something like that of a bluebird's. Like a young bluebird, the phoebe is growing in size, but no dramatic wing development has taken place as it did in tree swallows, chimney swifts, or Carolina wrens. The bird seems in no hurry to get to the point of flying.

June 2, 2006. Day 7. For the first time, the birds are beginning to look like phoebes to me. The head structure is more defined, and the bill has developed a raised culmen along with the somewhat flattened profile characteristic of flycatchers. Wing quills are lengthening, and the aspect is more bird now than lizard. I have a devil of a time discerning what's happening under the fine fuzz of down on this dark, rainy day.

June 3, 2006. Day 8. The chicks remind me of neat little packages yet to be opened. Their quills lie in orderly rows on back, wings, and sides. They're compact, not yet rangy, all curled around each other in the nest cup. Thick down makes a haze over them. Their eyes are still sealed shut. When I reach in to get one, I have to wiggle my finger deep into the warm mass of flesh and tease it out. I hate to disturb them. I wonder if they sleep a lot before their eyes open, and what it must be like to have one's

eyelids separate and let the world in for the first time. We are born seeing. They live for eight days behind sealed lids, listening, feeling, but unable to look.

June 4, 2006. Day 9. The eyes are open. There's so much happening on the bird's little body, I can paint only one study. All feathers are poking paintbrush tips out the end of the sheaths. The baby cocks its tiny spike tail when it's alarmed. I wonder when it will begin to wag that tail.

June 5, 2006. Day 10. The rather protracted nestling stage of these flycatchers is in sharp contrast to the Carolina wren, which would be fully feathered by now. The phoebes' eyes have been open for only a day, and their back and wings are cloaked in

5-6 pm Day 12 June 10 2006 (see above)
Avis (R) and Luther (L)—my hand-
raised babies from Winsett Run

halfway up its length was all that the big   snake needed to give it a
hitch the rest of the way up. I stared at   the contraption, wondering
how I could have been so stupid, how I could have overlooked that fatal flaw. Last year
I must have put it up correctly, because the nest fledged successfully. And last year I
wasn't painting these birds.

These weren't just any phoebes; they were my models. Sadly, I slipped the unfinished
sheet into the flat file, and wondered when I'd be able to follow a phoebe nest through
to fledging. The phone rang the next afternoon. The caller described tearing down an
outbuilding and finding a mossy nest atop a small relay box. Not twenty minutes later,
she pulled up in my driveway, the nest and its two ten-day-old chicks in a small box.
Phoebe chicks. They were weak and cold, having gone without food for eighteen hours.
I warmed them and force-fed them a bug omelet. Each one voided an enormous fecal
sac. Guts were still working; we were on our way. I ordered 5,000 mealworms and 1,000
crickets, gathered my syringes, ground kitten chow and vitamins, and girded myself for
the long haul of being a mother phoebe for the next few weeks, with feedings every
half-hour from dawn to dark.

In more than thirty years of avian rehabilitation, these two are the only eastern
phoebes that have ever come in. That they arrived on the very next day, at almost the
same age as the ones I'd just lost, felt like nothing other than divine intervention, a
cosmic nod to this odd and solitary pursuit. Someone or something, watching. Kandy,
the caller, said, "You're not gonna believe this, but I looked in the phone book under

1:05 - 2:20 pm Day 13 June 11 2006
Doing very well on cricket, mealworms
& egg food. All feathered now, just a
few sheaths. They usually take only
one insect per feeding. I warm them
first thing in the morning with the
hot water bottle, but they're
regulating pretty well now

Avis

Luther

'bird' and didn't find anything. So I just figured there ought to be an 800 number. I dialed 1-800-WILDLIFE and got somebody who gave me your number."

Assisted only by common sense, she'd figured out the toll-free number for the Ohio Wildlife Center in Columbus, which has me on its list as the only songbird rehabilitator in my county, two hours away.

Phoebe, nine, names the birds Luther and Avis, guessing at their sex. I concur, though I can't say why. It's a great luxury to be able to handle and paint birds that were they in the wild, wouldn't be safe to handle. I'd have had to stop painting the deck brood at around Day 12. I quickly sketch and paint the

Luther

Tail bob!

Avis

7:45 - 8:30 pm Day 14 June 12 '06
There was something going on with Luther
today - rapid breathing & anorexia. I gave him a
drop a Zithromax at about 4 pm and he felt
much better by 6 pm. They're bobbing their tails
today! Slowly and uncertainly. They're fledgy, too,
watching everything around them. I'm keeping them
well hydrated. They are not avis gapers, that's for
sure! I'd normally stop handling them today - but I
get to stay with them because I'm raising
them!

birds as they crawl around the top of my drawing table, flapping unwieldy wings laden with blood-filled quills. Soft olive brown feathers are emerging all along back, wings, and head, and cinnamon brown wingbars already show.

June 11, 2006. Day 13. We've settled into a routine. I warm them with a hot-water bottle first thing in the morning, then feed them a bug omelet, crickets, and mealworms. Thermoregulation has kicked in now that they're fully feathered, so I dispense with the hot-water bottle by Day 14.

June 12, 2006. Day 14. Even now, they are not avid feeders, and I often have to open their bills to get the first bit of food into them. They're a bit of a worry to me. They seem healthy enough. I sense that there's some signal they're looking for and not getting from me. I try a number of different phoebe-like whistles and chips, but they know I'm not their parent and remain suspicious. When they're hungry, they vocalize with the *chip* note that's an exact replica of an adult's alarm call.

The chicks are fledgy and nervous. I'm so happy to be able to paint them past the danger date in the studio. I wouldn't get away with taking them from a nest at this stage—they'd fledge prematurely and there would be phoebes hopping all over the ground. They finally have tails, in a manner of speaking, and on Day 14 they begin to bob them, another behavior hard-wired into their brains. Why phoebes bob their tail is anyone's guess; perhaps it's a signal to other phoebes, discernible at great distances in an otherwise olive-drab bird, that proclaims their identity. It's tempting to think that everything a bird does has some function, and fun to wonder why something that seems

10 – 11:20 pm Day 15. They're
standing, preening, stretching,
flapping – it won't be long now!
Such tiny feet and legs, such
heavy heads. Only the bases
of the flight feathers are
still sheathed – perhaps 1/3"

Avis

Luther

3:4 pm Day 16 June 14 2006.
Fledging time is very near. They're
refusing food, and their fecal sacs
are formless. They still void when fed
but also in between. A new call note
—a dry chiddick! and increased alertness.
I guess I'd better set up the screened
tent tomorrow.

Avis

Luther

like nothing more than a nervous twitch might be coded in their DNA. Every chick I study is a frail little bag of guts and why.

June 13, 2006. Day 15. I get overwhelmed by the work of young children and summer, and leave my painting until after we get home from Phoebe's softball game. I start working around 10:00 P.M. Of course, there's no light, and I can't see what I'm doing. I squint and cuss and finally get a passable but hardly brilliant painting out of the hour-and-twenty-minute session. I'm impressed by how tiny the birds' feet and legs look relative to the bulk of their heads and bodies. They're standing up, preening, stretching and flapping their wings now, but they'd still be in the nest, as they've shown no inclination to jump or fly. Only the bases of the flight feathers, perhaps a third of an inch, are still in the sheath. It's been my experience that, with the exception of indigo buntings and smaller sparrows, which fledge between Days 8 and 10, most songbirds don't leave the nest before their flight feathers are completely out of the sheaths.

June 14, 2006. Day 16. The big day is coming. It's going to happen tomorrow. I can feel it. The babies are fully feathered, restless, alert. They're preening and rearranging their feathers like crazy. They're giving a new call—a dry *chiddick!* They're no longer voiding fecal sacs: a sure sign of readiness to fledge. Their droppings are loose, small, and frequent. And most important, they're refusing food. Just like the chimney swifts before they fledged, they're trying to lose their baby fat before they fly. This is so cool. Thank goodness, they're still in their Tupperware bowl, swaddled in Kleenex. I decide

Avis (back) and Luther, Day 17.

to paint them in the nest they were brought in, and they settle in happily to its familiar confines. But I think I will be setting up the fledging tent tomorrow. I'm very glad I have a tent to put them in. What a mess they'd be, flying around the house.

June 15, 2006. Day 17. They've done it—fledged. Both have jumped from their Tupperware "nest," Avis in the morning, Luther in the afternoon. They refuse to gape, and must be fed by having their mouths pried open. I can't escape the feeling that this apparent anorexia is tied to some stimulus they need but aren't getting from me. And I suspect it may be auditory. This inflexibility that makes them so hard to feed has something to do with their hard-wired species-specific vocalizations, mentioned above. I wonder if they need to hear a real phoebe giving some kind of feeding call to be stimulated to gape. You need to blow on young chimney swifts to trigger gaping—it imitates the rush of air from their parents' wings in the dark chimney. After eight days of acting as their mother, I still haven't cracked the phoebes' code. I'm a slave to their needs, always wondering if I'm doing the right thing.

The family pitches in to help me erect the 15 × 17 foot nylon fledging tent in the side yard. The soft screening won't harm the birds' feathers. It's too flimsy to resist the teeth and claws of raccoons, though, so I must bring the birds into the house each night to sleep in a pet carrier. Because I know coons well, I leave the tent wide open, to let them come and go as they please, so they don't feel the need to rip their way in.

June 16, 2006. Day 18. Released into the tent, Avis flies strongly back and forth, clinging to the mesh walls. Luther is more circumspect, sitting on the ash branches I've provided, waiting to be fed. The anorexia continues. I have to pry their little bills open to give them crickets and mealworms, with a dropper of water to keep them from getting dehydrated. I'm praying that once they really start flying, this weight-reducing behavior (which doubtless makes perfect evolutionary sense) will cease. It's clear to me that there's nothing wrong with them; they're bright and healthy and active, preening and flying. They just aren't interested in food, at least not from me. It will be another ten days before they're able to catch their own food. I'm in the hoosegow until June 26.

Luther

Avis

June 15 2006
Day 17- fledging day? Both have jumped from their
"nest." Avis in the morning; Luther in the afternoon.
They won't gape, and must be fed by prying open
their mouths. I can't escape the feeling that there's
something I'm not providing - a stimulus to gape.
As such, they're a little more work to feed than
others. They preen, stretch, and flap constantly.

Luther shows Avis
how it's done, beating
a cricket into
submission. June 20, 2006
They're 22 days old, and
this is a first. .

If I'll be gone more than a couple of hours, I have to pack them into a pet carrier and take them and their mealworms and crickets along. If I go to a softball game, I have to bring the birds with me. The same goes for the grocery store, the bank, and the pool. No matter what I'm doing, I have to shuttle them along with me, as there's no leaving them in the car in June. And I must stop every hour or so and cram crickets down two birds' throats. It takes a kind of dedication, planning, and constant preoccupation that's not everyone's cup of tea. I have to admit, lugging two recalcitrant teenaged phoebes around makes me a special kind of cranky.

June 18, 2006. Day 20. It is hot as Hades. The phoebes spent the entire day in the flight tent. A new call emerged: a cricketlike *chiddiddit*. I'd swear it was a black field cricket if I didn't see them making it. Finally, after four days of force feeding, they're gaping for me again. In desperation, I had started syringe-feeding them a loose, watery mixture of ground kitten chow with spirulina, and they made a turnaround. I think they were running lean and dry, and in being dehydrated, lost their appetites. It made an immediate difference in them to be rehydrated.

June 20, 2006. Day 22. Today the phoebes started to process their food, beating crickets against the perch. They get better at it every day. They aren't able to knock the legs off them yet, but they will get there. It's amazing to watch a creature that's lived only three weeks figure out how to crush the life out of another organism, understanding that bashing its head works best.

June 22, 2006. Day 24. The phoebes are growing, flying, learning new things every day. We have a routine: I take them out to their fledging tent at dawn, feed them every hour until dusk, and bring them back inside, locked in a pet carrier, for the night. I put them in a dark stairwell so they won't flutter and fuss too much. After the freedom of the tent, they hate to be locked in the tote. But raccoons and black ratsnakes are ever vigilant. I looked out just in time to see a coon peering into the tent yesterday afternoon. Now that they're flying so well, there's little chance a raccoon could catch one, but after all this work I'd hate to lose them now.

Little things tell me their brains and neural connections are maturing. When a baby bird grabs a moth from forceps without having it stuffed down its throat, that's progress. It's a mental leap from being fed to feeding itself. Moths prove irresistible to these birds. They already know what they like.

Today Luther, the smaller, sweeter one, whirled out, grabbed a housefly off the tent wall, brought it back to the perch, and released it. Well, he's getting the idea, anyway!

Luther nails a moth in flight
June 22, 2006 – Day 24

My heart sang. Later that day, I watched open-mouthed as he launched, grabbed a little white miller off the tent wall, returned to his perch, and masticated and swallowed it. I can see the light at the end of the tunnel. They're acting like phoebes. They sit on high perches, bobbing their tails, sally out after nothing in particular or perhaps to peck at a moth, then return to the perch. They're flycatchers at last.

We've got maybe another week of this hourly feeding, until that magic day when they fly down and take crickets out of a dish. There are few things I've looked forward to so much. I did my huge weekly grocery shop at 5:30 A.M. today, so I would get back in time to put the phoebes in their tent for the 7:30 feeding. Grocery stores are weird places at dawn. I'm a weird person when I have baby birds to raise. I dream of the day that they're finally feeding themselves. I'll go out to dinner. I'll go for a bike ride. Maybe I'll see a movie. Or just climb in the car and drive.

June 26, 2006. Day 28. The birds are feeding themselves at long last. I left a lamp burning in the tent all night and a bunch of moths and gnats had gathered when I brought the birds in. Avis immediately spun up and grabbed a lightning bug, returned to a perch, and released it. They're toxic, so that was good to see. Luther grabbed a white moth and ate it. Today they seem offended by the forceps, even when loaded with cricket or mealworm. There's no force-feeding them now; I couldn't catch them if I wanted to. I have dishes of mealworms all over the tent, and today Phoebe finally saw Avis fly down to a jar lid and gobble down a mealworm. We high-fived and cheered.

I know they're eating them, because the supplies are dwindling, and they refuse to be fed now. They prefer moths and flies, though, and woe be the moth that tries to navigate across the tented airspace. It is immediately snapped up. Release day is almost here. This is the first day I haven't fed them every hour. I've fed them three times since dawn; it's 1:30. And the kids and I are going into town this afternoon and evening, and when we return, it is going to feel wonderful to drive up and see the birds there, fine and fed. I've been so pleased with how well they're progressing. It's been steady and natural. They crossed the threshold of grabbing a worm from the forceps instead of gaping at about Day 23. Then they progressed to picking it up off our open palms at Day 25. That's mostly how we fed them on Days 26 and 27. Gaping is becoming a thing of the past, though they still talk to me when I approach the tent. They're wild, quick, flighty, and uppity, and that's just how I want them.

June 27, 2006. Day 29. It's time. They don't want anything to do with me. I put a light in their tent all night, and in the morning it's full of crane flies and moths, gnats, and mosquitoes. And that's what they want. I tickle their bills with mealworms and they seem taken aback. "Why would I want that?" they seem to ask, then flash away on agile wings. They land, tails bobbing, looking at me balefully. Go away. We're feeding ourselves now.

I watch from the kitchen window as they whirl up after all the flying insects. One dips down and grabs a mealworm from the Pyrex pie plate, takes it back to the perch, bashes it, and eats it. They pile into a shallow bowl and bathe, preen, shake their feathers, and bathe again. Yes, it's time. They're twenty-nine days old. Their parents would have quit feeding them by now. They seem too proud to beg even when I know they're hungry. Their tails are almost full-length; their gape corners shrunken and almost gone. The soft phoebe *chip* has largely replaced the cricketlike begging calls.

It rains and rains. I hate to let them out when it's pouring. So I hold them, hoping for a break in the weather, some sign that it's okay to open the flaps. I admit to myself that I'm hanging on to them. I think I'm going to draw and paint them some more. I try to find the time to do that. I have to take the kids to a dental appointment; I have to do the grocery shopping; there's a book the library is threatening to make me pay for that I must find and return. The vacuum cleaner is broken, our closet shelves have fallen down with all the clothes piled on them. My car needs an oil change. A hummingbird plate is due in four days. The kids fight incessantly. I try to ignore them. If I broke up every fight that's all I'd do all day long. They'll work it out, I guess. It's lunchtime. They're hungry, that's why they fight. There's band practice tonight and tomorrow, a gig Saturday. We're so rusty; there's been no time to play music. I have to dream up dinner. I want to take more pictures of the birds. There's no light; it rains all the time. And so my days piddle away and the phoebes grow and whirl and hit the sides of the tent. It's time. I have to let them go. And so I unzip the tent this afternoon, rain be damned.

June 28, 2006. Day 30. The morning after release is always a cliffhanger. My charges have spent their first night outside with the raccoons and owls and weather. I was greatly relieved to find both phoebes at hand. Luther landed on my hand and gobbled down a good breakfast of mealworms. Avis flew closer but wouldn't eat. Uh-oh. I watched her closely that morning, and found her growing increasingly lethargic. I could approach her, but couldn't get her to take food. At noon I found her back in the fledging tent, so I zipped it closed. Luther sat just outside on a branch, as close as he could get to Avis. I let him in to keep her company.

I couldn't believe that here I was having to force-feed Avis again. Capturing her and prying her bill open after her hard-won independence just seemed so wrong. How could she have come this far and then fail? Her feathers got fouled with food. I had to wash and blow-dry her. As she continued to decline, I brought her in the house and started her on a broad-spectrum antibiotic, figuring it was better than watching her die. For his part, Luther continued to thrive, so I let him back out to make his way in the world. I left the tent open so he could return for food and water, and he took me up on the offer.

On his thirty-first day, I woke to the sound of a phoebe singing in a lilac just outside the bedroom window. Three times Luther sang, a hurried, high-pitched, slightly thin attempt. Phoebe had guessed his sex correctly! Better than that, he began to investigate all the eaves and awnings, instinctively drawn to the places he would choose to nest next spring. He ranged farther and farther afield, but kept coming back to the tent to feed. I smiled every time I caught him inside, making his way in the world, but still working the system.

I force-fed and medicated Avis for three days. On July 1, she seemed well enough to be taken back out to the fledging tent. She'd begun self-feeding, and was looking brighter each day. I emerged from the house with the pet carrier, Avis inside. When Luther saw the carrier he chipped excitedly and hovered in front of it, chittering and scolding. I released Avis into the tent and Luther hurled himself against its nylon sides, trying to get in. I was moved by his devotion to his sibling, and opened a flap to admit him. The two birds spent the day gorging on mealworms and sitting pressed together. Avis ate and bathed and preened. The next morning Luther was clearly bored, and asked to be let out. I opened the tent flap for him, but Avis stayed put until midafternoon. She left briefly, then returned around 6:00 P.M. to feed. I was delighted. Maybe she was out of the woods at last.

July 4 was a happy day, as I watched the pair come and go, feeding in their tent, then foraging in the yard. At dusk Luther tucked himself into a lilac by the house foundation. Avis couldn't settle; she was fluttering from tree to tree in the half-light, when she should have already gone to roost. It was raining again. She was wet to the skin, disheveled. I couldn't get her to come to me. Who could blame her? She likely knew there would be a blow-drying in her future. I was worried for my little truant, and I had a bad feeling of foreboding, as if I knew this would be the last time I'd see her.

July 5 dawned. I hurried out at first light to look for the phoebes. Luther flitted up to me, warm and dry as toast, but Avis never appeared. Carrying a bowl of mealworms, I mounted a search of the yard and surrounding woods, anxiously checking the ground for a pile of gray-brown feathers, but found nothing. I knew these birds well enough to know something must have happened to Avis in the night. All the dithering with formula and antibiotics, all the worry and intervention had been for naught. A bird has to be functioning at 100 percent to make it in the wild, and Avis simply never got there.

Luther hung around until the afternoon of July 9. I last fed him at 4:00 P.M. His eyes were bright, his wings were quick; his tail bobbed sassily. He had It, whatever it is that makes an avian rehabilitator sure that this one will make it. Vigor, star quality, the spark of life, barely contained in a bundle of olive-drab feathers. He didn't reappear until the morning of July 11, Phoebe's tenth birthday. She went out on the stoop with a palm full of mealworms and stood beaming as he gripped her fingers with his wiry black toes. He juggled a mealworm, dropped it, and swooped down to catch it before it hit the ground. Phoebe's eyes met mine. This bird would make it. Instinct would send him south for the winter, and instinct might just guide him back, but we knew our work was done.

Though I always hope to see my wild orphans again, I never have the temerity to expect it. So when a phoebe showed up in the yard on March 13, 2007, on Luther's favorite low-hanging ash branch, my brow furrowed. Could it be? I walked toward him, something that would make any wild phoebe retreat. He bobbed his tail and flew a few feet closer to me. From there, he flew to the birch by the birdbath, another of Luther's favorite perches from last summer. If ever there were a generic-looking bird, the phoebe is it. But there was something special in this one's eye. Call it star quality.

Phoebes, pondering.

H has no fecal matter visible when I start
the session - 25 min. and 7 mealworms
later, it's got a bolus eyed up & ready to void.
Imagine passing food this fast!
One eye slits open when I call to it
and it gapes. Day 7.

2:00 - 3:10 pm
May 11 - Day 6. A big change is now
boisterous. Look at those spiky flight
feathers! Everything's more defined - he's
looking less blobby, more anyone.
6 mealworms eaten. He doesn't peep,
but his bill gaps open when he hears
my voice. Very pleasant and calm to work with.
The tiny siblings still peeping and gobbling mealworms.

3:30 pm - 3:48 pm   Day 7
May 12. ate 7 mealworms. His pin feathers - lower 50%
still bloody. I carry the chick pressed against
my warm belly on the way from the box.
The cutie thing that seems to have grown is
its feathery girth - they're fuzzier on top. I fed
the smallest, and took a 1st bill & meal-back at
the box ring. Its feet have grown and strengthened.

3:15 - 4:00 pm

Day 5 May 10. Already preening. More pterylae on
head - two on either side of the central
tract. He was very quiet until I sneezed,
then said, "Excuse me!" in a very small
voice, whereupon he popped up with gaping
bill - style. Have said with a chickadee
to him. He took two slide-probed mealworms.
Most impressive is the variety of foot and
leg muscle development. Note wing pins too.

Day 4. May 9. More down on head and
shoulders; more fat laid down over
the pygostyle. 12 noon - 12:45

This is the larger sibling of the chick in the
three studies below. I have been slipping the
runt a few extra tender mealworms when I
replace the model chick each day. I
want them all to thrive.

Day 3   May 8 '06

Day 2. Impossibly tiny, but peeping lustily. They each ate
a mealworm, diced into bits. This one hatched later,
I think, but is determined to catch up to the
rest. It begs constantly. It has to!
May 8 '06
11:04 am - 11:57   I always wonder: How is this folded to fit in
that tiny shell: poison? The gray on either
side of its gape is its eyes, seen through the roof of
its mouth! Eeck!

The softest of
nests - a Carolina
Chickadee's.
Goldenrod fiber, rabbit
hair, green mosses and
the fluff of milkweed and
dogbane - the seven eggs gleaming
in the deep tunnel of softness. I've never
found parasites in a chickadee nest.

Carolina Chickadee, 2006

Day 8
May 13 1:20 - 1:50 pm It can sit on its tarsometatarsi
today and holds itself obliquely upright. It's
very restless. I imagine it's hungry after two cold
days, so I fed it five mealworms, and it produces
a nice fecal sac. Pectoral and flank tracts are bursting
sheathes. Its legs and feet are a bewitching lilac.

Day 9 May 14 6:45 pm - ?
Pouring rain. 54° I saw soaked through
just walking out. But the chicks are
warm and the female's been on them.
I see the black eye coming and today

Day 10 May 15 5:57 - 6:49 pm - a big
change. It's really looking like a
chickadee. It's sitting up and looking
around. I wish I could say it's easier to
paint but it's incredibly hard to tell
what's going on under all these quills
and fluff. Today, I paint the stunted
chick, who is also 10 days old but
mysteriously and profoundly retarded in
its development. For whoever developed
like a 7 day old chick, but its body is
the size of a 5 day old. I wonder and
worry what will happen to it when the
other two are ready to fly.

Day 10 - Stunted chick
No spinal or crural tract
showing. And yet the feathers
are bursting sheathes on the wings

1:25 - 3:48 pm Day 12 May 17. The two
chicks' gape flanges are almost gone, while
the stunted chick's are still prominent. Normal chick
is bigger and alert, almost flighty. It breaks
its tail and now shows spots, as in the
upper 60%. I will probably have to stop
painting tomorrow.

1:04 - 1:42 pm
Day 11 - May 16 Becoming a big bird. This is
really fun now. I like to watch it sit up,
and notice its increased eye. It's grown 5% legs
but it won't down mealworms. I put in six
inches of the morsel. It still smells of
butterscotch.

Carolina Chickadee, 2006

SPRING IS ALWAYS a time of both elation and frustration for me. Everything seems to happen at once, as if all the birds checked their watches and laid their eggs simultaneously. And that's my busiest work time, too; I speak and lead field trips at bird-watching festivals all over the country, and they all seem to fall when the birding is best at home. I had done the math, and knew that a clutch of six Carolina chickadee eggs was due to hatch on Saturday, May 6, 2006, while I was working at the New River Birding & Nature Festival near Fayetteville, West Virginia. When I returned late Sunday, I knew I'd have to get with it the next morning in order to catch as much of their lives as possible.

A chickadee nest is impossibly soft, beautifully composed of layers of dry green moss, plant fibers, inner bark, and nameless vegetal fuzz, with an inner lining of soft animal hair. This pillowy creation may stack 7 or more inches high, with a sort of tunnel leading down to the nest cup. The best part is the blanket the female chickadee weaves, which she pulls over her eggs when she goes out to feed. For years, I'd check my nest boxes and find no eggs, only

The softest of nests- a Carolina chickadee's. Goldenrod fiber, rabbit hair, green mosses and the fluff of milkweed and dogbane - the seven eggs gleaming in the deep tunnel of softness. I've never found parasites in a chickadee nest.

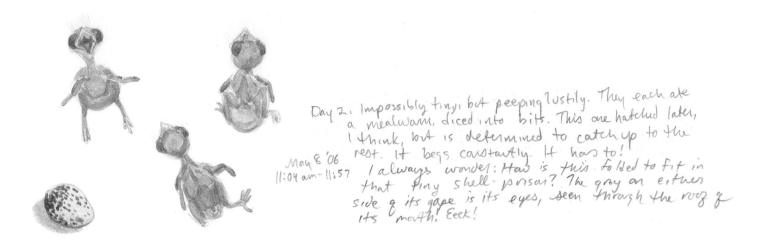

Day 2. Impossibly tiny, but peeping lustily. They each ate a mealworm, diced into bits. This one hatched later, I think, but is determined to catch up to the rest. It begs constantly. It has to! I always wonder: How is this folded to fit in that tiny shell-prison? The gray on either side of its gape is its eyes, seen through the roof of its mouth! Eeek!

May 8 '06
11:04 am - 11:57

to see a complete clutch of six in the same box when I'd surprise a female and get her off her nest. I learned to pull back the warm fuzzy coverlet to count the eggs, then replace it. How the female makes a retractable blanket with only her bill and feet, I can't imagine.

The tiny red-flecked eggs had been replaced by squirming pink flesh when I opened the box on May 8. Oh, they were impossibly tiny. I'd missed Hatch Day, though, and was delighted to find a chick that looked as if it had hatched a day or two later than the others, so for the first session I took two — the tiniest one, and a medium-size one. From the start, the smallest chick was active and vociferous, peeping loudly and standing up to beg. Helpless to resist its call, I diced up a small tender mealworm and fed it with forceps. The older chick lay quietly. It was visibly larger and better filled out than its sibling, and it didn't peep or beg.

May 8, 2006. Days 2, 3. On this first day, I paint both the smallest chick and a larger sibling, and trust that I've got birds aged two days and three days recorded for the book. Perhaps it's best I didn't try to handle them on Day 1. It would have been like handling a cochlea.

I'm quite surprised to find the chicks naked, with only a few strands of ineffectual down on head and spine. The abundance of plant fuzz and animal underfur in the cavity nest must make up for that deficiency. I think about house finches, which have such heavy down that only their yellow bills show beneath it when huddled in the nest. But

Day 3   May 8 '06

This is the larger sibling of the chick in the three studies below. I have been slipping the runt a few extra tender mealworms when I replace the model chick each day. I want them all to thrive.

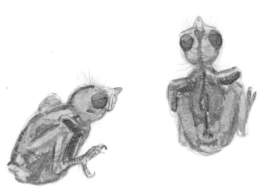

Day 4. May 9. More down on head and
shoulders; more fat laid down over
the pygostyle. 12 noon - 12:45

they're open-cup nesters, and need to grow their own insulation. Chickadees bring their insulation by the billful to snug cavities.

May 9, 2006. Day 4. The larger chick has almost doubled in size, and it shows a bit more down on head and spine. A little yellow fat has been laid down over the pygostyle (tailbone), and blue pterylae show on wings, spine, and head. The feet are amazingly strong and well coordinated for a four-day-old nestling. It grips the nest lining and takes some fuzz with it when I lift it from its downy cradle. Most songbirds are unable to do much at all with their feet at this age. I can already see minute scales forming on the legs and feet.

May 10, 2006. Day 5. I'm amazed to see tiny pinfeathers emerging on the wings on Day 5. It seems early. These birds are taking a typical cavity nester's approach — going from naked to feathered. Pinfeathers itch, and the tiny birdlet is already preening as I hold it in my warm hand. Calling what it does "preening" may be a bit generous; it's turning its head back over its back and wiggling its waxy bill over the offending pinfeathers. I'm always disarmed to see this behavior in such a tiny blob of flesh. This chick doesn't peep or beg. When I suddenly sneeze, I say "Excuse me!" in a tiny voice

3:15 - 4:00 pm
Day 5 May 10 - Already preening. More pterylae on
head - two on either side of the central
tract. He was very quiet until I sneezed,
then said, "Excuse me!" in a very small
voice, whereupon he popped up with gaping
bill! Must have sounded like a chickadee
to him. He took four white, peeled mealworms.
Most impressive is the amount of foot and
leg muscle development. Note wing pins too.

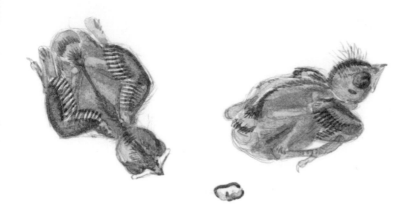

2:50 - 3:30 pm

May 11 - Day 6. A big change in wing maturation - look at those spiky flight feathers! Everything's more defined - he's looking less blobby, more angular. 6 mealworms eaten - he doesnt peep, but his bill pops open when he hears my voice. Very pleasant and calm to work with. The tiny siblings still peeping and gobbling mealworms.

to the chick, and its bill flies open. I guess to it, I sounded like a chickadee. I stuff four tender white mealworms in its gaping bill. By feeding my subjects abundant, age-appropriate food, I try to return the favor of their modeling for me. When I go back to the box, I feed the smallest chick, and any others that beg. It's the least I can do for them.

May 11, 2006. Day 6. This is getting fun. I'm painting only the older chick now. As they age, there is more and more to notice about them. Feather tracts are coming in, eyes are opening, fat deposits are spreading. Features are taking form. The chick is developing some angles, and its wings look like paddles, thickly spiked with feathers. I count nine minute spines that will be its primaries, nine that will be secondaries, and neat layers of smaller pinfeathers overlaying those that will be coverts. It wears its wings like an escutcheon or shield over its back, a delightful effect, then folds them down in a more birdlike position for the second painting. I'm struck by what a calm and pleasant little bird this is. Many nestlings wriggle and circle incessantly, but these chickadees lie quietly in my palm as if grateful for the warmth it holds. I suspect that has much to do with their demeanor; a cold nestling will move restlessly, trying to get comfortable. I know they're comfortable when they settle down. I move closer to breathe on the chick and warm it up. It smells like butterscotch, or brown sugar. Delicious. I know how bluebirds and robins, wrens, swallows, swifts, and even baby hummingbirds smell. These are the sweetest smelling yet.

I don't understand why Ohio Valley springs have to be so cruel. It's windy, cold, and rainy today, with the temperature dropping through the lower 50s by late afternoon. There's steady rain in the forecast for the next six days. My heart sinks for the chickadees, bluebirds, and tree swallows in my nest boxes. When I take my model back to its box, I feed as many of its siblings as will gape for me, then leave a stash of tender white

mealworms on the roof of the box for the adults to dole out. They don't hesitate for a moment.

Nor do the bluebirds on my box trail. I prepare a number of plastic jar lids with duct tape on their bottoms, and affix these, filled with mealworms, to the roofs of boxes that hold nestlings. I feel responsible for all of them, and I go to sleep worrying about them, and wake up thinking about them, too.

The hardest part of my painting project is not drawing wiggly nestlings from life. It's worrying about my subjects, which become more precious to me with each passing day, both as models and as individuals.

May 12, 2006. Day 7. It's still windy and cold, only 54 degrees, but at least it has stopped raining. The female is sitting tight when I arrive, and I'm amazed at the heat generated by her presence in the box. She flies out, right into my face. I take the largest baby and leave her a jar lid of mealworms, taped to the roof of the box. I carry the baby cupped against my warm belly, its tiny head between thumb and forefinger, to keep it from jostling as I walk. It squirms against my skin, reminding me startlingly of the flutter of Phoebe's first kicks — foreign and familiar at the same time.

In the twenty-five minutes I'm working with the chick, I stop seven times to give it a mealworm. Because food is scarce in the cold, rainy weather, these chicks aren't getting much to eat. It's in the low 50s all day today, so they're not growing as fast. The wing quills have doubled in length, and the feet are better developed and stronger than they were yesterday, but that's about all I notice. When I first start drawing, there is no fecal matter visible beneath the tissue-thin skin around the cloaca. By the end of the session, the bird has processed the first few mealworms into a bolus of feces, ready to void. I'm impressed. In this small, odd observation lies a clue to the mystery of nestling growth — the speed of its metabolism, and the souped-up, powerful insect-processing factory that is the digestive tract. More food: more growth. On cold days, there's less food, and less growth. I think of this nestling as a tiny race car, and insects are its fuel. On a warm day with plenty of food, it's pedal to the metal. The tiny bird's eye briefly slits open, and I see a glint of dark iris peeking through. I finish my painting and carry it back, feed the runt, and leave a lid full of mealworms on the roof of the box.

May 13, 2006. Day 8. There is so much going on with this chick's feather tracts today that I struggle to see and paint it all. I take off my glasses and squint like a mole to figure out what I'm seeing. The chick is able to sit up on its scaly legs — the tarsometatarsi — and it's extremely restless and active. I feed it five mealworms, and wonder if this brood would have made it at all without my subsidy. And yet — the cardinals and chipping sparrows I'm monitoring are doing fine in their open-cup nests. Cold weather is a double-edged blade. It reduces the amount of insect food available, but it keeps the snakes in their lairs and crevices, and out of bird nests — a gift to vulnerable sparrows and cardinals.

When I take the chick back to the nest, the female chickadee is brooding. She stands fast, gives a high-pitched purr-growl, and strikes at my hand like a snake. Six years later, I'll see the same striking behavior executed with more drama by a hen tufted titmouse nesting in one of my boxes. I smile at the courage of a 10-gram bird standing me down and, having nowhere else to put it, place the chick atop her back. She'll work it out once I'm gone.

Day 8
May 13 1:20 – 1:50 pm. It can sit on its tarso-metatarsi
today and holds itself obliquely upright. It's
very restless. I imagine it's hungry after two cold
days, so I feed it five mealworms, and it produces
a nice fecal sac. Pectoral and flank tracts are bursting
sweathers. Its legs and feet are a bewitching lilac.

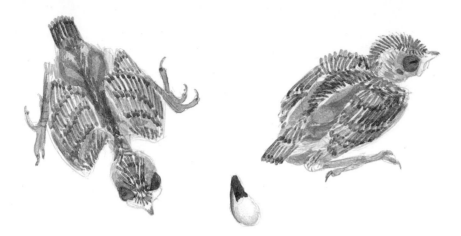

Day 9 May 14 6:45pm—?
Pouring rain, 54°. I am soaked through
just watching at. But the chicks are
warm and the female's been on them.
I see the black cap coming in today

May 14, 2006. Day 9. The day starts out nicely enough, if threatening, then disintegrates into cold lashing rain, 54 degrees by late afternoon. There's so much going on in my model's feathers that I am almost overwhelmed. They're bursting the sheaths all over. I can see the black cap and even the white cheeks forming. The chick can sit up for short periods. Once it starts to topple, and grips hard with its toes and rights itself. Its eyes are slit open, and it looks around. It seems happy to have mealworms to eat, and voids a large fecal sac after the fourth one. The female is sitting on the chicks both times I approach, and she waits until I'm actually removing the nest before flying out with a big flurry of wings. I must remove the nest from the box momentarily to be able to see and select the right chick. Then I put it back and head for the house. As always the smallest chick raises its head, begging, and is happy to be fed by me. I make plans to paint it next time, just to show how far behind it is.

May 15, 2006. Day 10. For the first time I admit I'm exhausted by this pursuit of suiting up in full rain gear, trudging out to the end of the orchard, abducting a chick, trudging back to the house, taking off my soaked gear, painting the chick as best I can given its wiggly nature, suiting up in wet gear, and trudging back to return the bird to the nest. Then I walk back to the house again. I drag myself out to the nest box in slicker, hat, and rain pants and find nestlings that are now more feathered than quilled. I pick the biggest and the smallest. I'm forced to realize now that the smallest chick, despite my generous mealworm subsidy, is truly stunted, and its prospects look poor. I paint it, noting that it lacks a complete spinal feather tract, has stunted tail feathers, no abdominal tracts—that it's the size of a five-day-old chick, although its wings look like a seven-day-old's, albeit in miniature. Ironically, its flight feathers are bursting the sheaths, as they should at this age, but it has no body feathers, barely the hint of them beginning to form. I feel bad for it, and feed it several tender white mealworms. It is

Day 10 May 15 5:57 - 5:49 pm - a big change. It's really looking like a chickadee. It's sitting up and looking around. I wish I could say It's easier to paint but it's incredibly hard to tell whats going on under all those quills and fluff. Today, I paint the stunted chick, who is also 10 days old but mysteriously and profoundly retarded in its development. Its wings are developed like a 7-day old chick, but its body is the size of a 5-day old. I wonder and worry what will happen to it when the other four are ready to fly.

Day 10 - Stunted chick
No spinal or coronal tract showing! And yet the feathers are bursting sheathes on the wings.

finally behaving in an age-appropriate way at ten days: active but suspicious. It doesn't beg as readily as it did yesterday. I wish I didn't worry so much about these birds, but at this point, for better or worse, I'm deeply involved: eye, hand, mind, and heart.

The bigger chick is sitting up for short periods, looking around for the first time through slitted eyes. It enjoys being fed and consumes five large white mealworms, then presents me with a large fecal sac. I paint that, too. It's all grist for the mill. I'm looking for answers in everything. How do they do it—grow or not grow? Why is one so stunted? Was the egg in its yolk too small to sustain normal growth? I keep the birds for almost an hour. God, I miss my eyes. I'm not used to my progressive lenses. It figures I would pick chickadees to paint on these dark, rainy days. It's so hard to see what's going on under the emerging feathers. The chicks are just a quilly mess now. I'm sure tomorrow will hold a great transformation, but for now, these chicks are perched on the edge of bird.

May 16, 2006. Day 11. When I walk up to the box (again in a 50-degree drizzle, pants soaked to my thighs, freezing—why didn't I wear rain pants today?) I see an adult chickadee in there, weaving back and forth, looking straight at me like a snake. The chicks don't know that something's going down, and they're yammering like crazy,

having just been fed. Their voices have changed today from a feeble peeping to a *dee-dee-dee-dee* call. Wow. They're beginning to be chickadees. When I open the box it's all feathers in there, black caps and yellow lips and half-open eyes. They really look like chickadees today. It's amazing how much the feathers have emerged since yesterday, all except those of the runt, which is still naked as a jaybird.

I take the baby I had yesterday and it sits up in my palm and looks around the studio, eyes half-open but bright. It eats a little reluctantly — gapes only once — but greedily sucks down worms that I work into the corners of its mouth. I enjoy feeding it up while I have it, for the forty minutes that it's in my care. I also much prefer to paint a clothed bird than a half-naked one. Yesterday's stage was very difficult for me — so spiky and hard to interpret. As the feathers emerge I am back in familiar territory. After the sixth worm the bird voids a huge fecal sac. I paint it, too. So far the weather's not bad enough to kill the chicks, and they seem to be doing all right. I leave a bunch of mealworms on the roof of the box and they are gone an hour later when I come back, so I leave a bunch more. There hadn't been much enthusiasm for my offerings until now. The adult chickadees would take the tender white newly molted worms, but no others. I suspect that the adults judged them too heavily covered in chitin — the slick, hard exoskeleton — for the chicks until Day 11. Bluebirds start feeding mealworms to their young around Day 6. Chickadees must need much softer fare.

May 17, 2006. Day 12. This feels like the last day for my work with these chickadees. I peer into the nest and it's all feathers (all except for the runt, who's trying mightily to catch up). I pick one and bring it out. It looks around expectantly, flutters its wings. Uh-oh. I know fledgy birds when I see them. Still, it settles down nicely in the Tupperware when I put a paper towel over it and stuff the container in my jacket. I add the runt for one final portrait.

3:05-3:48 pm Day 12 May 17. The big chick's gape flanges are almost gone, while the stunted chick's are still swollen. Normal chick is bright and alert, almost fledgy. A break in the cold and rain this aft.- its in the upper 60's. I will probably have to stop painting tomorrow.

I'm dying to know if it will make it to fledging. It's got so much catching up to do. I figure it needs at least nine more days to feather out. That would be Day 21. There's no way these birds will be in the box that long. But I'm impressed with how much better covered the runt is than it was yesterday.

May 18, 2006. Day 13. I take them back and am charmed at how the runt burrows under its sibling's wing, clinging to its leg like a perch. So I paint them that way, all bundled together. The runt shivers; the normal chick preens in my palm. Both eat a lot of mealworms; I lose count. The runt takes at least eight. Put that into growth, will you? Both produce a couple of fecal sacs in the fifty-five minutes I have them. It's hard, knowing this is my last session with them. I've got about thirteen hours in this brood of birds, solid hours of staring and peering and squinting and trying to get it all down on paper. And now I have to quit. How I wish I could keep going, because they'll just get

2:45-3:40 pm Day 13 May 18, 2006
Still there May 22 Day 17 - runt, too!

sleeker and more beautiful day by day. I have to keep checking the box to see if the runt gets left behind. I swear I'll take it in if they stop feeding it when all the others fledge. What have I got to lose? Maybe it will be sleek and lovely one day, too. I would like to know a chickadee personally, anyway. They have been wonderful subjects. I leave a gift of freshly molted white mealworms on the roof of the box and turn for home.

May 22, 2006. Day 17. Warm and sunny, with a bright breeze blowing. I walk out to the orchard, leaving my rain gear behind for once. The chickadees are scolding like mad around the nest box. That's a sign the chicks are ready to go. I stick a silent, tentative finger in to find four satiny feathered heads and one that's rubbery. So the runt still survives. It's Day 17, and almost time for them to go. I will check again tomorrow.

May 23, 2006. Day 18. The orchard is eerily silent, with no chickadees to be heard or seen. With great trepidation, I open the box, to find the mossy nest flattened and full of shiny feather sheath dust: sure sign of a normal departure. No chicks, no runt, nothing but two still-moist fecal sacs. I think I know who left them, and I smile ruefully. I was ready to finish raising that naked little creature if I had to. I'm astonished to think that the parent birds cared for and fed the runt through its development, but also that it found the wherewithal to leave with the rest of its siblings. Did it hop after the rest as they flew? And they managed to fledge the entire brood in the worst possible weather, with nonstop driving rain beating the dogwood petals to the ground. If any bird could pull that off, a chickadee could. Fearless, smart, and resourceful, chickadees are tiny packages, stuffed with fortitude. It's been an honor to help these into their big green world.

Ca. Day 19, fledged.
There is a toylike perfection
to baby chickadees that I
always find disarming. Tiny
but so self-possessed.

Carolina Chickadee, 2006 ～～ 171

8:30–9:00 Day 5 June 23. Here's the change in only 13 hours. I can't believe how his legs have grown. It's clear that this will be a bird that walks. We leave at dawn tomorrow for Chicago, gone Fri, Sat & Sun. Monday morning I will paint it again— and I expect it to be monstrous! I feel awful leaving it in the bluebirds' care for the next 3 days— but I'll raise it from Monday on.

7:30 AM
Day 5 June 23. The beginning: his second full day in the care of bluebirds, he obviously agrees with him (also grubs) he's strong and growing. So grubby I decide to wash him. He isn't sitting up a proper bird he's life peace & scrawny and I guess that's why he's such a mess.

Day 6 – unutterably weird, scurfy little blob. Pterylae darkening, quills sprouting on wings, then tight folded to body. I'm interested by how flat the orbitals are – not a goggle-eyed creature in the least.

Day 4 June 22. I didn't draw him yesterday - it was a bad day for starlings. I found his twin younger sibling dead, and him cold and curled, and several arsenic from a heavy mite infestation. I replaced the nest with a clean one but no adult returned at 1pm overly tried it was 11am. I held him for the scrambled egg I feed him had dry he scrambled it neatly. I put him a little. At 4pm I slipped him into the nearby bluebird box, and they're rather good hosts of him I changed his nest...

Colors much better now

10:16 AM –
May 5 2008 Probably Day 7.

Three years later I finally have another brood of starlings to paint. Healthy and mite-free, and in a much more salubrious spring–warmer and perfectly sunny but moist. The chick bears a strong yeasty odor from its already-funky, damp nest. No organized fecal sacs and a lot I could in the droppings foil the adults' attempts at hygiene. I'm impressed at the strength of its grip. Down is long and yellowish, voice a reedy squeaky chirp. Rt. Eye has just opened today. It's already taking an interest in its surroundings. What a huge chunk of gargoyly chick to enjoy! I hold it in my palm to keep it warm.

Day 3 beginning

There were 2 eggs

Day 1 (Chart 1°)
7–7:30 pm June 19 2005 from the incubator ground.

The blue-green egg is golding and stained, and the chicks first chirping is wet and fresh inside. The shell is ringed with tiny chirps – little like a porch from the chick's egg tooth. There are 24 chips. 24 pecks? It still rolls around straining to haul itself still trying to free itself. It responds to touch by... It flinches...

European Starling, 2008

THE WORD THAT comes to mind to describe my relationship with starlings over the years is "fraught." I'm always of two minds about them. Starlings act like boorish house-guests as they descend in the depths of winter to devour our suet and peanuts in a flurry of bickering, and decorate the stoop and deck with the copious exudate of their portly guts. And yet, the moment the sun breaks back out and thaws the pastures, lawns, and meadows, these sloppy hoboes disperse to go earn a living the honest way—by prob-ing for insect larvae.

And then there are starling aesthetics. The video-watching world is all atwitter over the jaw-dropping flock formations called "murmurations," in which starlings form blobs, loops, and wavering ribbons as they mass in migrating flocks. I've loved watching this phenomenon since I was small, and I still pull over to gape when I spy a murmuration forming. My heart leaps, throbs, tightens, and goes free with the flock.

And there is their song, one of my favorites, for its improvisational nature. Listening to a starling sing, hearing what it chooses to mimic, I feel closer to understanding what is important to a bird. Loping along a riverside trail on a dreary February day, I heard the song of eastern meadowlarks floating over the sodden brown pastures. The top of a tall white sycamore had leafed out in black starlings, each one practicing its version of this long-awaited spring sonata. It was a moment of transcendent beauty as the birds sang in concert. Who can say why they all picked the meadowlark's song to voice at once? Was it a singing contest? Or was there simply a birdy aesthetic at work, one that delighted their hearts and mine?

Starlings were introduced to North America in the late 1890s in a misguided homage to William Shakespeare, who mentioned them in *Henry IV*. It seemed like a good idea to businessman Eugene Schieffelin at the time. Alone among the birds that Schieffelin's society brought over, starlings burgeoned and seemed intent on blanketing the country. Being cavity nesters, but unable to excavate wood themselves, they actively usurp the homes of primary excavators such as flickers and red-bellied woodpeckers, and take used cavities from bluebirds, tree swallows, and purple martins, among others. Oh, thank you for these hordes of chubby invaders, just what we needed in America.

I didn't want to add to the world's starlings by hosting them in our martin nesting gourds, so year after year I hauled their nests out before eggs were laid. I hoped to be able to prevent them from nesting successfully and to clear the gourds for the birds I desired. I remember two starling nests that I pulled out of the gourds on April 15, 2000. One was decorated with a mushy jalapeño pepper, plucked from last year's still-standing plants in the garden. The other sported a freshly picked pale yellow narcissus blossom, tucked into the straw. The mushy pepper made me laugh; the flower made me sigh. Who was I to destroy their careful creations?

Starling nest with narcissus, last fall's mushy jalapeño pepper, and the promise of five eggs. April 23, 2006

When the male starling trying to nest in our yard learned to imitate my baby son Liam's voice, softly calling "Mommy? Mommy?" in between chatters, squeaks, grunts, and rattles, I folded. That summer, I allowed him and his mate to finish their clutch and raise five sooty young in a martin gourd. They'd worn me down with their potbellied charm, strutting around on the emerald grass like dusky penguins, speaking in my tongue. No purple martin had looked sideways at our nesting gourds in a decade, anyway. And then I discovered a side benefit of letting one pair of starlings nest in the gourds. Now, when the phone rings in the spring and someone on the other end sends a photo of a big, ugly, yellow-lipped orphan they've found, I know that I likely have a home for it. Starling nesting is a delicately timed thing, and the majority of the population seems to nest in almost perfect synchrony. Several springs in a row, I've been able to pop an orphan into our starling nest and leave the enormous time commitment of raising it to its own species, where it belongs. I know that there's a serious attitudinal disjunct here, but you try euthanizing a bright-eyed baby starling when it's brought to you in a shoebox.

The most amazing adoption was of a week-old orphan that came to me via a caller to *Bird Watcher's Digest* on June 5, 2012. It was dehydrated, lethargic, and weak; I built it back up with Pedialyte, food, and heat. There was one starling nest with two four-day-old chicks, and one with five eggs in our martin gourds. I planned to slip the orphan into the two-chick brood, but they were inexplicably dead the next morning, the parents nowhere to be found: another weird starling nesting event in a string of weird events. My elegant plan disintegrated before my eyes. I did not want to have to raise a starling! In desperation, I put the week-old chick into the nest with five eggs. Watching anxiously from inside the house, I saw the adult starlings come to their nest, register great surprise and consternation, then drop to the lawn to begin foraging. At 12:22 P.M., an adult entered the gourd with a caterpillar and came out without it. They raised the foster chick without incident, their own eggs left unincubated in the thrill of finding a huge chick, miraculously hatched, atop them.

The synchronous nesting in starlings, which helps me hoodwink birds into raising orphans, may be driven by food availability, or even by what happens on the other end of the cycle. For fledgling starlings, upon leaving the nest, get but a few days' care from their parents, if they're lucky. Some may get a day; some get none at all. The juveniles, forsaken by their parents, seek out each other and flock tightly together for the late summer and fall. There they find safety in numbers, and they quickly learn to find food together. I'm always amused to see the huge red mulberry tree on my dirt road fill up with a churring flock of newly fledged starlings when it fruits in mid-June. Something, likely day length, tells starlings exactly when to initiate their nests, perhaps so that all may fledge and flock together. I'm not at all sure what tells the newly minted starlings what they should eat and how to find it. Considering the weeks that most other songbird fledglings depend on their parents for subsidy, this feat alone is astonishing. Is there some cultural transmission of information in these highly intelligent birds? Do the adults give verbal instructions on how to find each type of food they bring, in the long twenty-three-day nestling period? I'm only half-joking, but that's because I have come to know starlings.

Of all the species of nestling birds I've painted, the European starling, ironically enough, was the most difficult to obtain. My quest for subjects has been fraught with difficulty and disappointment. Three grubby, pale blue eggs lay cold in the gourd nest on May 31, 2005 — extremely late, and out of synch with other area starlings. Though

Mites, full of blood

So very pale - anemic in fact. Later this day the parents abandoned them.

Day 2 - beginning
27 hours old 10:30 - 10:50 AM June 20
This is the firstborn bird, not the one I painted yesterday. (It's only 1st hrs old now). I'm struck by how pale the 2 elder birds have grown. The natal down is thick and gray, going white on the ... tract. I drew it through a haze of dawn.

The third chick hatched this morning, 9am June 20, 48 hrs after the first (pictured a left), which hatched 7am June ... Phoebe found the fresh eggshell. It's 27 hrs younger than the eldest.

the normal incubation period is twelve days, these did not hatch until June 19. Perhaps their parents were inexperienced. I lowered the gourd and borrowed one chick to draw just after it pecked its way out of the shell, counting twenty-four separate perforations where it had pierced its frail case. As I drew it, the chick kept rolling around and lifting its head upward, as if it still felt the need to peck its way out. It responded to my touch by gaping.

Painting the chicks on their second day of life, I was worried by how pallid they were, like pale ghosts of healthy starling chicks. Mites fell off them and crawled on the paper, bright red from the blood they'd ingested. On Day 3, I peeked in the gourd, intending to clean and change their nest, to find two of the three chicks dead, and my model clinging to life, severely anemic from the mite infestation. I quickly switched the infested gourd for a clean one with a new nest in it and replaced the chick, but the damage was done. I watched the gourd all day, and a starling returned but once, around 1:00 P.M. The starlings had decided their brood was doomed, and ceased feeding the living chick. It was clear that but for the scrambled egg I'd fed my model, it would have died as well.

What now? I was stuck with another orphaned starling I'd never intended to raise. If I were to paint this bird's growth, I'd have to find a way to keep it alive. My schedule was crammed and hectic, as it always is in spring. I wouldn't be home enough to feed this baby starling every half-hour. In desperation, I lit on the temporary solution of popping the orphan in a nearby box holding a clutch of bluebirds about the same age. It was an idea just crazy enough to work. The change in the orphan was apparent by

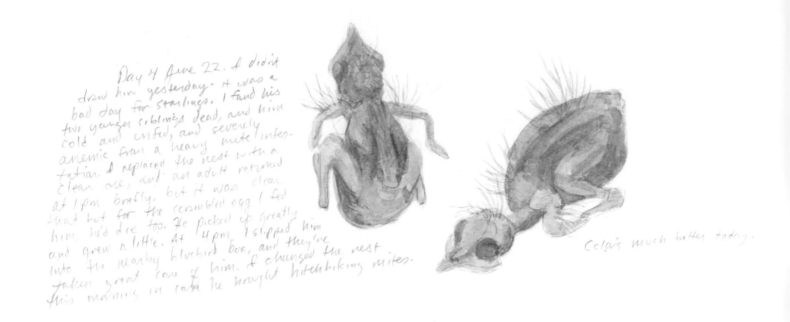

Day 4 June 22. I didn't draw him yesterday. It was a bad day for starlings. I found his two younger siblings dead, and him cold and chilled, and severely anemic from a heavy mite infestation. I replaced the nest with a clean one, and an adult returned at 1 pm briefly, but it was clear that but for the scrambled egg I fed him, he'd die too. He picked up greatly and grew a little. At 4 pm I slipped him into the nearby bluebird box, and they've taken great care of him. I changed the nest this morning in case he brought hitchhiking mites.

Cola's much better today.

the next morning—his color had improved and he'd grown visibly in the care of his unwitting foster parents. The irony of bluebirds raising a sworn enemy, a competitor for their nest cavities, didn't escape me. I promised the bluebirds this wouldn't be for long. I had to go to Chicago for three days, but when I returned, I planned to remove this grubby foster child and finish raising it myself.

7-8 AM
Day 5 June 23. The beginning of his second full day in the care of bluebirds. It's obviously agreeing with him. Cola's good, he's strong and growing, if grubby. I decide to wash him. This bird doesn't make a proper fecal sac—its feces is stringy—and I guess that's why he's such a mess.

the wingsac orangeish

no tooth still there but shrinking

On Day 5, its second full day in the care of bluebirds, the starling chick was strong and beefy pink. It was still dirty from its old nest, so I washed it in mild baby soap and warm water, towel dried it, painted its portrait, and replaced it in the bluebird nest. I had to smile at the energy I was expending to keep this bird among the living, to keep my odd little obsession for painting baby birds going. Because I would be gone the next three days, I decided to paint the chick at both 7:00 A.M. and 8:00 P.M. on Thursday, depicting a thirteen-hour span in its life. I was stunned by how much it grew in a half-day.

The change was most noticeable in its legs. They were suddenly longer, sturdier, the toes better formed. Clearly, this would grow up to be a walking bird. The changes taking place in the nestling had me completely in its thrall. I felt like calling the Chicago Flower Show organizers to tell them I wouldn't be there to deliver my seminar on gardening for native birds. I had a starling here to paint, and what could be more wonderful than that? I tucked the weird avian exchange student in among its small pink bluebird hosts and told it I'd be its new mama come Monday. Yes, I'd miss three days of its development, but a partial record would be better than nothing.

While I was in Chicago, a pair of house sparrows that had been lurking around the yard took their opportunity to attack the bluebird brood, pecking them and the baby starling to death. It's a hard, hard world out there for bluebirds *and* starlings. What a sad scene greeted me early Monday morning. I'd laid out my paper and paints and cooked up some scrambled egg. I was preparing to draw and paint, then take over raising my little model. It was not to be. Sadly, I cleaned out the box, set a sparrow trap for the interlopers, and put my starling plate away, until fate sent me another model. I hoped it wouldn't all be so difficult next time.

8:30 – 9:10 Day 5 June 23. Here's the change in only 13 hours. I can't believe how his legs have grown. It's clear that this will be a bird that walks. We leave at dawn tomorrow for Chicago, gone Fri, Sat & Sun. Monday morning I will paint it again – and I expect it to be monstrous. I feel awful leaving it in the bluebirds' care for the next 3 days – but I'll raise it from Monday on.

Three years would pass before starlings again attempted to nest in the martin gourds. I laughed at my glee when a pair began prospecting at the gourds in April 2008, thinking of all the years I'd clawed their nests out in my dreary spring housecleaning ritual. I wanted to see what happened next in a young starling's life! Once again, a work commitment kept me away from the nestlings until May 5, so I'd have to resort to photos for Day 6. I suspect the chick raised by bluebirds was necessarily skinner than one fed by natural parents. What a hulk this creature was.

Day 6 - unutterably weird, scurfy little blob. Pterylae darkening, quills sprouting on wings, here tight folded to body. I'm interested by how flat the orbitals are - not a goggle-eyed creature in the least.

On arriving home, I set to painting the seven-day-old chicks in their martin gourd nest. The spring of 2008 was much more salubrious—warm and sunny, and the chick I picked was vital and strong. Like the 2005 bird, it was a mess to handle, with disorganized droppings that quickly soiled its nest. I'd see the adults cleaning up after it, but their efforts were mostly in vain, as both starlings I'd observed seemed to lack the ability to tie up their droppings in a neat membranous disposable diaper for the adults to carry off.

The seven-day-old chick is a great big bag of guts, topped with an enormous yellow clown's mouth. I have never beheld anything like it. It emits a strong horsey odor. Reports that starlings are good to eat won't be tested by me. Phew!

By Day 8, its body odor has taken on pungent metallic overtones, reminding me of copperhead musk. I realize that not many readers will have smelled that, but here in southeast Ohio we become familiar with it fast. While I work at painting its stinky magnificence, I feed the bird three times with moistened parrot chow in a syringe, and take away three huge droppings in the fifty minutes I'm working with it. I need a triple layer of tissues for this model.

10:16 AM-
MAY 5 2008 Probably Day 7.

Three years later I finally have another brood of starlings to paint. Healthy and mite-free, and in a much more salubrious spring-warmer and perfectly sunny but moist. The chick bears a strong yeasey odor from its already-funky, damp nest. No organized fecal sacs and a lot of liquid in the droppings foil the adults' attempts at hygeine. I'm impressed at the strength of its grip. Dawn is long and yellowish, voice a reedy squeaky chirp. Rt. Eye has just opened today. It is already taking an interest in its surrandigs What a huge chunk of gargoyly chick to enjoy! I hold it in my palm to keep it warm.

On Day 9, I see the sentience creep into the starling's eyes. It feels like a hot-water balloon in my hand; its abdomen is so big and packed with guts and fat; its skin moist and a bit sticky, the strong odor still emanating. And yet it looks around with newly opened eyes and orients toward the sound of my voice when I speak softly to it. It begins to shiver, and I cover it with my hand. It cuddles up against my skin. I find myself responding in all the right maternal ways to its signals, and feel myself falling for it. Even though it poops five times in the half-hour I'm painting it. I decide to immortalize the droppings in watercolor. They're quite nice, now encased in membrane as a good fecal sac should be. I realize I sound like a new mother.

The bird is transformed by the next morning, Day 10, a glorious mess of feathers bursting their sheaths. Brown paintbrush tips end each sheath, and the back has sprouted in feathers. Although it's cool today, the nestling doesn't shiver, demonstrating the insulative power of even partially emerged feathers.

I'm called away by a West Virginia birding festival on Days 11 and 12, but someone serendipitously sends me photos of an eleven-day-old chick for identification, and I'm able to paint from those. It's a teddy bear of a chick, finally beginning to look like a bird instead of some monstrous naked pincushion. Once again, my starling painting project is sputtering along, punctuated by interruptions. I return from West Virginia on the evening of the starling chicks' thirteenth day, unpack my car, and rush out to the martin gourds to collect a chick. I'm relieved to find the brood alive and well, though beginning to be overrun by mites. Because I've missed some developmental days, I select the youngest bird, rather than the big fat one I've been working with. By doing this, I hope to have a smoother transition in my paintings, despite the missed days. The difference in the two individuals is immediately obvious. This bird doesn't know me. It won't cuddle into my hand. It hasn't learned that I mean warm food and gentle handling. It's frightened of me and tries to escape. It's a squirming, squirting, terrified little mess.

12:50–1:40 pm May 6 2008 Day 8. Phew! A strong, pungent, metallic, almost snakelike odor emanates from the chick today. Stroking the top of its head elicits gaping, and I feed it moistened parrot chow 7x, taking away 3 huge fecal sacs in 50 min.

10:20 - 10:50AM May 7 2008 Day 9. Boy, there
is really someone in those eyes today. He clings & almost
perches, voids 5x (where does it all come from?) eats 5x,
snuggles, orients to the sand of my voice, and gapes for
food when gently squeezed. He shivers until I cradle him
against my chest, then eats lustily and falls asleep.
    There is a consciousness in this bird
and I find myself falling for him.
His foot scutes are coming into focus
like developing film - yesterday they were
barely visible. The first tips of feathers
are coming at on rump, flanks and
flight feathers. A few miles.

Day 9, begging - it
turns from a quiet bag of
guts to a giant red maw.
Ya could stuff food in it all
day, and the adults clearly
do.

I paint its portrait with great difficulty and take the chick back to its nest. I decide to remove an older sibling to work from, to show the contrast in their development. I'm not sure which of the three is my original subject. To my dismay, the one I select shrieks and orients toward the exit hole of the gourd. Yikes! My painting days are over after this. I bring the bird inside and paint its portrait as it huddles in fear.

Their nest is a soggy mess, seething with mites. I have to do something about it. The gourd next door is clean and mite-free, with a starling nest already built in it. Quickly, I transfer the three nestlings to this gourd, and hang it where theirs had been. I take the stinking, infested gourd away and immerse it in a muck bucket full of hot water. Mites float up in a thin gray felt atop the water. Ammonia rises in a cloud to my nose. Phew!! It isn't easy being a starling. I feel good to have helped these babies on the last day I could safely handle them. Now to sit back and watch to see when they fledge.

To my relief and fascination, the adults are still feeding the brood on May 20, Day 22. That's a long time in the nest for babies that seemed quite jumpy and "fledgy" at Day 13: ten days more! It's two days longer than the longest stay I've seen in tree swallows. The starlings finally fledge on the morning of Day 23. They're flying well, and able to follow their parents around on the lawn with the characteristic throaty *churrr* call

8–8:35 AM May 8 2008 Day 10. He's a glorious mess today as all his feathers begin to burst the sheathes. Wow. Lots to do and draw. Very quiet, and although it's much cooler today I notice he is not shivering – the insulative power of feathers. Neither is he pooping. It's pouring and I doubt they've had much to eat. Gape flanges are shrinking back. Dan is shedding off the tops of the emerging feathers.

Day 11. From photos sent to me for ID by a Florida friend.

I'd been hearing from the martin gourd for the last week. Upon fledging, the adults' territorial boundary melts away, and the fledglings learn to forage for beetle grubs by probing into the grass, opening their bill, and grabbing whatever wriggles. On Day 29 I see a fledgling being stuffed with my homemade peanut butter suet dough at the dog dish on our deck railing, and on Day 30 I see one foraging alongside a parent on the lawn. I don't see them after that, and assume they've flown off to join flocks of other graduates of Starling School.

If the whole picture for starlings nesting in my yard seems, well, fraught with peril and difficulty, it's no illusion. When I hear someone complaining about starlings, I'll often wait for the right moment to interject this tidbit of information: in Britain, European starling populations declined 68 percent between 1965 and 2002 (Crick et al. 2002). The dramatic decline seems to be linked to lowered juvenile survival just post-fledging. Estimates of 50 percent juvenile survival in 1980 plunged to 31 percent in 1991, subsequently rising back to about 45 percent. Increased use of pesticides; decreased numbers of livestock kept on pasture; and changes in grassland management,

Day 13

Sun. May 11 2008 6:45 - 7:23pm. I'm back from WV, having missed Fri & Sat. Unpacked the car, grabbed the youngest baby and went to work. The nest and birds are seething with mites- ecch- and they streamed up both arms as I worked. This baby doesn't know me like my other subject did, and it is quite alarmed and tried to escape repeatedly. Day 13- it shows! I know my time's almost up but

I'll try to do one last painting of my original subject, who looks almost fully feathered this evening. If this painting's loose it's because the baby was a squirting, squirming, frightened mess to try to contain. Still has perukes of puffball down on sides of head & poking through wing coverts. There's a glint in its eye and resolve in its struggles. Fledgy. When I put it back it oriented toward the exit hole & chirped- not a good sign for continued artistic efforts. They're supposed to stay in the nest until Day 21- 8 more days- but I'd fledge early with a soggy, mite-infested nest!

including pesticide and fertilizer use, have likely reduced the birds' food base and foraging opportunities. Crane fly larvae, which eat the roots and emerging leaves of many crops, are a major component of the starling's food in Britain, and successful efforts to control this agricultural pest may also be knocking back starlings. Having fought this invasive bird for most of my life, it is slightly surreal to read British recommendations for habitat management to encourage starlings, including erecting nest boxes for this red-listed species' use.

Knowing that British bird watchers are deeply concerned about the decline of starlings makes me look at the birds with a more appreciative eye, and I decide to keep my eyes

Monday May 12 2008. Day 14.

Feet clenched in fear.
That's the hallux in front.

open for any observations I can make of starlings during the perilous post-fledging stage. I never know when I make my modest, self-piloted solitary studies whether I might be breaking new ornithological ground. I've found over the years that what I observe often differs substantially from published accounts, and I know that, even with the error that goes with observing unmarked birds, that can mean I'm on to something. Published accounts don't necessarily have the last word in ornithology—especially where the difficult-to-observe post-fledging behavior is concerned. That's what's such fun about getting to know the individual birds in my world. I'm happy to have been able to observe a starling family for a full week after fledging, to have looked into a bunch of their nests; to have drawn them as they grow; to take these drops of information from the sea of things we *don't* know about starlings.

Day 31 May 28 2008. Still being fed - here, a cranefly larva (leatherjacket).
Amazingly rotund, and loud, with incessant churring. By the next day
it was forging in the lawn alongside a parent. I never saw the
pair together - just one adult w/one chick.

Northern Cardinal, 2009

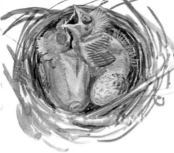

Day 4. Eyes are opening,
and wing quills are busy turning.
They stand up and beg lustily.
These birds seem in a hurry to
grow up.

Day 5. Impressive wing
quill growth - they are
turning into porcupines.
Developmental arc is
reminiscent of Carolina wrens.

Day 3 and at came
the wing quills.
They've taken a quantum
leap in size. The
egg won't hatch now.

Day 6 All quills, but
not a one open. I've never
seen a nestling so be-
quilled, except for a 6-day
old mourning dove. It has
to be uncomfortable to be
clad in floppy, spiky,
heavy armor.

Day 2. They've got a thick gray
down on head, wings and back.
Glued and begging from the whole time
I make poking my camera through
the maple twigs. This plate will be
an amalgam of nests I studied in
2009 and 2013.

Day 7. Such a different aspect between
the frightened chick huddled in the
nest, and the one who dances and
sings for its support. Feathers are
finally bursting the sheaths. Enormous
eyes, even by nestling standards. It
may have something to do with the
cardinal's crepuscular habits.

Day 8. Flight feathers
burst their sheaths. This is
the presage to Transformation
Day! All that feather growth
sets up a powerful hunger.
A lust for life. I can see
the big primaries inserting
into the wrist bone.

An infant cardinal in the
forsythia - I peek into its
cradle when the hen is away

Hard to believe they both even fit in this straw and stick basket. Feathers are all except atop the head, so they keep their goggle-eyed look.

Day 9 - In the morning they were huddled together and by noon this one is alone with the chalky old egg. Its sibling is perched about a foot away, looking at the great wide world.

Ten days old, this cardinal is out of the nest. It can't fly, can barely perch, but it's on its way. Its parents will feed it for up to two more months.

Day 11. All this baby needs to be able to do is clamber and flutter. Still stay hidden in dense vine tangles, and will be fed until long after she can fly perfectly. Cardinals have an extremely long juvenile dependency.

Based on her tail length (8.5 cm) this young female is about 23 days old. Still begging and being subsidized almost entirely by her parents. ♀'s don't seem to develop the black mask as early as males, which will show red in belly's crest by Day 23.

Hard to believe they both even fit in this straw and stick basket. Feathers are all except atop the head, so they keep their goggle-eyed look.

Cardinal parents care for fledged young an average of 35 days after fledging (32 in So. Ontario, 39 in S. Indiana), but they may still feed fledglings until 56 days after fledging. This is a very long juvenile dependency period.

Northern Cardinal, 2009

EACH BIRD SPECIES has its own model for reproduction. Look at enough models, and you begin to see the forces that shape the speed and process of nestling development. For instance, many of our eastern wood-warblers fly from the Neotropics to the boreal forest to breed. Why go so far north? Well, by traveling so far, warblers are exploiting the brief seasonal bloom of insects, mostly lepidopteran (butterfly and moth) larvae, in the northern forest. Caterpillars abound in the short boreal summer, and it's caterpillars that go into those yellow diamonds—the gaping bills of nestling warblers. Moreover, there are comparatively few nest predators in the boreal forest; no climbing snakes and far fewer predatory mammals such as raccoons and opossums. A bay-breasted warbler may lay eight eggs in a single clutch, banking on the seasonal flush of caterpillars in the spruce-fir forest to feed and fledge them all. One big brood, and then the birds are done and preparing to head south again.

Come down a bit in latitude, and things change. Warmer temperatures make for a longer growing season, and the booming summer flush of insects typical of northern climes is spread throughout a longer season. Songbirds have the time to raise two or more broods. But with that opportunity comes an abundance of nest predators, from furbearers to climbing ratsnakes. The northern cardinal, so named to distinguish it from its natty Neotropical cousins, has a nesting profile that fits the humid southern United States forest in which it evolved. A denizen of low shrubbery and tangled edges, it rarely nests much above eye level, which leaves it vulnerable to climbing snakes and small mammals. In fact, a dismal 15 to 37 percent of all cardinal nests ever fledge young. So the cardinal hedges its bets, building a quick, flimsy, but durable platform

An infant cardinal in the forsythia—I peek into its cradle when the hen is away.

of interwoven twigs with a shallow cup, and laying an average of only three eggs with each attempt. And attempt it does, nesting from March through September in most of the United States. Small broods follow one after another. I associate midsummer in my Ohio yard with the constant pippering of young cardinals, begging to be fed. The ones that make it, that is.

Because the cardinal nests in such vulnerable situations, so low to the ground, I had to wait for a special situation in order to be able to record its nestling growth each day. Finally, a female built her nest in a small Japanese maple that had started its life as a seedling in a Styrofoam cup, dug out from under a beautiful mature maple in Central Park and brought home in my backpack around 1982. You never know what you'll get when growing the seed children of hybrid Japanese maples. Sometimes you luck

Day 2. They've got a thick gray
down at heads, wings and backs.
Blind and begging from the vibrations
I make poking my camera up through
the maple twigs. This plate will be
an amalgam of nests & studied in 2002,
2009 and 2013.

out; sometimes you don't. I trained it as a bonsai, but its growth habit was too gangly and tall to make a pleasing subject. So after a decade or so of failing to shape it into a good-looking bonsai, I liberated the maple into our yard in Ohio. It took off, reaching for the sky as it had always tried to do. Finally, it started spreading laterally, getting big enough to throw a nice pool of shade in the yard. It attracted the attention of a nesting cardinal pair in 2009. The nest was a bit higher than my head, but I found I could stand on tiptoe and point my camera down into it to record its contents.

My dilemma then was how to record the nestlings' growth without endangering them. I couldn't risk losing them to a snake or raccoon. I needed to keep anything from climbing the trunk, which rose for a good 3 feet before any branches emerged. I had

Day 3 and at came the wing quills. They've taken a quantum leap in size. The egg won't hatch now

to baffle the tree against predators. Prowling the aisles of my local hardware store for the materials I needed, I found something called a "yard funnel," which was a 3-foot-long cylinder of green vinyl, designed to channel yard waste into garbage bags. I cut the plastic cylinder down the side with tin snips, wrapped it around the tree trunk, and taped it back together with aluminum duct tape. I crossed my fingers and prayed it would work to protect the nest from predation.

Day 4- Eyes are opening and wing quills are lengthening. They stand up and beg lustily. These birds seem in a hurry to grow up.

Day 5. Impressive wing quill growth—they are turning into porcupines. Developmental arc is reminiscent of Carolina wrens!

The next morning, I checked the nest: eggs still intact. On the homemade baffle, in the fresh summer dew, were the handprints of a raccoon that had tried to climb it that same night. Do anything out of the ordinary in our yard, and a raccoon will check it out. That includes visiting a bird's nest more than once. Hence the baffles on all my nest boxes, and now on my Japanese maple.

With the raccoon and snake threat defused, I now could walk up to the nest, point my camera down into it, and record the chicks' development each day. Though climbing predators were no longer an issue, I still wanted to avoid disturbing the birds, so I waited until I saw the female cardinal leave the nest before tiptoeing up to the tree, snapping a photo, and tiptoeing away. This was easy enough to do when the chicks were tiny, but as they grew and required more and more food, catching the nest unattended became a challenge. Cardinals are attentive parents.

Day 6. All quills, but not a one open. I've never seen a nestling so be-quilled, except for a 6-day old mourning dove. It has to be uncomfortable to be clad in floppy, spiky, heavy armor.

Day 7. Such a different aspect between the frightened chick huddled in the nest, and the one who dances and sings for its supper! Feathers are finally bursting the sheaths. Enormous eyes, even by nestling standards. It may have something to do with the cardinal's crepuscular habits.

Only two of the three eggs hatched in two nests I studied, the third egg being infertile in both instances. The chicks were covered in thick grayish down that stood over their heads like a fuzz halo. They grew by leaps and bounds. By Day 3, blue feather quills were sprouting from their paddlelike wings, and Day 4 saw their eyes opening. I was amazed to see the wings completely quilled out on five-day-old birds; their developmental speed reminded me of that of Carolina wrens.

By Day 6, a feature unique to cardinals comes to the fore: their enormous, goggle eyes. Concealed by feathers in the adult bird, these protruding orbs help them gather light, and allow them to keep rather odd hours. Cardinals are the first birds of the day to sing and begin foraging here in southeast Ohio, and the last to go to roost at night. They seem to thrive in the crepuscular light. And nestling cardinals have very prominent eyes, looking more like some kind of prickly toad than a bird at around one week of age.

Day 8. Flight feathers burst their sheaths. This is the presage to Transformation Day. All that feather growth sets up a powerful hunger. A lust for life. I can see the big primaries inserting into the wrist bone.

The effect is enhanced once their body feathers burst their sheaths on Day 9, for those great purplish orbs protrude to each side. They remain uncovered until about Day 13, when fledgling cardinals finally look more like birds than amphibians.

The cardinal's developmental arc is quite similar to that of the indigo bunting, which feeds its young insects and builds its nest in very similar low, shrubby situations. The same stressors are at work to speed the two species' development: the snakes and mammalian predators that are common in such edge habitats. The charge of young cardinals and buntings is to leave the nest, ready or not, by Day 9. Clambering and fluttering, the half-feathered fledglings make their way into the world. They need only to be able to cling and perch: to leave.

Hard to believe
they both even fit
in this straw and
stick basket.
Feathers are at!
except atop the
head, so they keep
their goggle-eyed
look.

Day 9. In the morning they were huddled together, and
by noon this one is alone with the chalky old egg.
Its sibling is perched about a foot away, looking out at
the great wide world.

Young cardinals can flutter short distances, low to the ground, by Day 11, looking more like an Easter decoration than a viable bird, but making their way nonetheless. Their movements are heralded by the frantic chipping of their parents, warning them to take cover, get out of sight. The adults stuff their young with insects, speeding their growth, development, and mobility with each meal.

Ten days old, this cardinal is out of the nest. It can't fly, can barely perch, but it's on its way. Its parents will feed it for up to two more months.

Day 11. All this baby needs to be able to do is clamber and flutter. She'll stay hidden in dense vine tangles, and will be fed until long after she can fly perfectly. Cardinals have an extremely long juvenile dependency.

Cardinals are not truly mobile until about Day 20, usually perching quietly in the vicinity of the nest, waiting to be fed. Sustained flight comes later. And both cardinals and indigo buntings enjoy a long juvenile dependency period, doing the bulk of their growing and maturation after leaving the dangerous confines of the nest. With the power of flight kicking in around Day 20, they also find their voice.

Constantly chippering young cardinals are fed by their parents for as few as twenty-five, and as long as fifty-six, days after fledging. It's humbling to witness their repeated efforts, against the near-certainty of predation. And should chicks fledge, three to eight weeks of intense parental investment are needed to take them from clambering puffballs to semiautonomous juveniles. Should a predator find the nest before the young climb out, the cardinal pair will try again—and again, small clutch after small clutch, well into late summer and even autumn, patiently working to add more daubs of carmine to the winter landscape.

Based on her tail length (6.5 cm) this young female is about 23 days old. Still begging and being subsidized almost entirely by her parents. ♀'s don't seem to develop the black mask as early as males, which would show red in belly & crest by Day 23.

Cardinal parents care for
fledged young an average of 35
days after fledging (32 in
So. Ontario, 39 in S. Indiana),
but they may still feed fledglings
until 56 days after fledging.
This is a very long juvenile
dependency period.

Day 6 June 17 2013. Babies are very wriggly.
The eyes are fully open today though
they keep them closed when they are
afraid. Pinfeathers are coming in all along
spinal tract - and 12 minute pins emerging
from tail. They're quite active, more so each day,
moving around when placed on the paper
towel.

"Does he know how
beautiful he'll be?"

Day 7 June 18 2013. So active now
that they need to be contained - crawling
everywhere! Spinal tract has a "mohawk"
look! and breast feathers are showing
tiny pale yellow paintbrush tips coming out
of sheaths. They act like birds, not sleepy
lumps now. Wing feathers are bursting as well.
Eyes wide and bright.

Day 5 June 16 2013. Amazing wing feather growth and spinal.
Feather tract is beginning to "raise" into a pad and erupt with
sheathes. The head is getting darker as feathers cover the skin
the face. All that blue is blood filled feather sheaths beneath
the skin. The male parents singing has slowed, but he sings after vanquishing
'a base' wren or tufted titmouse which
comes too close to the box. Eyes slitted.

Day 4. June 15 13. One baby
has disappeared but the remaining
3 are almost doubled in bulk. A base
wren which had sung atop the warbler
nest box may have raided it. Primary
feather sheathes are prominent and
growing quickly today. Slippers become
flappers. Eyes staying "green" skin
turning lucky pink. Good fat deposits
around tail. These birds are getting
plenty to eat.

Day 3 June 14 13. Babies are more
active, using wings like flippers for
locomotion. Eye slits are more
prominent as eye playoe or wings.
Bright coral-orange skin at its peak.
It will get duller from here on out.

Day 2 June 13, 2013. Perfectly
naked. Gape brilliant azure-red.
Fat in cloacal area. Minute
playoe visible on wings.

10:50 am June 12, 2013 - Hatching! First egg laid May 27, 16 days ago.
Incubation probably 14 days. 2 at, 3rd pipping (laura left). All
four eggs hatched. But one nestling disappeared on Day 4.

Prothonotary Warbler, 2012

Day 8 June 19 2013. A 12" gray
rat snake caused all hell to
break loose today until Cyndi
found it under a shrub and
tossed it over the fence. Adult
warblers didn't visit box for
over 1 hour, chipped constantly.
The box is baffled, thank goodness.
When adults finally brought (damselfly)
food, the babies' peeping was
audible from back deck. They
were hungry! Feathers are bursting
sheaths all over. Olive on back,
yellow on breast. They're practically
birds!

Day 9 June 20 2013. The transformation nears. Smooth feathers
on underparts, but wing feathers are still emerging from
sheathed. Cyndi began vigil at dawn and took photos
right after both adults fed the young. Peeping now
loud, audible from deck. Fecal sacs are so large the adults
fly as if weighted down when carrying them off.

June 21 Day 10. They're birds! Adults
making fewer trips, sometimes coming w/o food and
exiting w/ fecal sacs. Sacs have lost integrity, and adults are
having trouble removing them.
Male is singing at territory
boundaries, while ♀ chips
agitatedly.

Day 11 June 22, 2013. Fledging day! All 3 out by 1:50 pm. The young sat in box opening
most of morning until they left. At this tender age they max out at 15',
crash landing and teetering.

Prothonotary Warbler, 2012

SERENDIPITY GUIDES MY life and work, and most of my inquiry. Technology helps me along, mostly. E-mail has proven to be a mixed gift: convenient and fast, but capable of occupying much of my day if I allow it to. Social networking is even more insidious. It allows me to reach out, provide content, and present my offerings to thousands of people I have never met. But having a strong Web presence also opens me to near-constant questions and appeals for help, especially during what we wildlife rehabilitators call "baby season." Between the ringing telephone, the e-mails, and the Facebook messages, I realize that I've unintentionally started my own sometimes-worldwide Bird Help Hotline, with a staff of one, available 24/7. I've been asked about rescuing and feeding baby birds found on the ground as far away as India, California, and Canada and everywhere in between. When baby season ends, injured hawks and owls come to me throughout the rest of the year. I've learned to reply, "First, where are you, geographically?"

Lest I seem to be whining, which of course I am, I'll hasten to add that the same accessibility that sometimes vexes brings me great gifts as well.

It started like so many e-mails did in 2012:

Need some advice or a suggestion ASAP . . .

We have a pair of nesting prothonotary warblers that have all but finished building their nest in one of our nest boxes. Today to my horror I saw a male house sparrow hanging around the box. Is there anything I can do to "sparrow-proof" the box and in doing so not chase off the warblers?? I can't stand guard 24/7 even though I'd like to.

The box was made with a vertical "slot" type opening across the entire front of the box, not the typical round hole. It's in our side garden under the pussy willow tree.

I do have wire sparrow traps typically used with martin houses. Suggestions??? Thoughts??? Help??

Thanks . . .

Cyndi

The words "nesting prothonotary warblers" got my full and instant attention. These firebrands of wooded swamps are among the most stunningly gorgeous birds in a family with many worthy contenders. Because they are also one of the only cavity-nesting warblers, and a pair in a well-protected nest box could afford subjects for my work, I'd been dreaming of studying and painting their chicks for more than a decade. Not only that, but Cyndi Routledge is a terrific photographer, writer, and natural history educator in Tennessee. She'd earned my deep respect when we worked together to try to keep Tennessee from instituting a hunting season on sandhill cranes in 2011. The proposal eventually passed, but I gained a wonderful friend. I hurried to help:

Sparrows don't like Mylar or things that move in the wind. There's something called a Sparrow Spooker—you can Google it and make your own—basically a long thin stick with long stringers of Mylar fastened to it that blow around in the wind. You mount it on the roof of the box and one hopes that it will spook the sparrows but won't scare off the prothonotaries. HOWEVER . . .

Is the box on a pole that is baffled? Boxes under trees are vulnerable to snakes dropping down from above. I won't argue with site selection by prothonotaries—they might like being under trees—but I worry about predation in this situation should you be able to get rid of the sparrows.

By all means set out the sparrow traps baited with corn, millet, white bread. Get those suckers. Try that first before putting anything on the box. Nest building is the stage most vulnerable to abandonment by the birds. The spooker could cause abandonment, and you sure don't want that. Just start feeding the sparrows and then set out the traps, once they're coming to the food. Put the food in the traps only after you've got the sparrows hooked.

JZ

Cyndi answered my concerns about protection for the nest box, and we were off to the races.

THANKS!!!

YES the pole is baffled. First thing we did when the prothonotaries took an interest!!

I've set the trap. We'll see what that reaps. I'm on a mission, and if you know me that means I won't rest until it's accomplished.

Little did I know how prophetic were Cyndi's words. By the end of the next day, May 27, Cyndi had trapped three house sparrows, using waffles as bait. Two of the sparrows were males, which are most aggressive to native nesters, often killing them in competition for nest cavities. The male prothonotary was still singing and bringing nesting materials to the box. Fingers were crossed in Tennessee and Ohio, and a plan was hatching in my mind. I tried to sound casual about it:

Male house sparrows are the bad actors as far as throwing out eggs and killing female bluebirds, so you done good! This may end the chapter. Good luck.

Take pictures. I know you will.

Can you open the box easily? I'm hatching a plan . . . I have always wanted to paint prothonotary warbler nestlings but have had no opportunity. I know this is putting the cart before the horse, but what would you think of photographing the babies each day up to fledging?

It'd be a cool record at the very least, and might serve as reference for paintings. Just a thought.

JZ

I'm on board if it turns out we have babies!! Send details on the how's, etc. and we'll make it happen if possible!! Love it!!

CR

I had a hunch Cyndi would be on my suggestion like the white on rice.

There was a whoop in Whipple when I read this.

Like I said, let's not put the cart before the horse—I'm going to consider this a huge windfall if it can happen. Basically I'd just ask you to put the baby on a white background with a coin or ruler for scale—paper towel would be fine—and snap a couple photos of it from above and from the side each day. You could just stand under the box and do it in less than a minute I'd think. Then put it back in the nest and go out and re-peat around the same time next day.

If nothing else, you'd have a very cool photo record of prothonotary development. At best, I could paint from the jpegs and continue my baby series. I added tufted titmouse this year!! Gunning for white-breasted nuthatch . . . and prothonotary has always been a dream. I'm limited to birds that nest in protected nest boxes, hanging baskets, and the like—somewhere where my meddling won't endanger them. I've got all the obvious candidates and am getting into esoterica. Also dream of great crested flycatcher . . .

Very exciting!

JZ

Cyndi would capture four house sparrows by May 31. She watched the nest box as much as possible, and released the tufted titmice and downy woodpeckers that got into her sparrow trap. The male prothonotary sang lustily at the beginning and end of each day. "Such a glorious song and wonderful way to begin and end the day!" Cyndi wrote. Having heard exactly one singing on our land in the twenty-three years we've lived here, I could only dream about having a prothonotary warbler nest in one of my boxes.

Cyndi and I were on tenterhooks through the incubation period, firing e-mails back and forth. At least one male house sparrow continued to evade her traps, and a pair of house wrens, also egg piercers and home wreckers of the first order, checked out the box on the morning of June 3. The odds seemed stacked against success in the box, but Cyndi proved herself a fiercely vigilant protector. She finally captured a fifth, aggressive male house sparrow:

Guess what finally lured him into the trap? Leftover baby shower cake. Guess they're right when they say too much sugar and fat will get ya!

CR

Meanwhile, with the house sparrow infestation mostly under control, the house wren pair stepped up their campaign to take over the warblers' nest box. Cyndi and I were doing some anxious long-distance strategizing. All it would take to end the project before it began was a moment's inattention on the part of the warblers. In a matter of seconds, a house wren could slip into the nest and pierce all the eggs. While starlings can be excluded from nest boxes with a 1½-inch entry hole, there is no way to bar a house wren from any nest box, because they're smaller than any other cavity nester, able to slip into a hole only 1 inch in diameter. I advised Cyndi to put up a wren box with a 1-inch entry hole at some distance, in shrubbery, to give them a place to settle. Cyndi trapped two more house sparrows with cake on June 4. I was amazed but not surprised at her vigilance and dedication. She'd watched the box like a hawk every day since May 24, and there was no doubt in my mind that the warblers still had a clutch of eggs to defend thanks only to her efforts. By now, Cyndi was all in, and working overtime to defend her investment of time and caring. On June 5, she e-mailed me:

I must confess that last night as I tried to go to sleep, all I could do was think about my little nature "drama" that has been unfolding . . . so in my pajamas, with a pending thunderstorm, near midnight, I was out in the yard scouting out the best places to put more boxes (to lure the wren away)! And in doing so moving one of the two I placed over the weekend, deciding it wasn't the right spot.

I endured less stress raising my 4 kids!! And talk about a kick in the teeth if this fails. Goodness. Anyway, after hanging 3 new boxes to tempt the house wren out of the prothonotary's territory, or what I perceive to be such based on where I see the male warbler singing, I sat and kept vigil on the nesting box. Prothonotary male continues to sing loud and proud this morning. Female has come out three times to preen and stretch, get a drink, take a bath, and then is quickly back inside. I would suspect she's incubating.

Anyway when she zipped to the water feature I was ready with camera and step stool and zoomed over to photograph the eggs. I'm exhausted, but LOVING every minute of it.

I tried to think like a house wren, and offered more suggestions:

It occurs to me that the wren might be particularly attracted to the warblers' slot box because it's so easy to get his twigs into it (should he try to start building). And it also occurs to me that fitting little blocks of wood into the slot until you have just enough room for a warbler to get in and out might help discourage him should he start hauling twigs in. This is ONLY should he really press the assault. It might be a good idea to be ready with Plan Wren just in case.

JZ

Sure enough, the very next day a fight broke out:

> After dinner tonight I heard a horrible ruckus. Went flying out the front door to find the two house wrens "battling" it out with the male warbler. He must be an experienced male with good DNA because he was giving them hell!! They all scattered when I arrived on the scene, but the male prothonotary continued to chase after one of the wrens and then arrived back with a victorious song. Thankfully all is well; Momma was inside the box; eggs are safe and sound. Daddy did a good job of defending his territory, and the sun has set on this day. How's a body to even leave home without worrying about what's going to happen while I'm out?!
>
> Trapped house sparrow #7!

Cyndi sent photos documenting warblers coming and going from the nest box, now fitted with blocks to narrow its entrance and perhaps make it less attractive to house wrens hoping to haul in sticks. It was hard to know which of Cyndi's multipronged efforts would help save the prothonotary eggs from destruction, but neither of us could rest until she'd done everything possible to discourage the nest competitors. It hit me how very rare and fiercely contended are good nesting cavities. I hoped hard that Cyndi's lightning responses to these threats would result in a successful nesting, with fledgling prothonotary warblers chipping in the pussy willow someday. Nearly two weeks had passed since Cyndi found the first tiny, red-speckled egg in the warblers' nest. Hatching time was imminent. As of a quick box check on June 8, all four eggs were intact and warm, but a small twig lay atop them—chilling evidence that a house wren had succeeded in entering the box. Cyndi removed it and shifted the blocks in the entry hole to make it even smaller, then watched as the female prothonotary slipped in without trouble. To Cyndi's relief, the male wren was singing and building a twig nest in one of the three boxes she had provided on the far side of her house. She spent all day on June 11 sitting guard over the box from her porch and reported the following the next day, June 12.

> As I sit on my "perch" this morning I've observed a somewhat different behavior by the warblers this morning. Both are a bit on "edge," staying close if not inside the box, "guarding" the box together if anyone dare come near it, and the male although ever visible is singing less. I think we are on the cusp of hatching babies or perhaps it has begun!!

10:30 AM June 12, 2013 – Hatching! First egg laid May 27, 16 days ago. Incubation probably 14 days. 2 out, 3rd pipping (lower left). All four eggs hatched, but one nestling disappeared on Day 4.

Hatching had indeed commenced. Cyndi began photographing the four tiny pink nestlings each day, first shooting directly into the nest cup, and then, when the chicks were more substantial (which isn't saying much for minuscule blobs of protoplasm), lifting one gently from the nest, placing it on tissues, shooting several angles, and then replacing it. She'd e-mail the photos to me each evening, and I marveled to see the chicks growing before my eyes, if only on a computer screen.

Day 2 June 13, 2013. Perfectly nude. Gape brilliant orange-red. Fat in cloacal area. Minute pterylae visible on wings.

Day 3 June 14 '13. Babies are more active, using wings like flippers for locomotion. Eye slits are more prominent as are pterylae or wings. Bright coral-orange skin at its peak. It will get duller from here on out.

By June 15, the house wren had returned. If Cyndi had ever relaxed, she couldn't now.

A check of the box this morning and a few pictures to follow . . . found only 3 babies. But those 3 have almost doubled in "bulk" since yesterday morning and seem to be well.

Protho Mom and Dad come and go all day, and I get more and more anxious each day until I know all is well, as Dad has all but quit his singing. And this morning didn't help my worry as the house wren is BACK! Singing and carrying on and this morning checking out the nest box. So once again I'm perched on the porch, ever vigilant.

Day 4. June 15/13. One baby has disappeared but the remaining 3 are almost doubled in bulk. A house wren which had sung atop the warbler nest box may have raided it. Primary feather sheathes are prominent and growing quickly today. flippers became flappers. Eyes slitting open! Skin turning dusky pink. Good fat deposits around tail. These birds are getting plenty to eat.

I had a strong suspicion that the missing warbler chick had been removed by the wren, but I didn't voice it, knowing that Cyndi likely suspected it, too. House wrens are like cat burglars—silent, quick, and deadly. But there were to be no more incidents, and Cyndi's joy came through in her next e-mail, on June 16.

Good Morning!

Today finds all well with our 3 babies. Watched daddy Protho dive-bomb a titmouse yesterday afternoon who happened to get a bit too close to the box for his comfort. He then triumphantly sang for all to hear. It surprises me that he continues to sing, a bit less each day and I have to laugh when he tries to sing through a beak full of bugs—what a muffled funny song. I've watched both parents carrying away fecal sac after sac to-day. Well-fed babies for sure!

More good news followed the next day, June 17.

It's Day 6 and all is well here at Prothonotary Central. Babies continue to grow, more squiggly today than yesterday, the nest cup fuller. Pinfeathers appearing more and

Day 5 June 16 2013. Amazing wing feather growth, and spinal. feather tract is beginning to raise into a pad and erupt with sheathes. The head is getting duskier as feathers near the skin surface. All that blue is blood-filled feather sheathes beneath the skin. The male parents singing has slowed, but he sings after vanquishing a house-wren or tufted titmouse which comes too close to the box. Eyes slitted.

more; I even noticed them on the "tail bump" today. Eyes open in round circles instead of slits, and they're starting to move a bit when I place them on the paper towel.

I find myself taking longer breaks from staring at the nest box with each passing day but always with an ever-vigilant ear listening for those house wrens! Who, from the sounds of it, have established a new territory and sing daily from across the street. Regardless, I still don't trust the little suckers!

And so this morning finds me once again perched on the porch watching. It continues to be the first thing I do every morning and the last thing I do at dusk. Makes me wonder what I'll do after babies have fledged and I've scanned the treetops 'til I see them no more? I suspect the rest of the year will be a long one for me, as I wait, ever hopeful, that come next March I'll hear that *wheat, wheat, wheat, wheat* once again ringing through my yard!!

Guess there's no need to dwell on that right now . . . I have days of "good watching" yet to do, pictures to take and babies to get fledged!

CR

Day 6 June 17 2013. Babies are very wriggly. The eyes are fully open today though they keep them closed when they are afraid. Pinfeathers are coming at all along spinal tract - and 12 minute pins emerging from tail. They're quite active, moves each day, moving around when placed on the paper towel.

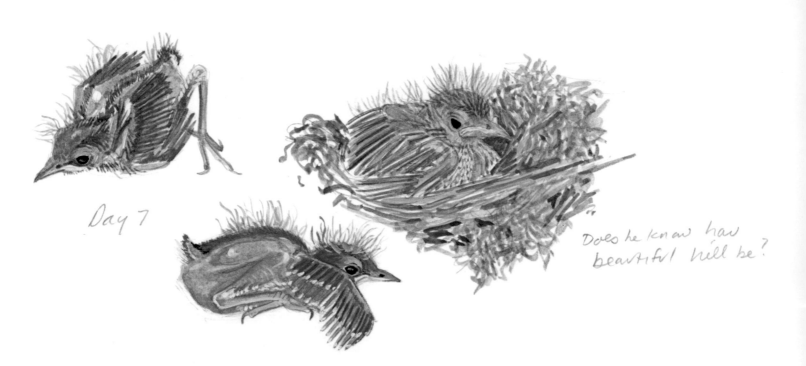

Day 7

Does he know how beautiful he'll be?

As the nestlings grew, they became more fidgety, crawling around on Day 7 until Cyndi had to contain them in a Tupperware box. She noted that they weren't displaying fear, just more active than before, and we discussed the cutoff day for any further photos.

We both knew Cyndi was dancing a fine line. If she handled the birds after their fear response had kicked in, she could risk causing premature fledging by the precious brood. Since prothonotary warblers can fledge as early as Day 9, handling them on that day (June 20) might be contraindicated. I was aghast to get an e-mail from Cyndi on the morning of June 19, describing a tumultuous scene in her yard:

> Having a moment here. Not quite sure what's happening. About an hour and a half ago I was sitting here on the porch and it seemed like all hell was breaking loose. There were eight crows in the side yard hollering and flying all over the place. Three squirrels were screaming, jabbering and carrying on in panic mode. The titmice and chickadees were going crazy screaming. Mom prothonotary was plastered to a branch on the tree near the nest box and Dad prothonotary was clearly alarmed, flying hither and yon looking for his mate, whom he found eventually hanging out under the bushes around the corner from the nest box. They have not fed the babies or gone near the box for over an hour. If I didn't know better I'd swear the babies were under the bushes, which they're NOT. The prothonotaries are clearly agitated and on edge.

Day 8

A few minutes later, Cyndi sent a photo of a gray ratsnake (a major nest predator) wound around a branch not far from the nest box. It had doubtless been attracted to the vicinity by picking up vibrations from the pippering nestlings, and the frequent comings and goings of the adults. I found myself thinking that if this much drama attends every nesting attempt birds make, it's no wonder most of them have such short life spans! Cyndi relocated the snake, and added another task to her day: beating the bushes around the nest with a rake to discourage snakes. She managed to get a photo of an eight-day-old prothonotary, briefly placing it in a basket, then back in the nest.

Day 9 - June 20 2013. The transformation nears. Smooth feathers on underparts, but wing feathers are still emerging from sheathes. Cyndi began vigil at dawn and took photos right after both adults fed the young. Peeping now loud, audible from deck. Fecal sacs are so large the adults fly as if weighted down when carrying them off.

On the tenth day, June 21, knowing the nestlings were too old to be handled, she stood on a stepstool and aimed her camera into the nest box.

Good morning. As you've probably discovered I was able to get pictures of babies today on Day 10. As I walked away from the nest box tears came out of nowhere, for I knew in my heart today was the last day I'd make that trip.

My adventure with these prothonotaries is drawing to a close. My heart is full yet breaking. But for now it will be as it was before they hatched. I'm back sitting on my "perch," watching and listening.

June 21 Day 10. They're birds! Adults making fewer trips, sometimes coming w/o food and exiting w/ fecal sacs. Sacs have lost integrity, and adults are having trouble removing them. Male is singing at territory boundaries, while ♀ chips agitatedly.

My response:

OMG!!! THEY'RE BIRDS!!!

You did it!!! They'll go today or tomorrow morning I'd think.

INCREDIBLE. Beautiful. What an experience!! I couldn't be happier or prouder of you and that gallant pair of warblers. What a gift they've given us, what a gift you've given me. I'd be bawling too. I can't believe you were able to do that on Day 10. And what an incredible change from Day 9. Just amazing. But that's birds for you.

See that superwatery semi-fecal sac/dropping? Big sign of impending fledging. When they stop using disposable diapers, Mom can't clean the nest anymore—they have to

get out of there. Maybe this afternoon. I'm so thankful you'll be there to see them off.
   WAY TO GO, CYNDI!!

On June 21, Day 10, Cyndi noted that the adults' trips had dropped in frequency, and that twice an adult entered the box without food and exited with a fecal sac. These sacs had lost integrity, and the adults were unable to simply lean into the box, snatch a fecal sac, and fly off. They'd enter the box and come out headfirst with a bill full of long gooey strings. The adults lingered near the box, chipping insistently, without feeding the young. One of two things could have been happening: the adults may have decreased the frequency of feeding to goad the young birds into fledging, or the chicks may have been refusing food just prior to fledging, a behavior I've seen in hand-raised chimney swifts.

On the morning of June 22, Day 11, Cyndi spotted a young warbler sitting in the nest entrance, looking out. It was fledging day for sure. All three had left as of 2:00 PM, apparently unhindered by complete lack of a visible tail. As Cyndi watched, they made their way in short flights of about 10 to 15 feet at a time through her wooded lot, until they were lost to view. "They flap like little puffballs that crash on landing, or land on a branch and teeter back and forth." She saw all three get fed before losing track of them in the woods.

Hard not to keep checking. I might need detox! I am a bit sad . . . it comes in waves.
Took that long shower before dinner. Going to have that beer in a bit.

Day 11 June 22, 2013, Fledging day! All 3 at by 1:50 pm. The young sat in box opening most of morning until they left. At this tender age they max at at 15', crash landing and teetering.

Thus ended an adventure, guided by serendipity down the perilous life path of a pair of warblers and their young. Far from disturbing the birds, I feel certain that Cyndi's constant vigilance and lightning-quick intervention sent three more prothonotary warblers into the world than otherwise would have survived. That I got some otherwise unattainable painting reference out of it seemed secondary to the rollercoaster of wonder, joy, and stress, and Cyndi's total commitment to seeing her brilliant golden tenants through from nest building to fledging. That's one way to make the world a better place.

Day 8. Cooler 70's sunny 11:50-12:30
All knees and angles today, the
eyes slit open, and the feet much
better developed. He's flapping and crawling
and protesting silently! I can see the
rufous flank feathers coming in. His top-
knot's falcon shape, too. He's much less
downy than a typical passerine. More
woodpecker-like in that respect.

Day 7. Hot! 85° and sunny. Babies all eyed
& hopping. This too pile knew better after
a few minutes. Good fat deposit evident, pygostyle
plainly, air chubby slate-grey pads on hand & heel
feet much better formed today. Scutes apparent. His
feet much better formed today. Scutes apparent. His
more active and climbing more. Notice two nestles so
I dusted the rest of Diatomaceous earth. Will probably
need to replace it - use of the nest chicks right wasn't equal.
3:15-4pm

Day 6 4/29/12. Really downy today
with the big bogo'gar's feet, and
reptilian feet & feathers now out on
the wings. He snuggles into the warmth
of my hand, still blind. Here in the 70's and
sunny today, and all six babies are live & warm.

4/28/12 Day 5. A big change (Hairsan 11:20-1:45)
Pterulae much more evident. Glad to see not
deposits indicating the pygostyle, even though
the bare skin's sure w/ one of cols asking
the air's evident very and a bit of pigmentation
The air's evident very and a bit of pigmentation
has appeared on the maxilla. A huge feral rac
is visible in the caecum - kneading to have to see
gut that transparent they skin is the feet are much
larger & better developed today. This is getting so interesting!

He was here now the sharper. Day 4
Feet are scaly and contour feather
Pygostyle & feather forming & flat his
hair, and 6" in. They looked alternately
more scrawly today & today I was amazed
at a splendidly blonde which I had so have
Suddenly crust is the cup to eat his mite
He was crawling today. I was sure well too
out the other. Sunny 60° 3:15-3:45pm

April 26 2012 Day 3. Even a huge
change, legs & bill longer, and the down is
ruffling. I fed him 5x about 1x each much
for begging. I was surprised when I raised
him and I had to leave him & it was so
clouды & warm 65° 3:15-3:45pm

April 25 Day 2. A bit darker redder than
Day 1. All 6 have hatched. I wasn't on
plate I arrived, nor was the time when
I brought it back, Mom! Fed him 3x regrettably.
They are very live food and swallow a Jam like a snake.

Hatch Day
April 24, The hen titmouse is so defensive,
2012 snake-striking, that when the leaves
I just snap a photo and go home.
4 of the 6 have hatched, and I don't
want to mess about.

Tufted Titmouse, 2012

Day 9 May 2 2012 Oh my gosh he's got wings! Rubbery spiky bits, but wings! Eyes fatten again, tho' he keeps them closed. "Paintbrush" upper tail coverts, tail tips and tertials, also spreading rectrices. Primaries still in sheaths. 1st tantalizing hint of rufous on flanks. Really quite a change today. I can't wait till tomorrow!

May 3 2012
Day 10. A feathier version of Day 9. I notice much stronger toes today. He perches on my hand rather than rolling helplessly. His eyes are open. His legs are strong. I'm off to WV. Sheila will care and photograph him on Day 12, and I'll be back on Day 13. Had to leave 12:40 - 1:10 pm. Only time for one.

They struggle to sit up. Wings are heavy with blood-filled quills.

May 4 Day 11 Lots of sheaths bursting here. Abdominal tracts are not warm like a 1 to 4 nest.

May 5 Day 12. Natal down trails like smoke off the tips of emerging crest feathers. Consciousness is up - he's looking around and sitting up to take in the world. I think he'll feel a lot better when these feathers have all emerged from their sheaths.

Day 13 May 6 2012 I knew he'd have changed, but you still would expect a bird. After glancing around w/ head still rigid & turning, he screwed his eyes shut for the duration of the sitting, he curled like a dog & fell asleep through the painting. He could. He was. He's not going anywhere. Reach halfway forward and still in sheath. He scrambled from my hand back into the nest when I put him back.

ca Day 19 - out of the nest, but spending time on the ground. Sustained flight being yet to be attained.

Day 14 May 7 2012 7:15-7:45 pm. Phoebe said, "Are you going to take Tezt? So grown up and perching. Crest erect but not fuzzy crouching & stand. Today is probably it. I'll miss these birdlets! Still in the box on Day 13 May 11, giving the simulation I made a video. Very jumpy.

Literature states that Tufted Titmice self-feed entirely by Day 42. This bird looks to be close to that age, but still showing colorful gape and rictal flanges. And still begging!

Tufted Titmouse, 2012

As I write, I can hear the echoing *Peeto peeto! Wheat! Wheat! Wheat!* of an amorous titmouse. Of all the "mystery" bird songs I'm asked about, the tufted titmouse's is number one, because it's loud and insistent enough to penetrate even the least observant person's consciousness. Chasing down a mystery song to see what bird might be making it seems to have fallen from the repertoire of human behavior, perhaps because it's so much easier to ask me. Titmice have just started thinking about cavities and soft, fur-lined nests. Their whistled calls ring through the dreary February woods, taking some of the chill out of the raw air. Thanks, titmice.

I love titmice, so much so that I hung a little Plexiglas dome feeder handy by the kitchen window, tailored for titmice. In it, I put my homemade Zick dough, a nutritious concoction of fortified chick starter, rolled oats, cornmeal, and flour, held together with melted peanut butter and lard. Two titmice, the only birds thus far bold, pioneering, and agile enough to enter the small, slippery plastic feeder, help themselves all day long. Carolina wrens should follow their lead before long.

When nesting season nears, I offer alpaca fiber and mohair wool in special dispensers, and love to watch the titmice make great white Santa beards for themselves as they tug and shuttle wads of animal hair to their secret nest cavities. We've had tufted titmice land on our hammock and pull our hair as we snooze on spring days, so eager are they to line their nests with the finest. One of the best things I ever saw was a turkey vulture, feeding on a road-killed opossum. A titmouse was darting in between the vulture's scaly red legs to pull hair from the possum's hide.

I like the titmouse's smooth, subtle, clean colors, the eyeliner ring of tiny black feathers around those luminous onyx eyes, which gives it a look of permanent surprise.

A very ticked-off titmouse.

I know a woman who got "permanent eyeliner" tattoos around her eyes. I secretly think she looks like a titmouse, which isn't such a bad thing after all.

Adaptability is a hallmark of titmice. A trait that serves them well in invading suburban and agricultural areas is their ability to eke out a living in small, fragmented forest patches, at least in winter. Titmice glean along tree limbs and large branches, also hanging upside down from twigs and leaf clusters, searching for dormant insects, egg cases, larvae, and pupae. They will also land on the ground and toss through leaf litter, something chickadees don't often do, effectively scouring the entire habitat for hidden food.

Tufted titmice (*Baeolophus bicolor*) are a bit of an anomaly in their family, the Paridae. Oh, how I miss their old genus, *Parus*, but I see why they should be a different genus from chickadees (*Poecile*). They're big and strong, more like miniature jays to my eye than chickadees. Not only that, but tufted titmice are dominant to Carolina and black-capped chickadees in the mixed feeding flocks these species join in winter. The tufted titmouse's social structure sounds pretty familiar to me: males are dominant to females, adults are dominant to juveniles, and dominance within the flock depends on when a bird joined it. Birds who joined earlier preside over latecomers.

Also in contrast to chickadee social structure, tufted titmice tend to hang together as families through their first winter. It's nice to know that that little flock of titmice bickering at the feeder might all be related. Not only that, but titmice from the previous year may help feed their parents' brood in their second spring! At one nest, the helper was one of the nesting female's offspring from the previous year, though from a different father. I find myself wondering if titmouse societies might be matriarchies. Why not? The "tiny corvid" analogy kicks in again, as I think about the social structure of Florida scrub-jays and American crows, which also help at the nest. We're naturally attracted to creatures that share aspects of our own social structure. Having good eye makeup and a peppy little crest doesn't hurt, either.

So imagine my excitement when I found a mysterious nest, composed of bark fiber, moss, and grass, and distinguished by a telltale foundation of dead, crumbled leaves, in a nest box at the far end of our long scraggly meadow in April 2012. Only two birds that might nest in a box use dead leaves in their foundation: Carolina wren and tufted titmouse. I was used to hosting Carolina wrens, but in twenty-two years of monitoring nest boxes in Ohio, I'd had only one titmouse use a box. Until, perhaps, now. I photographed the nest and left it alone. The next time I opened the box, something flung itself at me with a ferocious snarl and a percussive, snapping sound. *Skroww! Skroww! Skroww!* I

Hatch Day
April 24, 2012. The hen titmouse is so defensive, snake-striking, that when she leaves I just snap a photo and go home. 4 of the 6 have hatched, and I don't want to mess about.

leapt back, heart pounding, fighting my urge to cut and run home screaming. The nest was occupied by an incubating female tufted titmouse with an extremely convincing snake act. I closed the box and crept away, bursting into laughter as soon as I was out of earshot.

The next time I opened the box, I had my iPhone camera set to record video. The hen titmouse obligingly repeated the display, and I captured what I believe is the best existing video of this amazing behavior. Alone among the birds whose nests I host in my boxes, titmice and chickadees will actively defend their eggs and chicks, biting (chickadees) or performing this elaborate and frightening "snake strike" display. With each strike, the female titmouse fans her tail, opens her wings, and lunges forward with bill wide open, voicing the harsh *skroww!* call at a frequency of one lunge per second. Though the titmouse weighs only 21 grams, this display is highly effective in scaring the bejabbers out of a human perhaps 3,500 times her weight. A picture pops into my head as I do the calculation: a burlap sack full of 3,500 broody female titmice. I would not want to have them mad at me.

I stayed away from the nest box, not wanting to elicit further striking displays from the hen titmouse. I waited until I figured incubation would be complete. When I opened the box, her chicks were hatching, and she lunged and struck at me again, then left the box. This presented a dilemma. I didn't want to upset her by absconding with a chick to draw on hatching day, and risk possible injury to the tiny nestlings as she defended them when I brought the chick back. So I snapped a couple of quick photos of the hatching chicks and left her alone. To my great relief, on Day 2 and each subsequent day, the female titmouse left the nest as I approached, perhaps having decided that the snake strike act had lost its efficacy. I was clear to draw!

April 25 Day 2. A bit darker reddish than Day 1. All 6 have hatched. I wasn't as white I arrived, nor was she there when I brought it back. Whew! Fed him 3x - naglanedfly. Then grip the food and swallow - Jaw like a snake.

April 26 2012 Day 3. Here a huge
change, just a bit bigger, and the down is
stiffer. I fed him 3x though he isn't much
for begging. She was on nest when I returned
him and I had to leave him next to her.
Cloudy & warm 65° 3:15-5:30 pm

By Day 2, all six eggs had hatched. I took a tiny pink nestling to the studio to paint it, and fed it three times while I worked. Unlike most other nestlings I'd worked with, which won't swallow unless food is pushed deep into the throat, the tiny pink titmouse bit down on the bits of "bug omelet" I offered, actively grabbing the food and swallowing it down like a snake. Well!

On the third day, the female titmouse was off the nest when I took a chick, and sitting tight when I returned with it. She didn't strike but refused to budge, so I had to leave the chick next to her, confident that she would pull it under her as soon as I closed the box. Titmice are good parents. There was a quantum leap in the chicks' size on Day 4; they'd doubled in bulk and length.

Another leap on Day 5—the chicks were showing dark pterylae (feather tracts), and despite frigid April rain and temperatures in the 40s and 50s, the chicks were warm

4/27 2012 Here came the pterylae! Day 4
Dark blue tracts are emerging; five
pinpricks & feathers forming under the
transparent skin. They looked different today
more robust, gaping lustily. I was worried
about yesterday's chick, which I had to leave
beside Mom in the nest but not in the cup-
she was striking windily. I knew she'd roll it in
w/ the others. Sunny 60° 3:15-3:35 pm

4/28/12 Day 5. A big change (Husband 4:30-4:45)
Pterylae much more evident. Glad to see fat
deposits bracketing the pygostyle, even though
it's been 40's & 50's w/rain off & on all day.
The ear's evident today and a bit of pigmentation
has appeared on the maxilla. A huge feral sac
is visible in the caecum - bringing it home to me
just how transparent the skin is. The feet are much
larger & better developed today. This is getting so interesting

and laying on fat. Generalists like titmice tend to do better in bad weather than birds that rely on only one kind of food; titmice and chickadees can keep their broods going through cold rainy spells that readily kill bluebird and tree swallow hatchlings. The titmouse nestlings' ears, which had been sealed, opened up on this day—another thing I hadn't seen in other species I'd worked with, all of which seemed to have open ears from hatching on.

One chick's eyes were slit open on Day 7; the others' remained sealed. Spotting two mites on the chick I painted on Day 7, I decided to dust the nest box with diatomaceous earth, a nontoxic way to kill soft-bodied mites. The sharp silica-based fossil diatoms of which it's composed abrade the mites' exoskeletons, eventually killing them. I was reluctant to replace the nest, as I would not hesitate to do with the simple grass nests of bluebirds and tree swallows, because I wasn't sure how fussy titmice might be about such interventions. They seem like fussy birds to me—birds who know what they like and could take exception to my messing about with their work. The diatomaceous earth seemed to do the trick, and no mite infestation followed.

Day 6 4/29/12. Really rowdy today
with the big bag o'guts look, and
reptilian pads & feathers coming out on
the wings. He snuggles into the warmth
of my hand, still blind. It's in the 70's and
sunny today, and all six babies are fine & warm.

Day 7. Hot! 85° and sunny. Babies all keyed up and begging; this + this are knew better after a few moments. Good fat deposit around pygostyle. Pterylae are rubbery slate-grey pads on head & back much better defined today. Scutes apparent. It's Feet more active and climbing more. I noticed two mites so I dusted the nest w/ Diatomaceous earth. Will probably need to replace it. One of the bigger chick's eyes was slit open. 3:15 - 4 pm

Throughout the chicks' development, I marveled at the strength and size of their feet; they seemed to gain clutching strength and maneuverability very early. Feet are very important to titmice. They spend a lot of time hanging upside down, as well as clutching food in their toes for hammering apart.

There comes a point in most songbirds' development when they "shoot up" like a teenage boy, all their rounded corners turning into angles. Sometimes they look pallid and starved, as if their growth were outstripping their food supply. That tipping point seems to be Day 8 for these titmice.

Day 8. Cooler 70's sunny 11:50 - 12:30 All knees and angles today, one eyes slit open, and the feet much better developed. He's flapping and crawling and protesting silently! I can see the rufous flank feathers coming in. His top- knot's taking shape, too. Still much less down than a typical passerine. More woodpecker-like in that regard.

Day 9 May 2 2012 Oh my gosh he's got wings! Rubbery spiky ones, but wings! Eyes farther open, tho' he keeps them closed. "Paintbrush" upper tail coverts, tail tips and tertials, also secondary coverts, Primaries still in sheath. 1st tantalizing bits of rufous on flanks. Really quite a change today. I can't wait till tomorrow!

On Day 9 the birds are suddenly cloaked in their own wing quills, and a spiky Mohawk has sprouted on their heads, running all the way down the spine. It's a presage to feathering out, and after nine days of painting nakedness, I'm eager to see the transformation of gawky duckling to swan. Flank feathers are coming out, too, with rufous tips showing.

Meanwhile, the wing quills are lengthening dramatically, and by Day 10 paintbrush tips are popping open on wing quills. The chick's toes are much stronger today, and he wraps them around my fingers and perches instead of rolling around helplessly.

May 3 2012
Day 10 - A feathered version of Day 9. I notice much stronger toes today. He perches on my hand rather than rolling helplessly. His eyes are open. His legs are strong. I'm off to WV. Shila will come and photograph him on Day 12, and I'll be back on Day 13. Hate to leave. 12:40-1:10 pm Only time for one.

They struggle to
sit up. Wings are
heavy with blood-
filled quills.

May 4 Day 11 Lots of sheath bursting here.
Abdominal tracts are out. Worn like a little vest.

I'm painting from photos taken by my best friend, Shila, who has driven out to the farm on Days 11 and 12 to fill in the gaps with photos while I'm away at a birding festival. There's so much going on here that I hardly know where to start. I'm glad to have the luxury of studying it closely. All flight feathers are making paintbrush tips, and the crest has emerged comically. The chick looks like a woman in curlers, a bit embarrassed and waiting impatiently under the dryer hood for her new look.

May 5 Day 12. Natal down trails
like smoke off the tips of emerging
crest feathers. Consciousness is up—
he's looking around and sitting up to
take in the world. I think he'll feel a
lot better when those feathers have
all emerged from the sheaths.

Day 13 May 6 2012. I knew he'd have changed but you
still never expect a bird. After glancing around w/ head
turning, he screwed his eyes shut for the duration 3/4 of
the way through the painting he circled like a dog & fell
sound asleep. Primaries still in sheath. 1/2 way. He's not going anywhere.
But he crawled from my hand back into the nest when I put him back.

The bird has emerged in the reptilian mess of quills and spikes. There's someone in those wide-open eyes, and the feet are strong and capable. A new layer of feathers gives a tantalizing glimpse of the bird to be. I note that titmice proceed at roughly the same pace as do bluebirds—feathered enough to be identifiable titmice at Day 12 but nowhere near ready for the outside world.

With Shila's photo portraits in hand, I got home from West Virginia to resume the series at Day 13. I couldn't believe the little feathered being in my hand was the same bird I'd left only three days earlier. It was extremely alert, turning its head and looking around the studio as I worked. Like a dog preparing for a nap, it then described a little circle, screwed its eyes shut, and fell sound asleep, its tiny bill drooping into its tissue bed. When I carried the chick back to the nest, it kept its eyes shut, and looked for all the world as if it had died. But when it heard the box open and the tiny rustling of its siblings, it raised its head and crawled from my open palm into the center of the soft, warm ring of gray feathers. Clearly, this birdlet knew where it belonged, and meant to return on its own steam.

Day 14 May 7 2012 7:15-7:45 pm
Phoebe said, "Are you going to take That?"
So grown up and perching, crest erect
but not fledgy- crouching & scared. Today's
probably it. I'll miss these birdlets!
Still in the box on Day 18- May 11, giving the See-wer call.
I made a video. VERY jumpy.

With that kind of sentience and mobility, I knew that taking a chick on Day 14 would be pushing it. My daughter, Phoebe, then fifteen, accompanied me out to the titmouse box to collect a chick. We opened the box, looked at the bright-eyed chicks, and Phoebe gasped, "Are you going to take *that*?" Well might you ask, Grasshopper. I knew that my success would hinge on whether the chick cheeped when I picked it up. One cheep of distress, and the entire nest could explode. Then Phoebe and I would be scrambling to gather them back up, stuff them in the box, and plug the entry hole until they all settled back down. To our relief, the chick closed its eyes and remained silent, and Phoebe and I crept away with our last model on the last day I dared to depict it.

In the end, the titmice remained in the box through Day 18, completing a rather

ca-Day 19- out of the
nest, but spending
time on the ground,
sustained flight being
yet to be attained.

leisurely infancy, as is the wont of cavity nesters. They have the luxury of taking their time, being less exposed to wind and weather and the attention of predators than do open-cup nesters. I walked out to clean their box and was surprised to be met with a battery of bright black eyes. "Wow!" I breathed, and the chicks instantly flattened themselves down into the nest material at the sound. This box was full of avian shrapnel, waiting to explode. I closed the box, grinning like a pirate who'd found treasure. Another brood of birds would be headed out into the warm May air tomorrow morning, and I'd been there the whole way to see them grow up. Watching songbirds develop is like speed parenting: as if your infant stood up, walked, talked, graduated from high school, and asked for the car keys, all in the space of eighteen days. Or twelve, if you're a Carolina wren or a mourning dove. I watch it, I draw it, I study it, and I still don't get how it happens. Witnessing it is as close as I can get to understanding it.

Literature states that tufted titmice self-feed entirely by Day 42. This bird has to be close to that age, but still showing colorful gape and rictal flanges. And still begging!

Day 2- August 16, 2012. Clear the 3rd egg won't hatch. I can see the growing gas space from the decomposing contents. I won't remove it - It's a good pillow for a sweet baby's chin. And I don't want to leave a trace & scent at the nest. The babies think I'm Mom, and gape at the slightest jostle.

their eyes are just lines

August 15 2012- Hatching Day! I wonder what first-time parents must think when their smooth blue eggs are replaced with Martians. Thick grey natal down on heads & backs.

August 17 2012
Day 3- beneath the leaf canopy the nestlings are huddled down, heads bowed. I can see enough to see their wings have gone blue with sheathes beneath the peach-coral skin. There is some change in size, but it's not dramatic. They look like they're conspiring.

I didn't know where she'd gone until I reached in to pull a tall white lettuce plant and spooked her out of the perennial hibiscus on Aug. 15 2012. Two eggs would hatch that very day. I saw an opportunity in the hot cement sidewalk. I could photograph them without touching anything!

July 30, 2012- I looked down from the studio window to see Piper's mate carrying cocoon fiber gleaned from a hanging basket liner, toward the front yard garage. O lucky day! Serendipity favors the prepared mind- L. Pasteur

Indigo Bunting, 2012

We call the place Indigo Hill, for the small blue buntings that sing from the meadow's edge through the hottest summer days. Yellow-breasted chats and prairie and blue-winged warblers have come and gone as the habitat has matured, but indigo buntings have more catholic habitat preferences, and have somehow stuck with us since we planted our flag on these 80 acres in 1992. For that I am grateful, and I'm more grateful to have known three of them personally in the years we've been here.

First was a male with an odd little divot of feathers missing from the back of his head. The not-very-creatively named Baldy would show up on an April day in the rain, eating at the first dandelion flowers to blow their seeds, and he'd help himself to sunflower seed at the feeder all summer long, always identifiable by that patch of missing feathers. It's a thing to have an indigo bunting you can recognize year after year, and when he finally vanished I was bereft. Buntings still sang from the meadow's edges, but I missed our yard bunting.

In the spring of 2011, another male showed up and staked his claim to our yard, and this one had a penchant for singing at first light from the most marvelous of perches: an antique cast-iron farm bell just outside the bedroom window. For someone who already loves indigo buntings, it hardly gets better than that. It's all right to be awakened at 5:15 A.M. on a Saturday if it's a brilliant blue bird sounding the alarm.

I named him Piper, for the Piper at the Gates of Dawn in my favorite chapter in *Wind in the Willows*. And Piper did me one better, taking to the bubbling Bird Spa bath just beneath the studio window as if it had been put there just for him. On a hot July day, he could be counted on to take at least three full, soaking baths, delighting me as his sodden feathers turned from lapis to black, to blue again as he preened and dried.

Piper
on the farm-
hase bell 7/14/12.

And in between his baths, a delicately tinted cocoa brown female sneaked in, a glaze of cerulean on her shoulders, tail, and crown: Mrs. Piper.

I couldn't put an estimate on the hours I spent watching these birds, smiling fondly down on them as they broadcast silver droplets from the Bird Spa; foraged in the plains coreopsis and foxtail grasses; sang against the shimmering white sky of late summer. In the summer of 2012, I decided to try to get photographs of Piper in the near-dark he prefers for his dawn song. He started singing before it got light, and he'd come to the farm bell, which is about 20 feet from my bedroom window, just as shivering Dawn was dragging herself out of her eastern bed. I wanted a picture of that. The first couple of times I shot through the glass, and it was terrible. It's hard to find a setting on your camera for oh-dark-thirty that doesn't involve flash, which was the last thing I wanted to do to a bird with the courage to sit and sing his heart out on a farm bell just outside my bedroom window. So I removed the screen and slept with the window wide open all night so I'd be awakened by Piper's first note.

I put my Canon 7D on a monopod and kept it at bedside. When Piper's ringing notes stirred me awake, I crawled from the bed and stealthily glided, camera and monopod in hand, toward the open window. I shot and shot, fighting vibration, Piper's spookiness, and deep darkness, for three mornings in a row. I finally got some images of a barely discernable bird, his silvery mandible standing out like a Christmas bulb, singing his heart out to the dark meadow. I'd always wondered about that reflective silver mandible. It looks nice against the brilliant blue plumage, but its function may be to serve as a visual display for predawn song, when the bird itself is but a midnight blue shadow. Follow the bouncing silver ball.

Chance oversees my work, none more so than my bird studies, for I gather encounters with my subjects only as their whims allow. Just before 10:00 on the morning of July 30, 2012, I was trying to write a column, but couldn't tear my eyes or lens away from the steady parade of birds at the bubbling Bird Spa. A white-eyed vireo, then Piper, then a male eastern bluebird took their toilettes. Two juvenile brown thrashers sunbathed gawkily on the lawn, looking deader than dead until they'd raise their heads to pant and preen. A pair of juvenile hooded warblers flirted just beneath the window. A young scarlet tanager dropped in for a bath, and Piper joined him for a second go. A worm-eating warbler perched prettily a few feet from my flabbergasted face, and was promptly knocked off its perch by the pugnacious white-eyed vireo. At 12:08, the prize of prizes: Piper's mate, perching briefly in the cardinal flower, her bill stuffed with long brown coco fibers from my hanging basket liners. That sighting capped a never-to-be forgotten two hours of my life, and started a line of inquiry that led to these paintings.

I sat perfectly still and watched her dart in a straight line toward the garage. I was burning to know where she would build her nest, but she was too smart to let me see

July 30, 2012 - I look down from
the studio window to see Piper's
mate carrying cocoa fiber gleaned
from a hanging basket liner, toward
the front yard garage. O lucky day!
Serendipity favors the prepared mind.
— L. Pasteur

her at work. I didn't figure it out until August 15, when I reached to pull a weed from the flower border along the garage. A small brown bird fluttered out of a shrubby pink hibiscus right by the door. I've seen enough birds leave their nests to know the way they fly—a slow, fluttery course, the tail spread, designed to draw attention to the flier and away from the nest. Peeking into the hibiscus, I saw three eggs of the palest blue in a neat, thick-walled grass and leaf cup about 3 feet off the ground. That very day, two of them hatched, and the chicks raised wobbly heads to the sky as they begged blindly. I always wonder what goes through a bird's mind when it finds a smooth blue egg has

been replaced by a squirming pink blob. Perhaps that's why new hatchlings raise their heads and gape as soon as they can. The brilliant orange mouth lining stimulates the parent birds to stuff it with food, perhaps derailing any thoughts such as, "Hey. Who are you and what have you done with my egg?"

I couldn't believe my good fortune at having Piper's little family just off the garage sidewalk. In any ordinary circumstance, you can't touch, much less borrow, nestlings from an open-cup nest without seriously endangering them. Leaving a scent trail to the nest, and touching the vegetation around it, invites predators like snakes, raccoons, opossums, even mice. As luck would have it, I could stand on the cement sidewalk, aim my little Canon camera into a small window between the hibiscus leaves, and get a lovely shot of the nest contents—all without touching a thing. Because the sidewalk is a high-traffic zone, any predator finding my scent there would think nothing of it. In a matter of a few seconds, without touching anything, I could lean over, take a couple of shots of the nestlings, and no snake or raccoon would be the wiser. This is how I elected to record the nestlings' growth. I'd miss drawing the wriggling babies from life, with all the wacky poses they strike, but I was thrilled to get so much as a single photo each day from which to work.

Mrs. Piper's choice of nest site leads to discussion of an interesting propensity of birds to nest in close proximity to humans, smack-dab in the middle of high-traffic areas. I'll never forget seeing an American robin stoically incubating in a bird's nest spruce (!) planted directly behind the loudspeaker at a drive-through hamburger stand in Marietta, Ohio. Her "habitat" consisted of a narrow strip of soil, studded with three small shrubs and a loudspeaker, and covered with dyed red pine-bark mulch. Of course, Mrs. Robin wasn't foraging there; this was strictly a nursery, albeit an unlikely one. And she pulled it off, raising three youngsters that had the privilege of fledging into an asphalt desert. One hopes they managed to hop and flutter to decent cover in the rough lot behind the Kmart. Oddly enough, nesting in a place where no predator in its right mind would want to be (or think to look for a nest) works well for robins, song sparrows, and many others. That phoebe that spooks off the porch light every time you open the back door isn't stupid. She is a bit afraid of you, but in the big picture she wants to be near you; she wants your activity, your hustle and bustle around her nest. She's chosen it precisely because predators are much less likely to find her there by your front door. When I had my epiphany about birds nesting in high-traffic areas, I became a great deal more relaxed about my comings and goings as they affected phoebes on porch lights and Carolina wrens in hanging baskets. As long as you mostly ignore the birds, they adapt very well to being your closest neighbor. Coming on and off the nest is the price they pay for your protection, and totally curtailing your activity defeats their purpose in being there.

This being said, I was careful to time my visits to the bunting nest when a binocular check revealed the female to be away. There would be no sense in stressing her unnecessarily. Because Piper did not help feed the hatchlings, his mate had to leave them for considerable periods while she was foraging. Indigo buntings nest in late summer—here it was mid-August! As I thought about it, the elegance of their plan—if plan it be—became clear. The buntings wait until weed seeds are ripe and insect prey is abundant before breeding. It's usually hot, so leaving the chicks uncovered during the day isn't a problem. If you're a female bird who has to raise chicks all by yourself, hot, usually dry mid-August is probably the best time to do it.

As the buntings' family life unfolded, Piper had vanished, but I didn't suspect foul play. Male indigo buntings tend not to feed their incubating mates or their young until after fledging. Why would this be? Given the male's brilliance, he'd be an electric blue beacon to the whereabouts of the nest. Conspicuousness is his stock-in-trade. While the female indigo bunting is rather rarely seen, living her life within about 6 feet of the ground, the male seeks out the tops of small trees as song perches. He sits like a musical note on power lines, singing continually through the heat of the day, when the sun's spotlight falls on him alone.

One might look at this behavior as guarding mate and territory, but indigo buntings of both sexes appear to have a broad philandering streak. Females will leave the territory in search of neighboring males, just as males seek out neighboring females for "affairs." Eleven of forty-four Michigan broods whose chromosomes were analyzed by David Westneat (1987) had young that were not the offspring of the putative father. Perhaps the

August 15 2012 - Hatching Day! I wonder what first-time parents must think when their smooth blue eggs are replaced with Martians. Thick grey natal down on heads & backs.

Day 2 - August 16, 2012. Clear the 3rd egg won't hatch. I can see the growing gas space from the decomposing contents. I won't remove it— It's a good pillow for a sweet baby's chin. And I don't want to leave a trace of scent at the nest. The babies think I'm Mom, and gape at the slightest jostle.

preanylae are just lines

bunting's ceaseless song can be viewed in a different light. "Here is my territory," he announces, over and over. "This is my mate. However . . . available females, I'm ready when you are!"

With this two-way opportunism going on, the male bunting's slim contribution to the care of his own brood becomes a bit more understandable. Only seven of thirty-four adult males in Westneat's study fed their nestlings at all. Once the

August 17 2012
Day 3- beneath the leaf canopy the nestlings are huddled down, heads buried. I can see enough to see their wings have gone blue with sheathes beneath the pinkish-coral skin. There is some change in size, but it's not dramatic. They look like they're conspiring.

brood fledged, eleven of twenty-seven males fed the young at least once. Subadult males (known by their patchwork brown and blue plumage), despite being the most vigorous singers, seemed to have trouble holding females. Their mates left the territories in search of neighboring males more often. None of the subadult males in Westneat's study were observed feeding their young. Why bother to invest in them if you're not sure they're yours? It's a rough-and-tumble relationship world for indigo buntings!

By August 16, it became clear that the third egg would not hatch. I could see a whitish gas space at the large end, becoming larger each day as the contents decomposed. It was likely infertile. I would have removed it were it in a protected nesting box, but I couldn't risk touching anything in this open-cup nest, so I left it. I'd find the chicks' heads resting on it, a smooth pillow for their small heads, this sibling that was not to be.

August 18·Day 4, and a vast transformation from Day 3's pink blobs. They're paler, much more angular, all jutting bones, almost skeletal, as if they're growing so fast they put it all into their framework. Wing quills have gone from fleshy pads to rapidly elongating baleen-like curtains of blood-rich quills.

Filling the nest cup! and all but covering the unhatched egg.

Day 5, August 19, 2012. Wing quills are dramatically longer. Scapular & spinal tracts are emerging. Eyes are slit open, and the chicks are seeing their world for the first time. It's brutally hot, heat reflecting off the pale garage siding, and they pant all morning. Foliage provides shade, at least.

Not much changed until August 18, Day 4, when the chicks underwent an explosive growth spurt. Wing quills sprouted where none were the day before. Feather tracts erupted in blue quills along spine and abdomen. The chicks looked paler, almost skeletal, as if the tremendous effort of growing that fast had sapped some of their strength. Their eyes had begun to slit open. I was relieved to see them pinker and better rounded on August 19, their wing quills still tracking meteoric growth.

By Day 6 the chicks' eyes were wide open, but they still did not register that I was anything out of the ordinary, and they gaped as my camera lens neared.

August 20, Day 6. Eyes are wide, but the chicks aren't yet afraid of me, and still hope I'm Mom. Blue quills might be thought to show future plumage color, but that's just the blood showing through. Neck feathers are the first to burst sheaths.

Sometime in the night, their fear response kicked in, and by the morning of Day 7 they huddled down into the nest, eyes squinched shut, at my approach. Tiny brown feather tips were bursting the sheaths on neck and wings.

August 21 Day 7 The Age of Awareness is here. Now, instead of begging, they huddle down and peek when they think I'm not looking. Paintbrush tips on most feathers, body and flight. And a first look at the tail!

Even more feather tips showed on Day 8, and the chicks' fear response was even more marked. They watched my every move, and huddled down with little shivers in response to the slightest motion or sound. All this presages fledging. Buntings may fledge as early as Day 8 if disturbed; it's good for an observer to be wary.

I was a little concerned by the nestlings' appearance on Day 8. Their heads stayed resolutely bald even as their wings and bodies had begun to feather out, and for a panicked half-hour I wondered if I'd been lovingly observing the daily growth of two brown-headed cowbirds! Indigo buntings do not eject cowbird eggs and willingly raise the young of these brood parasites. I turned to my books and a Google image search to review gape color in cowbirds: it's pink to red, with white rictal flanges (the "lips"). These birds had bright orange gapes and yellow rictal flanges. Still, it's a close call, and not one easily made. I made myself sure, though, that they were indigo buntings, and breathed a sigh of relief.

Day 8 August 22, 2012
Oh boy is there somebody in there!
Nest cup is packed with bird.
Their eyes are wide and afraid, and
they squinch down into the nest
with little shivers at my motion.
Right-hand bird has lesser coverts
tipped in buff, and his back and
scapular tracts are out. At
this stage they look so much
like cowbirds I double-
check my books—gape
color is orange in indigos,
red in cowbirds. Whew!

I knew that my time with these birds was growing short. I could tell by the look in their eyes. On Day 9 they glared at me, no longer shutting their eyes and huddling low. That look seems to say, "Come any closer and we're out of here!" The nest at this point was a grenade, ready to explode. I disallowed any further evening games of Wiffle Ball or Frisbee in the yard, lest a stray missile land in the border and launch these little rockets too early from the nest. It wasn't a popular stance with the family, but a bunting steward will do what she must.

Day 9 Aug 23. They've got that look in their eyes. Aware, ready to boot out of here if they have to. O I wish I could see their lower bodies, but I can only peek and withdraw.

Day 10 August 24
8:58 Am. Nest
Check shows them in
place, but very wary.

A morning nest check on Day 10 showed the chicks still in the nest but very wary. Their backs and wings were almost fully feathered out, though their foreheads stayed bald, and they looked like they were wearing bluish goggles. A half-hour later I peeked from a distance with binoculars to find one chick up on the nest rim, perched proudly and preening.

I watched it for a while and was charmed to see it stop in midstroke and stare at its own wing, as if it had never seen one before. I wondered if it knew that this brand-new appendage was its ticket to the sky, or wondered how the fleshy, quill-studded limb had morphed into a feathery sail.

By midmorning, I spotted a chick about 8 feet from the nest, sitting in the black-eyed Susans. It was gaping, but not for food. It was so hot—in the mid-90s—that the little thing was panting nonstop. I was stunned at how tiny it was, not even as long as my thumb, smaller than a *Rudbeckia* flower. Some of its wing feathers weren't even fully out of the sheaths. It wasn't flightworthy, lacking all but the stub of a tail. But an indigo bunting, equipped with strong feet and the ability to flutter-climb, doesn't need to be able to fly in order to leave the nest. As long as it can perch and clamber, it's good to go. The entire developmental cycle of these birds is geared toward getting out of the nest as soon as possible, beating the predators to discovering the nest. And against seemingly insurmountable odds, these birds had pulled

Day 10 Aug 24
just a few minutes
after, one is
perched up on the
nest rim! There's
no going back for
this goggle-eyed babe.
Don't know where the
2nd bird is.

And here is the second chick, in the Rudbeckia, panting in the blazing sun. Midmorning Aug 24 Day 10

it off. I don't know by what grace they had escaped the garage-dwelling ratsnakes or the coons that patrol the sidewalks each night, but they had, and I was elated to see Mrs. Piper ferrying grasshoppers to her young, and unsurprised to find no trace of the little family by evening. She had taken them off to the shrubby woods' edge, and I knew I might not see them again. I felt as if I'd stolen a little magic, painting these open-cup nesters, birds I never had any real expectation of studying closely.

Sixteen days went by. Though Piper was nowhere to be found, I continued to see his mate at the Bird Spa, so I figured all was well. I didn't expect to see the young. The morning of September 9, I spotted Mrs. Piper with her bill full of grasshopper. She flew to a young ash, its leaves coloring up for fall, and was joined by two fledglings—full size and perfect. What a difference two weeks make! They were birds! Soon these two would migrate, following nothing more than instinct and the stars to get them to the Gulf Coast and beyond. I wondered how long she would continue to feed them.

Another eight days went by. On September 17 a male indigo bunting rose up out of the prairie patch and gave a brief but indescribably sweet flight song, something I hadn't heard since late July, when Mrs. Piper was just building her nest. The bird landed in Piper's favorite cherry tree. Could it be the long-AWOL Piper? I ran for my binoculars and got him in my sights. What a motley character! He had a blue head, brown back, blue chest streaked with brown, bright white belly, and blue wings and tail. As I stood amazed, Mrs. Piper and the two fledglings flew up from the prairie patch and joined the mottled male in Piper's cherry tree. They chipped and fluttered little loops, acting for all the world like a happy family reunited.

It was Day 34 of their young lives, and the fledglings were still being fed. I had no idea they'd have such a long juvenile dependency period. And now my mind raced with questions about the mystery male's patchwork plumage. Could it be Piper? I wrote my molt guru, Bob Mulvihill, who has run a banding station for many years at Powdermill Nature Reserve in western Pennsylvania. I couldn't think of anyone who has handled more indigo buntings in more stages of molt than Bob. He assured me that in mid-September, Piper would be starting his prebasic molt, replacing his bright breeding plumage with brown basic, or "winter," plumage. He'd keep bright blue highlights on wings and head, just as I'd witnessed.

To see Piper with his family on September 17 was a fine, fine thing. To have seen the pair through an entire nesting cycle, and painted daily portraits of their offspring, was even better. When Piper returned to his bathing station at the Bird Spa in the spring of 2013 and sang briefly on the farm bell that July, I welcomed him like an old friend. I've had enough of these temporary liaisons with yard birds to know that they can be heartbreakingly brief. Longevity studies of indigo buntings show that, while two banded females were still breeding at nine and ten years of age, adult males survive on average less than two and a half years. No wonder the boy buntings sing so vigorously and mate so indiscriminately! I plan to enjoy Piper as long as he's with us. Knowing him personally is like opening a treasure box, and finding a bit of lapis inside.

The ash leaves are coloring when next I see the bunting family — two perfect fledglings, still being fed by their worn mother on Sept. 9, 2012! It is Day 26, and I am ecstatic to see them so near independence.

What a
difference
16 days makes!

Indigo Bunting, 2012 ⌒ 255

Day Seven 06/23/13
Growth seems to be concentrating
on feathers, which burst their
sheaths today. I have to think
it's highly uncomfortable to be
covered in spiky quills. Come on,
feathers! Adult not still on young
all day long, has left them
unattended only once. Wing-slapped
K 3x before spread-eagling
w/ quivering wings at two feet.
When 1st uncovered, both young
gaped briefly.

Day Six 06/22/13 Porcupines! The poultrings are nothing but
spiky quills. Down has fallen - a stringy afterthought.
The directionality of the quills is instructive, telling me how
the feathers will flow when they emerge, starting tomorrow.
Although BNA states the young will be left largely unattended after
Day 6, this close-sitting male refused to leave, and did a
distraction (wounded) display on Day 5, as well as perch-
cooing, which is thought to accustom squabs to his voice
so they can find him after fledging.

Feathers are
whitish as the
blood pulp turns to feather
inside them.
The young wheeze with a sibilant
wheeze. Both gaped at K when approached.

Day Five 06/21/13 Egg teeth are tiny and disappearing (resorbed?)
Eyes wide and birds alert and bright. Mouth has narrowed
into a diagonal slit. They look much darker overall, the
down taking a yellowish tint. Down is being shed off the tips
of the emerging feathers. You can see seeds through the
crop walls. Adult sat very
tightly - gave 8 wing slaps before
hurling about K's head then
giving a wounded display and a
whisper song of alarm. Male is
cooing from nest, sitting tight today.

Day Four 06/20/13
Eyes are open! Wing quills
greatly elongated. Today is the
Big Leap. A real head to paint.
I think to paint the purple-blue
wing and the crepe branche am
to capture this fantastic
unfinished down. Ad H gave
wounded display.

Down is
shedding
tips on these
growing forms.

06/19/13 Day Three Still
largely covered with yellowish
down!

06/18/13 Day Two You can see it last meal
through the size of its crop - the yellow sac
meal. Down looks less overall than Day
One simply because it's stretched thinner.

[egg measurements note]
27mm wide x 28? long, dove eggs
are almost perfect ovals with
no big end. Incubation runs
for 15 days.

06/17/13 Day One - The left hand bird has been
fed; it wears its crop like a neck pillow, its wobbly head
nestling atop it. The "hairy stringy down" is typical of
pigeons and cuckoos; so is the dark skin. Egg teeth
and the white tips on the mandibles. Does
having such soft, pliable, rubber bills they'd need two
start egg teeth - most birds have one at maxilla.

Mourning Dove, 2013

THOUGH I DOUBT they rank high on many people's list as favorite feeder birds, being subtle in color and flighty of nature, mourning doves hold a special place in my heart. Over the years I've been foster mother to three orphans, the first (Woyzek) when I was a high school senior. That bird was famous around our Virginia suburb for unexpected landings on neighbors' heads; my mother, the bird, and I even made the front page of the *Richmond Times-Dispatch*.

These chance opportunities to look under the hood of a common and sometimes maligned bird have given me an appreciation for its intelligence and resourcefulness. Perhaps due to their somewhat pinheaded look, and a propensity for waiting until the last moment to flee oncoming danger, mourning doves are popularly believed to be slow-witted. My own sister refers to them as "dippies," for their habit of getting inside a Plexiglas-topped feeder and repeatedly bumping their little heads before figuring out how to exit. Well, unlike cavity-nesting Carolina wrens, which can figure their way in and out of anywhere, mourning doves never evolved with the necessity or concept of being *inside* anything, so their confusion on finding themselves contained is understandable. And their habit of suddenly springing into the air with thundering wings is a good way to confuse and startle a predator, giving the doves precious seconds in which to arrow away.

So, if my paintings of mourning dove chicks hold a *je ne sais quoi* of affection and sweetness, it's because young squabs have nestled under my chin to sleep, or sought me out for a chat and a kiss on their knobby heads as I worked around the yard after their release. Libby, the 2010 foundling, fell from her nest on the slender branches high in a white pine at around Day 8, and was raised on parrot hand-rearing formula, fed from a syringe. A plush chipmunk was her substitute mother at first, but the affectionate and social nature of doves came to the fore, and she spent a great deal of time on my lap and shoulder and perched atop my computer screen as I worked. She picked up her first seeds on Day 12, and by Day 15 I'd cut the frequency of her feedings as she picked up more and more seed and chick starter on her own. Day 21 saw her continuing to beg for syringe feedings, but I'd finally weaned her by Day 27.

Weaning is considerably easier for the rehabilitator to accomplish in granivorous or frugivorous birds such as doves, finches, grosbeaks, and waxwings than in insectivorous birds. There seems to be more time involved in forming the neural pathways to capture and process live prey than in picking up seeds and fruit. Mourning dove fledglings, separated too early from their parents, in fact will pick up and swallow almost anything. I observed one young fledgling wandering wanly around our Ohio patio, eating pebbles, chaff, and bits of dirt, before I took pity on it and took the emaciated bird in for hand feeding. In the ensuing weeks, Cookie became a cherished part of our family. After being fortified with hand feeding, she transitioned easily to eating seed in a hopper feeder on our deck and was a fixture around the yard for much of the rest of the summer.

Libby, the 2010 foundling, spent the final nine days of her confinement in a nylon flight tent in our yard, getting used to self-feeding and becoming accustomed to outdoor sounds, wildlife, and weather. I opened the tent on the morning of May 23, 2010, when she was forty days old. Libby hung around the yard until noon, flew to the top of our weathervane, then took off flying high, hard, and fast due north. She was gone for eight hours. The sun was setting when Libby dropped back out of the northern sky. Trembling with hunger, she filled her crop, drank deeply, and flew right back into her fledging tent. Seeing this naive young dove navigate back home after disappearing over the horizon was nothing short of miraculous to me.

Libby executed the same maneuver on the following day, taking off headed northwest

at around 1:00 PM and returning before dark, to enter her tent again. On her third day of freedom, she stayed in the open tent until 12:30, then took off for parts unknown for the rest of the day. When she returned at dusk, she landed on the front porch and perched on a hanging basket until she got my attention as I stood inside at the kitchen sink. I opened the front door, and Libby flew into the house and to my studio, where she spent that night and the next three on the back of my drafting stool. Whatever she'd found out in the big world, she clearly preferred this shelter of wood and glass to the owl-hoot night woods. On her forty-fifth day, I dismantled the fledging tent and put a hopper feeder, with a dish of water, on a tall pole in the yard. Though she fed and drank there, Libby did not come into the house after Day 46.

On June 2, Day 50, I found Libby in the company of another juvenile her age in our vegetable garden. They stayed together while foraging, and perched close together in a birch, preening companionably. I was glad to see Libby learning vigilance behavior from a wild dove. When I walked out onto our deck to refill a feeder, the small flock of mourning doves there took off with a thunderous roar, leaving one puzzled immature alone, jerking her head back and forth, looking for the threat. It was Libby, failing to see me as such. June 4 saw Libby coming in to keep me company as I weeded the garden. She settled onto the mulch nearby and began arranging straw in a pile around her: a play nest! And possible corroboration on my hunch that this dove was a female. I last saw her on Day 64, just before we left to spend a week on the North Dakota prairie. The last apron string had been severed, and Libby was on her own.

In a turn of fate, I got to know fellow guide Keith Corliss while leading field trips at the Potholes & Prairie Birding Festival in North Dakota in 2012. In the spring of 2013, he had mourning doves nest successfully in a wreath on his back patio. This was not a coincidence, for Keith, a corporate pilot, North Dakota Rare Bird Records Committee member, and outdoors columnist for the *West Fargo Pioneer*, had consciously engineered just such an event. He wrote: "I relish the idea of birds nesting on or around my urban property. It keeps alive the notion that I can still maintain at least a thin thread of contact with the natural world even in a mostly unnatural setting. However bare that connection might be, it's worth salvaging. With that in mind I have taken steps to attract likely nesters to my property by offering a couple of nest boxes and by planting numerous cover trees and shrubs.

"After seeing several examples of house finches nesting in wreaths on neighbors' doors, I thought I might be able to get into the house finch nest business too. I had a willow in the back that produced countless long wispy twigs annually. Simply by cutting these and fashioning these into a wreath-like circle I had the substrate for a nest. By wiring a cheap, cheesy, plastic flower wreath to the outside of my homemade one, I now had a potential nest site that would a) provide fertile potential for some urban nesting birds (while avoiding house sparrows) and b) offer at least a modicum of visual appeal for my wife who no longer had to stare out the back window of the kitchen at a cluster of dead willow branches.

"It turned out to be quite productive. In the ensuing seasons we twice hosted nesting American robins and mourning doves. Alas, I have watched with eager anticipation while house finches check out the site every spring, but the birds have yet to nest there. It's there waiting for them next spring just in case" (Corliss 2013).

27mm wide × 28" long. dar eggs are almost perfect ovals, with no big end. Incubation ran 14-15 days.

06/17/13 Day One. The left hand bird has been fed; it wears its crop like a neck pillow, its wobbly head resting atop. The hairy, stringy down is typical of pigeons and cuckoos, as is the dark skin. 'Egg teeth' are the white tips on the mandibles. Doves have such soft, pliable rubber bills they'd need two stout egg teeth. most birds have an air maxilla.

At the June 2013 Potholes festival, Keith mentioned that the mourning dove pair had started another clutch in his West Fargo wreath two days after their first brace of squabs had fledged. My eyes lit up as I beheld a fresh victim for my nestling project. I asked Keith if he'd be willing to photograph the squabs each day as they grew up. And upon returning from the festival on the evening of June 17, 2013, he found the two tiny chicks, furred in yellowish down, just hatched.

Kismet had kicked in; this was meant to happen. For the next two weeks, despite a demanding flying schedule, Keith got home every day to faithfully photograph the squabs and adults in their stick nest in his homemade wreath, e-mailing the cell-phone shots to me in Ohio. So accustomed was I to sketching and hurriedly painting my nestlings from fidgety, constantly moving live birds, it was a pure luxury to paint the chicks from photos.

06/18/13 Day Two. You can see its last meal through the side of its crop—the yellowish mass. Down looks less dense than Day One simply because its stretched thinner

06/19/13 Day Three Still largely covered with yellowish down!

For his part, Keith fell into the thrall of the family just outside his back door:

"As much as I try to avoid anthropomorphism in my dealings with birds, there comes a point when playing host to a family of birds—in this case mourning doves—when a person inevitably starts to call them their own, as in 'our doves.' As I observed the comings and goings of the adult birds, and the meteoric growth rate of the young, a certain sense of intimacy became inevitable. I found myself becoming protective. Wind or rain became a concern—how are the doves doing? Are the parents still feeding the young? I checked on them daily as a parent does their own child."

Day Four 06/20/13
Eyes are green! Wing quills
greatly elongated. Today is the
Big Leap. A real bear to paint.
I have to paint the purple-blue
body and use opaque gouache over
it to capture the fantastic
curlicues of down. Adult gave
wounded display.

Down is
stretching
thin on their
growing forms.

On Day 5, Keith heard the male cooing from a nearby perch before he came to feed the young, a behavior called "perch cooing" that readies the young to recognize and orient to the male's voice after fledging. On this day, a parent dove performed a "wounded" display, hovering briefly before flopping about on the ground in an attempt to draw Keith from the nest. The parent doves were such close sitters that Keith usually had to gently nudge them off their chicks in order to get a quick photo. Despite mild weather, only after Day 10 were the squabs left unguarded for any appreciable length of time.

As I write, I have a 20 × 30 inch sheet of watercolor paper propped before me. It's covered, corner to corner, with life-size paintings of the twin mourning doves, from egg to Day 20. I'm a linear thinker and doer. I must finish one task completely before turning to the next. And I find that painting fully occupies my right brain, and while it's engaged, I have trouble getting the left half (the writing half) in gear. So I finished most of the paintings for this book before I could start writing it. What hits me in looking at the mourning dove sequence is the meteoric rate of their growth, especially in the first six days. After that, growth is still impressive, but the changes have more to do with plumage maturation than a great change in size. What could be going on? With my experience in aviculture and avian rehabilitation, I knew that the first place to look for an explanation would be diet.

Day Five 06/21/13 Egg teeth are tiny and disappearing (resorbed?) Eyes wide and birds alert and bright. Nostril has narrowed into a diagonal slit. They look much darker overall, the down taking a yellowish cast. Down is being shed off the tips of the emerging feathers. You can see seeds through the crop walls. Adult sat very tightly - gave 8 wing slaps before hurtling about K's head then giving a wounded display and a whisper song of alarm. Male is cooing from nest, sitting tight today.

Pigeons and doves, distributed worldwide, are in perhaps the most exclusive of all sets of birds: those that can produce crop milk. Imagine! The mourning dove and the rock pigeon, head-bobbing smartly down a New York City sidewalk, share this ability only with other pigeons, flamingos, and *male* emperor penguins. Knowing that there are currently estimated to be 10,000 known species of birds in the world casts that tiny subset of milk-making birds into an even more wondrous light.

Sheaths are
whitish as blue
blood pulp turns to feather
inside them.
The young whistle with a sibilant
wheeze. Both gaped at K when approached.

Day Seven 06/23/13
Growth seems to be concentrating
on feathers, which burst first
sheaths today. I have to think
it's highly uncomfortable to be
covered in spiky quills. Come on,
feathers! Adult ♂ still on young
all day long. Has left them
unattended only once. Wing-slapped
K 3x before spread-eagling
w/ quivering wings at his feet.
When 1st uncovered, both young
gaped briefly.

Day Six 06/22/13 Porcupines! The poorthings are nothing but
spiky quills. Dawn has fallen— a strangy afterthought.
The directionality of the quills is instinctive, telling me how
the feathers will flow when they emerge starting tomorrow.
Although BNA states the young will be left largely unattended after
Day 6, this close-sitting male refused to leave, and did a
distraction (wander) display on Day 5, as well as perch-
cooing, which is thought to accustom squabs to his voice
so they can find him after fledging.

06/24/13 Day 8. Another in a series of transformations. This done late in the day - but in a little over 24 hours, all the feathers have burst & emerged. The squabs must be much warmer and more comfortable now. Heads are still in pin curlers. Had to shoo adult of at 6:30pm - did spread - wing *grunn* display on ground.

What is crop milk? Perhaps more properly described as "crop cheese," it is a curdlike secretion produced by parent pigeons and doves, and fed exclusively to their young for the first five days after hatching. Parent doves are influenced by the hormone prolactin, which is secreted during incubation. Neutered pigeons are unable to produce the prolactin to stimulate the secretion of pigeon milk. When a sitting bird of either sex feels the movement of chicks in the developing eggs, and hears their faint vocalizations, prolactin flows, and the adult's crop undergoes further dramatic changes (*The Natural Winning Ways*, Vol. 10). Physiologists have investigated the unique buildup of the epithelium of the pigeon crop, the baglike food-storage pouch in the upper esophagus. Biochemists have analyzed the milk's chemical composition, dry and wet. Pigeon fanciers and behaviorists have determined what specific stimuli govern the onset of prolactin secretion, and subsequent crop milk production. And it's all a miracle in my eyes.

The incubating pigeon's crop, under the influence of prolactin, acts something like a uterus, its walls building and thickening to provide nutrition for offspring. On the eighth day of incubation, the crop wall starts to thicken and become congested, and glands within it develop until they are ready to secrete milk on hatching day. The crop epithelium thickens by a factor of five from its nonbreeding condition to the point where it is ready to produce crop milk. The volume of the crop's glandular system increases by a factor of twenty between egg laying and hatching. The parent doves in effect become milk machines, a transformation that any nursing mother can appreciate.

Day 9. 06/25/13. Smoothing out. White outer tail feathers are at. The squab in back, which keeps its position in the nest, is consistently behind in development and will fledge second. The adult ♂ will not leave today, perhaps sensing they might fledge too early.

The "milk" itself is composed entirely of fat-loaded epithelial cells, which are sloughed off into a cheesy mass that fills the crop of the parent dove. Dry analysis reveals a composition of 57.41 percent protein and 34.19 percent fat, and no carbohydrates. On a wet weight basis, pigeon milk contains 9 to 13 percent protein, 9 to 11 percent fat, 0.9 to 1.5 percent carbohydrate, and an energy content of 5.6 to 6.8 kilocalorie per gram. Whereas cow's milk is 92 percent water, crop milk contains about 70 to 75 percent water, giving it a consistency more like that of bread crumbs than of milk. Rock pigeon squabs fed pigeon milk increase their body weight twenty-two times in their first three weeks of life. Crude extracts of pigeon milk stimulate the growth of cultured hamster ovary cells (Shetty et al. 1992).

Day 10
06/26/13
"They're birds!"
And no adult. Acting
antsy. This is
the first day they
have been left alone.

Day 11 – young are a bit jumpier when adult is away. One gave a defensive bill snap when approached.

It is this homemade rocket sauce, then, that spurred the incredible growth I noticed in mourning doves from Days 1 to 6. Production of crop milk, in an evolutionary sense, would seem to be the dove's unique response to the need for its young, raised on a vegetarian diet, to grow rapidly and leave the nest as soon as possible. The threat of predation, as always, is the driver for this urgency. Indeed, I was stunned that the mourning dove, with its plant-based diet, had a developmental arc even faster than that of the Carolina wren, which feeds its young protein-rich insects. Mourning doves are largely covered in feathers by their eighth day, when the super-speedy wren chicks are still quilly pincushions. Thinking about this, I realized that in order for squabs to grow big and be ready to fly as fast as possible, there had to be a dietary afterburner in the parent doves' arsenal. And that afterburner is crop milk. After Day 5, increasing

Day Twelve. 06/28/13
Still in the nest for now.
Looking at the 12 days of growth,
I want to know the secret ingredient
in pigeon milk! This morning the
larger (right) bird dropped to perch on
the handle of a weber grill. On Day 13,
the elder went back to the grill top directly
beneath the nest wreath, as if to coax its
sibling down. It worked—nest was empty that
afternoon.

amounts of grain and seeds are mixed into the crop secretions, until production ceases. Though the parents still regurgitate food for them, the squabs are receiving a diet very much like the adult's by the time they fledge around Day 12.

Keith wrote, "On the morning of Day 12, the larger, bolder of the two young birds was perched on the handle of my Weber grill. It wasn't all that far from the nest, a drop of perhaps three feet, but it had indeed fledged. It's a big deal, the equivalent, I suppose, of the young teen getting the keys to the family car for the first time. The following day its sibling joined it in leaving the nest, which has gone entirely unused since."

Day 12. The faster-growing sib perches proudly on the roof. Only one way to get up there! I've seen them huddled up for so long I'd forgotten they have necks.

On Day 12, one sibling remained in the nest, watching the bolder one make its way from grill lid to rooftop. The first to fledge returned to the grill top on Day 13, as if to coax its sibling out of the nest. The wreath was empty the same afternoon.

"After successfully fledging the family stayed nearby. I would see a parent on the roof of our garage while in the shade of a tree the two squabs preened, walked, and picked at the ground. For several days the young were rarely left without at least the adult male keeping a watchful eye on his family.

"Finally they were gone. Various mourning doves continued to come and go from the yard and young became harder and harder to distinguish from adults as the summer waned. Still, when two birds with crisp fresh feathers would stop to bathe in our bird bath, I always wondered, 'Are those our birds?' I believe they were. I sometimes complain about the boring outdoors experiences to be had within city limits in general, my yard

Day Fifteen 07/01/13. Out and trucking around the yard. Still watched over and subsidized by their folks. The Grand dak stage

in particular. Occasionally, I need to be reminded that most of us don't get to walk in wilderness every day, but there is quite a bit of natural wonder to observe. It might not be as grand as a pack of wolves hunting in Yellowstone Park or the spawning of Chinook salmon in Alaska. But every day, all around us, dramas big and small are taking place. Even in our own back yard."

Adult plumage emerging on right hand shows as b show ide

Day 20 07/06/13 The last pair of them, still hanging together, still being tended by their parents, but picking up some food on their own. A fine pair of doves. They were fed by the male this Day, and will be fed until Day 30 at least.

Raising mourning doves on parrot formula produces a vastly inferior finished product, in both form and feather quality, than does the constant attention and unique nutrition afforded by a dove's biological parents. I did the best I could with what I had at hand, and Woyzek, Cookie, and Libby all lived to fledge and go their own way. Still, I'd saved their lives, and I was privy to much about mourning doves that I'd never have understood without being pressed into service as a foster mother. With Keith's contribution to the project, I was afforded a vicarious daily peek into an accessible and well-protected nest of wild doves, which is a rarer thing than one might imagine.

As I reflected, I realized that kismet has had a hand in my doings with doves since 1976. As I finished this chapter, I went to my files and dug out the *Richmond Times-Dispatch* clipping, with my fifty-six-year-old mother and seventeen-year-old me smiling at a sleek fledgling mourning dove perched on her finger. With nothing more than common sense, my parents and I had invented a liquid crop milk substitute for this foundling, whose parents had been shot by a neighborhood boy. I recall mixing half-and-half, ground oats, and pulverized sunflower hearts into a liquid slurry, which I administered from a rubber ear syringe. I wondered how a chemical analysis of our rich homemade formula would stack up against natural pigeon milk. That fledgling looked darn good in the photo. So did my mom: the same age I am now, when the photo was taken. Tears welled up; my mother had finally left us at ninety-four, just ten days earlier. I noted the date of publication: Sunday, July 11, 1976. Twenty years to the day later, our daughter Phoebe, named for a bird, would enter the world. And birds were and always would be a part of my life, wound inextricably into its fabric, flying through it all.

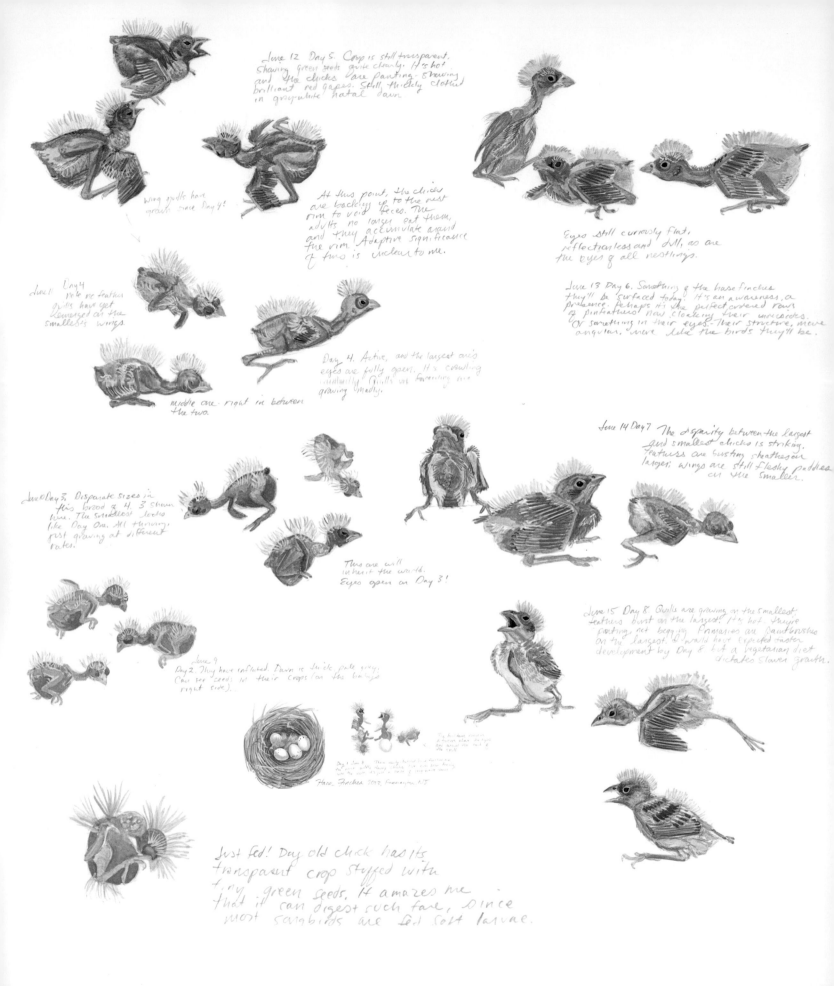

June 12 Day 5. Crop is still transparent, showing green seeds quite clearly. It's hot and the chicks are panting, showing brilliant red gapes. Still thickly clothed in grey-white natal down

Wing quills have grown since Day 4!

At this point, the chicks are backing up to the nest rim to void feces. The adults no longer eat them, and they accumulate around the rim. Adaptive significance of this is unclear to me.

Eyes still curiously flat, reflectionless and dull, as are the eyes of all nestlings.

June 13 Day 6. Something of the House Finches they'll be surfaced today. It's an awareness, a presence. Perhaps it's the perfect covered rows of pinfeathers now cloaking their wingcoverts. Or something in their eyes - their structure, more angular, more like the birds they'll be.

June 11 Day 4 Note: the feather quills have yet emerged on the smallest wings.

Day 4. Active, and the largest one's eyes are fully open. It's crawling vigorously. Quills not emerging are growing madly.

middle one right in between the two.

June 14 Day 7 The disparity between the largest and smallest chicks is striking. Feathers are bursting sheaths on larger; wings are still fleshy paddles on the smaller.

June 10 Day 3. Disparate sizes in this brood of 4. 3 shown here. The smallest looks like Day One. All thriving, just growing at different rates.

These will inherit the world. Eyes open on Day 3!

June 15 Day 8. Quills are growing on the smallest; feathers burst on the largest. It's hot. They're panting, not begging. Primaries are paintbrushes on the largest. I would have expected faster development by Day 8 but a vegetarian diet dictates slower growth.

June 9 Day 2. They have inflated. Down is thick, pale grey. Can see seeds in their crops (on the baby's right side)...

Day 1 June 8. These newly hatched House Finches are translucent, mottled, downy chicks. You can hear them peeping from the nest, as just a cloth of skin and bone.

Hare Finches 2012, Pennington, N.J.

Just fed! Day old chick has its transparent crop stuffed with tiny green seeds. It amazes me that it can digest such fare, since most songbirds are fed soft larvae.

House Finch, 2013

While the larger chicks'
feathers continue to burst the
sheathes as they pass through the
paintbrush stage, the smallest
is still mostly a bundle of
quills (far right)

June 16 Day 9

There is a sweet,
blank bird-eyed
innocence to their gaze
that the adults share.

June 18 Day 11. There continues
to be a disparity in size and
development, but the gap is
closing slowly. Overall, house
finches are the fastest-
growing. Must be the vegetarian diet.

Lots of retained down and
bare skin on the youngest,
especially. But it's catching up.

Day 10 June 17. Fluffing up, at
least 3 of the 4 are. The smallest.
still a collection of quills. But there's
hope. There's a sentience in their eyes - less flat.
still and lizardlike - brighter. Streaking shows on the big one.

June 19 Day 12.

This is the last day
they'll be able to be
handled. Looking like birds
now, aware, sentient, suspicious and afraid. A precise
down is about all that's retained. Tail still in
paintbrush stage. Still in sheath and a ways from
flying.

June 20
Day 13.
Still not
flight-ready
(tails still in
sheath) but too
jumpy to handle.
One cheep & distress
from one today and
they'll all go. So, a nest
parasit, a veritable
saturn of ringed finch shit.
Perhaps only their plant-based
diet saves them
from predation despite
this filthy habit. Not enough
smell to attract attention?

← youngest →

Compare the nest to Hatch Day!

House Finch, 2013

I'M SMILING AS I write to think that for the first year or so I lived among house finches, I had no idea what they were. I'd grown up bird watching by myself in the suburbs of Richmond, Virginia, where purple finches were the closest thing, but rare: an occasional dead-of-winter treat, along with evening grosbeaks and pine siskins. I moved to Cambridge, Massachusetts, in the fall of 1976 to attend Harvard, and the spring of 1977 found me peering up at the buildings, thickly clad in Boston ivy, focusing my father's ancient Zeiss binoculars on the small bird with the red foreparts and the rich, cheery, wandering warble. I'd neither heard the song nor seen the bird in my life.

I kept coming back to the house finch in my *Birds of North America* Golden Guide but was confounded by the range map, which placed it firmly west of the Rockies. I found the bird and its nest in my National Geographic *Song and Garden Birds of North America* and wondered at the description of its western desert habitat. What on earth was going on here? In the Internet Age, I wouldn't be left wondering for more than a few minutes, much less a year. It took some asking around and a good deal of digging in current ornithological literature to learn that house finches had undergone an assisted range expansion from their historic haunts west of the Rockies to the East Coast. As a college freshman, I was witness to an avian explosion.

The story goes that a small number of "Hollywood linnets," trapped in Santa Barbara, California, for the cage-bird trade, were released from a pet store on Long Island, New York, in 1939. The Migratory Bird Treaty Act of 1918 had made it illegal to cage and keep native migratory birds; perhaps the dealer was trying to avoid being cited. A male house finch was seen near Jones Beach in April 1941; the first nest was found in July 1944 near Babylon, New York, and a bird was seen in Tarrytown in May 1948. Fifty years later, the species had spread throughout most of the eastern United States and southeast Canada. Interestingly, western populations were expanding naturally at the same time. Like the Transcontinental Railroad, the two groups met somewhere in central Kansas, in the 1990s, though it's likely that nobody was around to drive a golden spike to mark the convergence. Current range maps paint the entire United States with breeding house finches from coast to coast.

After seeing those first house finches in Cambridge, I became accustomed to their cheery song; it was part of my new aural landscape. In the summer of 1984, I was driving on a suburban road in Harvard, Massachusetts, when a family of house finches flew low in front of the car ahead. I saw one get hit and roll to the side of the road. I stopped and picked up the juvenile male, whose broken wrist left him unreleasable. Glenn lived and sang in a spacious cage for the next nine and a half years as I moved from Massachusetts to Connecticut to Maryland and finally to Ohio. His pinkish red plumage faded to a rich gold in captivity. His nature was gentle, incurious, and somewhat fearful; he was slow to investigate new situations and foods. But his rich, tumbling song and the hollow percussive beat of his hops from perch to perch were welcome music in my studio as I worked. I could appreciate why, before the Migratory Bird Treaty Act made it illegal, house finches were kept as cage birds. Some of the most profoundly beautiful bird music I have ever heard was produced by a house finch nesting inside a parking garage of a hotel in Baltimore. His meandering warble, amplified by the cavernous concrete structure, took on rich, fruity overtones as it bounced through the space. I stopped in my tracks and closed my eyes until the concerto ended.

When I moved to my first little cottage in Salem, Connecticut, in 1983, I was happy

June 9
Day 2. They have inflated. Down is thick, pale grey. Can see seeds in their crops (on the baby's right side).

newly established house finch populations, their young rarely survive more than three days on the finch's vegetarian diet. That's one way to foil a nest parasite: feed it food it can't digest.

The low-protein fare of weed seeds, buds, flowers, and leaves likely keeps nestling house finch development to a measured pace. The indigo bunting, which is fed insects, is ready to clamber out of the nest at eight to nine days; house finch young begin to perch, preen, and flap their wings around Day 13 but may be nestbound for several days after.

Newly hatched chicks are distinguished by long, grayish white down, so full and thick that they are almost completely obscured by a whitish fluff cloud as they lie in the nest. Just as striking is the transparent skin over the crop, which clearly shows the nestling's current meal of tiny seeds. This would provide a useful clue to the parent birds as to which have been fed last.

Day 3. Disparate sizes in this brood of 4. 3 shown here. The smallest looks like Day One. All thriving, just growing at different rates.

These are will inherit the world.
Eyes open on Day 3

Day 4. Active, and the largest one's eyes are fully open. It's crawling constantly! Quills on forewing are growing madly.

June 11 Day 4
note no feather quills have yet emerged on the smallest's wings.

middle one - right in between the two.

The three nestlings I painted displayed striking differences in the speed of their development, with one well out in front of the other two in size and strength. The largest chick's eyes were fully open by Day 4, and it was crawling strongly when removed from the nest.

Up to Day 5, the adult finches removed and ate the young birds' fecal sacs. It's likely that the comparatively inefficient digestive systems of very young chicks leave some nutritional value in their droppings. Starting on Day 5, the chicks backed up to the rim of the nest, elevated their tail nubs, and deposited fecal sacs on the nest rim. A circle of droppings soon formed, which became thicker and more impressive as each day passed. The nest, once a neatly woven grass cup, was almost completely covered by a great ring of black and white feces by Day 10. I could only wonder at the adaptive significance of this odd behavior on both the nestlings' and adults' parts. Buntings and sparrows, which feed their young insects, assiduously remove their nestlings' fecal sacs throughout their development.

The conventional wisdom that adult birds remove fecal sacs to prevent the odor of droppings from attracting predators to their nest may not apply to birds feeding a vegetarian diet to their young. It's possible that higher-protein insect fare produces a smellier dropping, one that mandates quick removal, while a vegetarian diet results in

June 12 Day 5. Crop is still transparent, showing green seeds quite clearly. It's hot and the chicks are panting, showing brilliant red gapes. Still thickly clothed in grey-white natal down.

Wing quills have grown since Day 4!

At this point, the chicks are backing up to the nest rim to void feces. The adults no longer eat them, and they accumulate around the rim. Adaptive significance of this is unclear to me.

low-odor droppings and less risk of detection by predators. Purple finches and goldfinches feed their young much the same vegetarian fare, and the chicks also deposit droppings on the nest rim, which can accumulate to towering proportions. It occurred to me, as I laboriously painted each dropping ringing the nest of a brood of nearly finished house finches, that this dirty habit might just have something to do with the species' susceptibility to *Mycoplasma*.

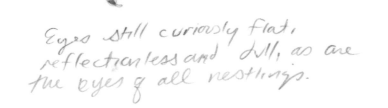

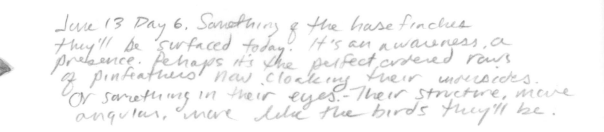

June 13 Day 6. Something of the house finches they'll be surfaced today. It's an awareness, a presence. Perhaps it's the perfect ordered rows of pinfeathers now cloaking their undersides. Or something in their eyes.—Their structure, more angular, more like the birds they'll be.

Eyes still curiously flat, reflectionless and dull, as are the eyes of all nestlings.

June 14 Day 7 The disparity between the largest and smallest chicks is striking. Feathers are bursting sheathes or larger; wings are still fleshy paddles on the smaller.

June 15 Day 8. Quills are growing on the smallest,
feathers burst on the largest. It's hot, they're
panting, not begging. Primaries are paintbrushes
on the largest. I would have expected faster
development by Day 8, but a vegetarian diet
dictates slower growth.

While the larger chicks'
feathers continue to burst the
sheaths as they pass through the
paintbrush stage, the smallest
is still mostly a bundle of
quills (far right)

June 16 Day 9

There is a sweet,
blank, round-eyed
innocence to their gaze
that the adults share.

Day 10 June 17. Fluffing up, at
least 3 q the 4 are. The smallest.
Still a collection of quills. But there's
hope. There's a sentience in their eyes - less flat.
dull and lizardlike - brighter. Streaking shows on the big one. less flat.

June 18 Day 11. There continues
to be a disparity in size and
development, but the gap is
closing slowly. Overall, house
finches aren't the fastest-
growing. Must be the vegetarian diet.

Lots of retained down and
bare skin on the youngest,
especially. But it's catching up.

To my amazement, the young are still in the nest, albeit sentient, alert, and very jumpy, on Day 13. This is a developmental arc that's closer to that of a cavity nester than an open-cup nester. The tail feathers of even the fastest-growing nestling are still in sheath, suggesting that these birds would have trouble flying much. Natural fledging may commence as early as Day 12 if the birds are disturbed; a single alarm call from a nestling can cause the entire brood to boot, instantly transforming them into fledglings. In the absence of disturbance, chicks linger in the nest until Day 16.

June 19 Day 12.

This is the last day
they'll be able to be
handled. Looking like birds
now, aware, sentient, suspicious and afraid. A peck &
dart is about all that's retained. Tail still in
paintbrush stage. Still in sheath and a ways from
flying.

Purple finches and American goldfinches, again, display the same protracted developmental arc. Once fledged, theirs is a long apprenticeship, and when feeders are near, they provide the birds with a gentle segue to foraging for themselves. Fledglings will try to pick up their own food as early as Day 26, and most are able to support themselves starting at Day 35. Where populations are strong, juvenile house finches form large flocks to seek out food sources; this is probably the phenomenon I observed in the early years of Connecticut's colonization by the species.

I'm no longer annoyed by house finches; in most years, they're absent from my Ohio yard, and what finches do appear are quickly cut back by *Mycoplasma* infections. Rather, I'm bemused that in my adult lifetime, I've seen this species explode to colonize the Midwest, the East, and southern Canada; I've seen it beaten back by disease; and I'm now watching its numbers slowly stabilize into something more ecologically sustainable. It all makes me realize that we're living in a vast laboratory, and before my eyes, this gentle little bird has thrown itself into a continent-wide experiment in overpopulation and checks and balances. With wild abandon, it went forth and multiplied, but thanks to a microbe, we've probably seen the last of the conquering flocks.

youngest →

June 20
Day 13.
Still not
flight-ready
(tails still in
sheath) but too
jumpy to handle.
One cheep g distress
from one baby and
they'll all go. So, a nest
parasit, a veritable
Saturn of ringed finch shit.
Perhaps only their plant-based
diet saves them
from predation despite
this filthy habit. Not enough
smell to attract attention?

Compare the nest to Hatch Day!

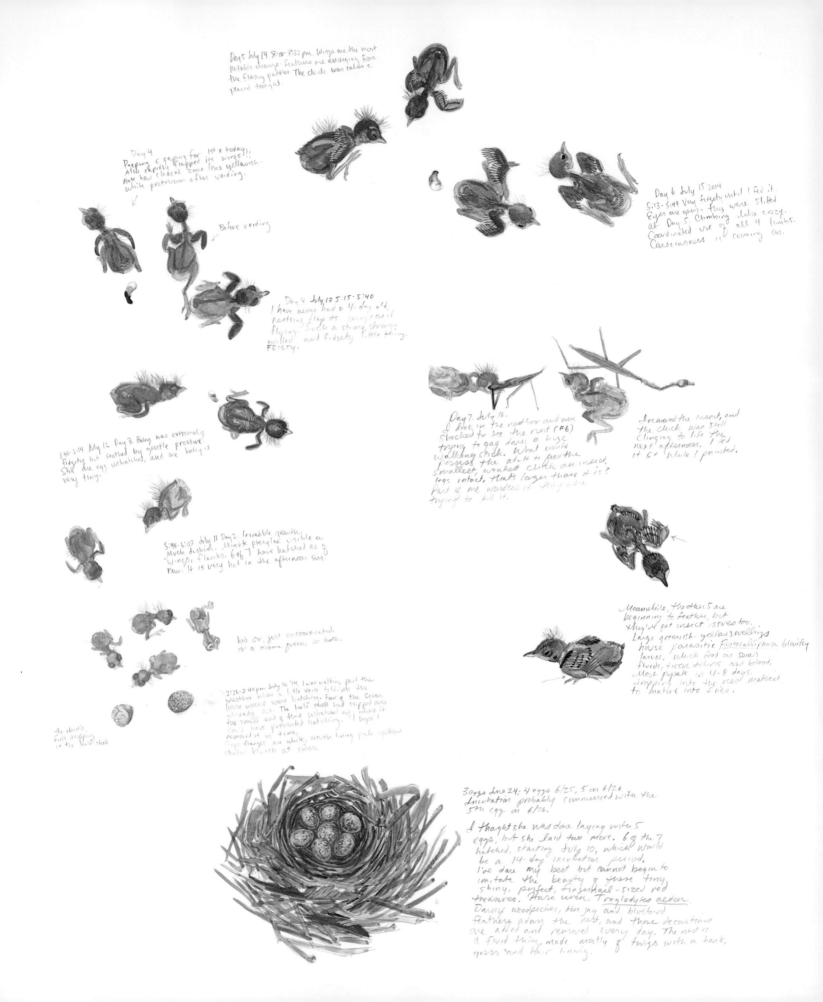

Day 5 July 14 8:00-8:32 pm. Wings are the most notable change. Feathers are emerging from the fleshy paddles. The chick was calm & placid tonight.

Day 4 Peeping & gaping for 1st x today. Also rapidly flapped its wings. Note how cloacal zone loses yellowish-white protrusion after voiding.

Before voiding

Day 6 July 15 2014 5:13-5:44 Very fidgety until I fed it. Eyes are open. They were slitted at Day 5. Climbing like crazy. Coordinated use of all 4 limbs. Carsicrasners is coming on.

Day 4 July 13 5:15-5:40 I have never had a 4-day old nestling flap its wings as if flying. Such a strong, strong-willed and fidgety little thing. FEISTY.

1:46-2:14 July 12 Day 3. Baby was extremely fidgety but soothed by gentle pressure. Still one egg unhatched, and one baby is very tiny.

Day 7. July 16. I look in the nestbox and am shocked to see the runt (#6) trying to gag down a huge walking stick. What would possess the adult to give the smallest, weakest chick an insect, legs intact, that's larger than it is? Part of me wonders if they are trying to kill it.

I removed the insect, and the chick was still clinging to life the next afternoon. I fed it 5x while I painted.

5:48-6:07 July 11 Day 2. Incredible growth. Much duskier. Minute pterylae visible on wings, flanks. 6 of 7 have hatched as of now. It is very hot in the afternoon sun.

Meanwhile, the other 5 are beginning to feather, but they've got insect issues too. Large greenish-yellow swellings house parasitic Protocalliphora blowfly larvae, which feed on serous fluids, tissue debris and blood. Most pupate in 4-8 days, dropping into the nest material to mature into flies.

he's OK, just uncoordinated, or a drama queen, or both.

2:26-2:40pm July 10 '14. I was walking past the nestbox when a little voice told me the babies were hatching. Four of the seven were already out. The half shell had slipped over the small end of this unhatched egg, where it could have prevented hatching. I hope I removed it in time. Egg flanges are white, mouth lining pale yellow, shinier blueish at sides.

the chick's first dropping in the half shell

3 eggs June 24; 4 eggs 6/25, 5 on 6/26. Incubation probably commenced with the 5th egg on 6/26.

I thought she was done laying with 5 eggs, but she laid two more. 6 of the 7 hatched, starting July 10, which would be a 14-day incubation period. I've done my best but cannot begin to imitate the beauty of these tiny, shiny, perfect, fingernail-sized red treasures. House wren, Troglodytes aedon. Downy woodpecker, blue jay and bluebird feathers adorn the nest, and these decorations are added and removed every day. The nest is a fluid thing, made mostly of twigs with a bark, grass and hair lining.

The runts still with few living Day 8.

Day 8 July 17 2014
4:12-4:50. Phoebe and I removed about a dozen Protocalliphora blowfly larvae from these poor birds. Fat larvae got under the skin- just a tip showing which we pulled out with nails or tweezers. (spiracle) breathing tube
They're easy to remove by squeezing the cyst then tweezing out. One bird has four in it's underwing. I'm so glad I could help them. Probably Protocalliphora braueri. These are subcutaneous parasites of House wrens.

Larvae are very mobile and crawl rapidly despite having no legs.

life-sized

2¢

These tiny flies, here shown life-sized and greatly magnified, hatched from pupal cases collected in the wren nest. I put the capsules in a jar on my desk and heard flies buzzing one August morning. Adults were identified as Protocalliphora deceptor by Terry Whitworth of Puyallup WA.

Day 9 July 18 '14. 4:50 - 5:25 pm
Alert, cheeping, not jittery or moving much tonight. I fed it 4 mealworms. The last one it reached toward and almost snatched the tweezers! I get an extremely precocious vibe off these birds. An attitude of "if I don't like my situation, I'll change it."

9:15-9:50AM Day 10 July 19 '14 Feathers have emerged overnight. Day 11 will hold a great change. If these two studies seem slapdash and inexpert, it's because he faced in a different direction every few seconds. Precious little bare skin showing now.

4pm July 21 '14
Day 12. The party's over, at least my study. The babies react strongly to every movement and sound by huddling tight. And when I remove one it squalls and leaps at my hand and scuttles across the driveway like a warm brown mouse. I catch it with difficulty, immediately tip it back in the nest, then plug the hole w/tissue until it settles down. Adult gives a rasping scold that tells it to flee. They may stay in the nest til Day 17, but I won't risk so much on a peek. They fledged July 22, Day 13! Nest was crawling w/tiny mites when I peeked July 23.

Feathered shrapnel, just waiting for an excuse to explode. My last look at my beloved subjects.

House Wren, 2014

THE SECOND COMING of house wrens on our Ohio sanctuary, where they'd been absent since a single nesting in the early 1990s, did not start auspiciously. On June 14, 2014, I heard the mechanical sputter-chatter of a male wren along our driveway. He moved from there down the border of pines out our meadow. I knew he was singing to attract a mate to one of the bluebird boxes there. Having monitored bluebird boxes since 1982, I've learned to associate the house wren's cheery song with trouble. I was saddened but not surprised to find three bluebird eggs, due to hatch in the next couple of days, pierced in a meadow nest box, the doomed embryos visible within. The house wren was doing his dirty work.

House wrens have nesting behavior that can kindly be described as acquisitive. At worst, it is deadly. A male house wren advertising for a mate will pierce eggs and throw nestlings out of all available cavities in his chosen territory. He will even seek out and pierce eggs in open-cup nests in the vicinity. One house wren can wreak havoc in a yard full of active nest boxes. He will then escort a female to several potential nest sites, which he's marked as his by emptying them of their rightful occupants and decorating them with a pile of twigs. I view the house wren as sort of a tiny, murderous, lame North American bowerbird.

And yet. . . . I had never had the chance to paint house wren nestlings, and I was eager to see how their developmental arc compared with that of Carolina wrens, which do not indulge in nest pillaging as part of their breeding biology. Carolina wrens nest in a variety of situations, constructing elaborate grass and twig nests in nooks and crannies in garages, outbuildings, under eaves, and occasionally in stumps and tree cavities. As it turned out, the house wren developed on almost exactly the

3 eggs June 24; 4 eggs 6/25, 5 on 6/26. Incubation probably commenced with the 5th egg on 6/26.

I thought she was done laying with 5 eggs, but she laid two more. 6 of the 7 hatched, starting July 10, which would be a 14-day incubation period. I've done my best but cannot begin to imitate the beauty of these tiny, shiny, perfect, fingernail-sized red treasures. House wren, Troglodytes aedon. Downy woodpecker, blue jay and bluebird feathers adorn the nest, and those decorations are added and removed every day. The nest is a fluid thing, made mostly of twigs with a bark, grass and hair lining.

same twelve-day schedule as a Carolina, with an interesting twist.

After clearing the bluebird nest of eggs, the 2014 house wren settled on an unoccupied nest box along our driveway, nearly a quarter of a mile away. That he had managed to attract a female was evident when the pile of twigs he'd stuffed into the box (often called a "dummy nest" or "cock nest") was lined with soft grasses and decorated with white spider egg cases and downy woodpecker, blue jay, and bluebird feathers. Though a male house wren may construct several such undifferentiated twig masses, only the

the chicks.
first dropping
in the half-shell.

2:26-2:40pm July 10 '14. I was walking past the
nestbox when a little voice told me the
house wrens were hatching. Four of the seven
have hatched already out. The half-shell had slipped over
the small end of this unhatched egg, where it
could have prevented hatching. I hope I
removed it in time.
Gape flanges are white, mouth lining pale yellow
shaded bluish at sides.

female will choose one and line it with soft grasses to prepare it for her eggs. The others are then abandoned. By June 28, 2014, the wren's mate had laid seven impossibly tiny, high-glossed eggs, heavily freckled with brick red. I was amused to see the nest decorations being moved around, removed, and replaced each day as the wrens fussed about their little PVC nest box home. I had to admit I was getting fond of these birds, whatever their past criminal record.

A little reading revealed that the small white spider egg cases I find in house wren nests belong to predatory jumping spiders. When the spiderlings hatch, they feed (in laboratory experiments, at least) on nest-dwelling mites that would otherwise attack the young birds (Pacejka et al. 1996). How elegant! And I'd thought wrens merely had a penchant for white spider egg sacs. One of my own maxims came to mind: wild things do nothing without a good reason.

I was eager to try my hand at sketching and painting the nestlings. I couldn't imagine how tiny they would be, hatching from eggs about the size of my ring finger nail. On July 10, I was walking by the nest box when a little voice told me to check. Four of the seven had

he's OK, just uncoordinated,
or a drama queen, or both.

5:48-6:03 July 11 Day 2. Incredible growth.
Much duskier. Minute pterylae visible on
wings, flanks. 6 of 7 have hatched as of
now. It is very hot in the afternoon sun.

hatched. And the half-shell of one of the eggs had slipped over the small end of an as-yet-unhatched egg, a rare occurrence that could prove deadly for the chick inside. Looking closely has its rewards. I removed the offending shell, hoping I'd caught it in time to allow the chick to hatch unimpeded. In all, six of the seven would hatch.

There followed eleven days of sketching and painting the house wrens, which distinguished themselves by being the most fidgety, restless, and hard-to-contain babies

Day 5 July 14 8:00-8:32 pm. Wings are the most notable change. Feathers are emerging from the fleshy paddles. The chick was calm e placed tonight.

Day 6 July 15 2014
5:13-5:44 Very fidgety until I fed it.
Eyes are open - they were slitted at Day 5. Climbing like crazy. Coordinated use of all 4 limbs. Consciousness is coming on.

of any species I'd handled. On Day 4, one flapped its tiny bluish proto-wings as if to take off, which would have been a neat trick for a bird equipped with fleshy flippers, innocent of feathers. I'd never seen any nestling, from bunting to hummingbird or swift, make such a maneuver at only four days of age.

As often happens in larger broods, one bird was dealt a losing hand, remaining pink and featherless through Day 8, when its siblings' feathers were beginning to burst their

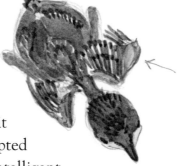

Day 7. July 16.
I look in the nestbox and am
shocked to see the runt (#6)
trying to gag down a huge
walking stick. What would
possess the adult to feed the
smallest, weakest chick an insect,
legs intact, that's larger than it is?
Part of me wonders if they were
trying to kill it.

I removed the insect, and
the chick was still
clinging to life the
next afternoon. I fed
it 5x while I painted.

sheaths. It never developed visibly beyond about Day 4, and remained stunted. On Day 7, I was shocked to find this sixth and weakest chick gagging on something long and brown. Thinking it had accidentally swallowed a grass stem from the nest material, I removed the chick and found it had half-swallowed an enormous walking stick.

Gently, I backed the insect out of the chick's gullet, to find the insect's total length considerably exceeded the chick's. The tiny bird was starving, with its mouth stuffed with food. I wondered why a parent wren would try to feed a baby an insect larger than it was, and shook my head. Had I interrupted attempted infanticide? With the highly intelligent

Meanwhile, the other 5 are
beginning to feather, but
they've got insect issues too.
Large greenish-yellow swellings
house parasitic Protocalliphora *blowfly*
larvae, which feed on serous
fluids, tissue debris and blood.
Most pupate in 4-8 days,
dropping into the nest material
to mature into flies.

house wren, well versed in murder most foul, it's worth wondering. I kept the chick in the studio for the rest of the afternoon, keeping it warm and giving it five small feedings, before replacing it in the nest that evening. By the ninth day, the runt had disappeared, probably thrown out by a parent for failing to thrive.

On Day 7, five healthy chicks were beginning to feather, but it became apparent they had insect issues as well. Bizarre greenish yellow swellings on their heads and wings popped up. Close examination revealed writhing fly larvae under their skin, something I'd never observed in over thirty years of nest box management. My daughter, Phoebe, and I were repulsed but fascinated, and we found that we could remove the larvae by gently squeezing the swelling while pulling on a larva's head, which protruded from a small opening in the bird's skin. We removed a few from one chick, then fetched tweezers and sat down in the driveway to perform quick field surgery on all five birds.

I was glad to be able to remove the larvae from my study brood. One chick's wing was so heavily infested as to be misshapen and hanging from the

The runt's still with the living Day 8.

Day 8 July 17 2014
4:12 – 4:50. Phoebe and I removed about a dozen Protocalliphora blowfly larvae from these poor birds. Fat larvae just under the skin—just a tip showing which we pulled out with nails or tweezers. They're easy to remove by squeezing the cyst then tweezing out. One bird has fur in its underwing. I'm so glad I can help them. Probably Protocalliphora braueri. These are subcutaneous parasites of House wrens.

breathing tube (spiracle)

Larvae are very mobile and crawl rapidly despite having no legs.

life-sized

These tiny flies, here shown life-sized and greatly magnified, hatched from pupal cases collected in the wren nest. I put the capsules in a jar on my desk and heard flies buzzing one August morning. Adults were identified as Protocalliphora deceptor by Terry Whitworth of Puyallup WA.

weight of the larvae. Out with them! Within a matter of minutes of removing the larvae, the swellings receded and exit holes seemed to close. I imagined how good it must have felt to be rid of several writhing subcutaneous parasites half the size of one's head. I took the larvae and some puparia (brown, beanlike pupal cases) that I found on the bottom of the box back to my studio, where I put them in a jar on my drawing table to mature. A couple of weeks later, furious buzzing in the jar announced the adult flies' emergence. They looked like bluebottle flies: metallic blue with dark red eyes. I sent them to a bird blowfly expert in Washington, who identified them as *Protocalliphora deceptor.* Though infestations of this bird blowfly have been documented to cause only slight reductions in growth and maturation rates, infestations of young chicks before Day 6, especially on the birds' heads, may kill affected birds (Johnson 1998). Female blowflies are long-lived and overwinter, waiting in spring to enter bird nests and nesting cavities, to lay their eggs directly on nestling birds (Sabrosky et al. 1989).

*Day 9 July 18'14. 4:50 - 5:25pm.
Alert, cheeping, not jittery or moving much though. I fed it 4 mealworms. The last one it reached toward and almost snatched it off the tweezers. I get an extremely precocious vibe off these birds. An attitude of "if I don't like my situation, I'll change it."*

9:18-9:50AM Day 10 July 19 '14 Feathers have
emerged overnight. Day 11 will hold a
great change. If these two studies
seem slapdash and inexpert, it's because
he faced in a different direction every few seconds.
Precious little bare skin showing now.

By Day 9, the nestling wren I chose for painting was a mass of silver feather sheaths with paintbrush tips of warm brown. It accepted mealworms, almost snatching them off the tweezer tips, in a highly precocious move.

On Day 10, the nestling was so restless that it faced in a different direction every time I started to sketch it. By Day 11, I had to work from quick cell-phone snapshots of a bird briefly held in the hand, for it was much too active and jumpy to sketch with any authority. On Day 12, a nestling I was removing for its sketching session gave a squall, leapt from my hand, and scuttled across the ground like a tiny brown mouse. I caught it with some difficulty, popped it back into the nest box, and stuffed the entry

Day 11 July 20 '14
Phoebe photographed them for me. Very jumpy—
she had a hard time containing the nestling.
Probably the last day it could be safely
handled, so I was to find at July 21!

hole with tissues to keep the entire brood from booting out of the nest. I could hear an adult wren giving a rasping scold that likely spurred the nestling to flee. My time with the birds was emphatically over. After creeping up to remove the tissues plugging the box hole when the young birds had finally settled down, I stayed well away from the box. They fledged the next day, on Day 13. Some house wrens stay in the nest until Day 17, but I'd have been surprised to see these wigglers remain much longer, as mobile and fidgety as they were.

I never know what I'll encounter when I embark on a relationship with nesting birds. There might be attempted infanticide by walking stick (she did it in the bedroom, with a walking stick!), nightmarish larval infestations, bright-eyed restless chicks in perpetual motion. The charming and the bizarre are all part and parcel of peeking into a bird's nest.

4pm July 21 '14
Day 12. The party's over, at least my study. The babies react strongly to every movement and sound by huddling tight. And when I remove one it squalls and leaps at y my hand and scuttles across the drive- way like a warm brown mouse. I catch it with difficulty, immediately drop it back in the nest, then plug the hole w/ tissue until it settles down. Adult gives a rasping scold that tells it to flee. They may stay in the nest 'til Day 17, but I won't risk so much as a peek. They fledged July 22, Day 13! Nest was crawling w/ tiny mites when I peeked July 23.

Feathered shrapnel,
just waiting for an
excuse to explode.
My last look at my
beloved subjects.

Trying to show wing motion with multiple poses- maybe not so successful.

Day 1: When I jostle the nest they erupt with a sizzling rattle, waving their heads and wings frantically. I can't tell if it's begging or threat- they're so weird and snakelike! The bluish-white pearls on the roof of the mouth glow. The overall effect: startling.

Sitting up already, the shards of their enormous eggs still beneath them. The vigor of these new chicks is incredible. 8-9 gm in weight.

14-15 gm Day 2

Day 2: Startling display—this has to be a defensive reaction, rather than begging. Also startling is the growth of pinfeathers—especially on wings—in only 24 hours! Eyes wide open Day 2—doesn't happen in others. May climb to nest rim and snap at flies.

Day 3: Wing feathers are longer and tipped buff. Chicks can perch on rim of nest, eject fecal sacs outward.

18-19 gm Day 3

Day 4: Pinfeathers have a two-toned look, lighter distally, as they begin to dry out and split. White chin and breast is evident. They're changing into birds!!

Yellow-billed Cuckoo defends its eggs with a weird side-to-side rocking and a clock-like purr

Yellow-billed Cuckoo, 2015

Day 7. In the space of two hours, all feather sheaths burst. Feces became loose and splattery. Chicks leave the nest, running along limbs to meet parents incoming with food. May lose 3-5 gm making these instant feathers.

Making herself as big as possible

Day 6. If there's a bigger mess than a 6-day old Yellow-billed cuckoo, I haven't painted it. These chicks are exploding with new feathers. This defensive pose, exactly like the adults'— I couldn't resist the comparison! The feathers emerge in a matter of hours. And chicks can clamber away from the nest.

and small as possible... 26-29 gm Day 6

Day 8. 32-34 gm and gone from the nest, clambering through the foliage

Sheath bits are everywhere.

Day 5. On the nest now, prickling with quills, which are beginning to turn into wings. 27-30 gm. Already more of a danger— crouches motionless in response to unfamiliar threat.

Young yellow-billed cuckoo, virtually grown, still begs and is subsidized. Though they leave the nest around Day 8, they don't fly reliably until about Day 21, and they're doubtless fed at least that long. Cuckoos are so secretive that we can only guess. Yellow eyering is a sign of youth; adult (left) has grayish orbital ring!

Yellow-billed Cuckoo, 2015

It isn't an orchard anymore, any more than the paths are paths, some years. Once, there were peaches, cherries, apples, even apricots; and people came and picked them here—here!—on our land, and it's said that they left their money in a country honor system by the mailbox. When the huge red oak that sheltered our mailbox leaned and finally toppled in 2011, I found a battered Liberty dime in the tossed duff at her roots. Through tears, I made out the date: 1903. All this is to explain the fact that the orchard is no more, with the rotting trunks of once-grand apples, the memory of peaches. In the spring of 1993, the hollow ghost of an old peach tree gave up one miraculous, softball-size fruit—its last—that remains the finest we've ever enjoyed.

Bill was trimming honeysuckle from a tangle that blocked one of the narrowing paths out there when he dropped his shears and ran to the house. "Julie. I think I found a cuckoo's nest!" We'd heard them in the orchard, winding their clocks, marking the hours until rain with a hollow *tock tock tock*. But we'd never dreamt of finding a nest. I grabbed my little camera and, in a moment of unusual foresight, set it to video and stealthily pushed it through the honeysuckle until it pointed down into the nest. I didn't know and couldn't see what I would capture, but I figured it would be good.

A pair of day-old yellow-billed cuckoos lay still in the shallow twig platform, breathing peacefully atop the sky blue shards of their eggshells. Stringy yellowish down lay across charcoal skin. Their eyes were sealed shut. By chance, the camera bumped a twig, and the weird, reptilian chicks instantly transformed, lifting themselves high on their haunches, standing erect. They flapped their paddle-stub wings rapidly as they opened cavernous gapes. Brilliant red mouths, studded with white protuberances called "pearls," opened wide. Two heads waved wildly as the chicks emitted a sizzling rattle that startled me. I've watched this video dozens of times, and I can't decide if the chicks are begging for food or pretending to be rattlesnakes. In the weird world of cuckoos, it could be some combination of both. If the nest-bumper were a predator, perhaps it would be scared away, as I was. If a cuckoo, perhaps it would stuff some masticated caterpillar in those pearly maws.

After that electrifying moment of discovery, we stayed far away, not wanting to disturb this precious family. We heard cuckoos calling in the nest vicinity, and hoped all was well. A few days later, I peeked into the nest, hoping hard to see something wonderful. It was empty. My heart sank. Something had gotten the chicks. Hoping I was wrong, I turned to Birds of North America (Hughes 2015). There, in Dr. Janice M. Hughes's elegantly condensed writing, I found something that made me sit up on my haunches and flap my wings.

"Growth rapid, 17d from start of incubation to fledging—among shortest for any species of bird; young gain an average of 4.9 g/d while in nest. . . . At 2d . . . can perch on side of nest and snap at flies." The account goes on, describing a preternatural rate of development that, for one who has looked into a lot of bird nests, defied belief. Wait. Seventeen days from start of incubation to *fledging*? Incubation is only nine days, and the young stay in the nest only eight. How could that be? Yellow-billed cuckoos feather out completely on Days 6 to 7. By Day 8, they are able to run along branches and *fly* to safety. My brain refused to wrap itself around such a thing.

Now, I'd seen nine-day-old indigo buntings leave the nest, half-naked and clambering clumsily in what for them is a normal fledging process. How could a cuckoo be fully feathered and clambering, even flying a bit, by Day 8? I riffled through my mental catalog of cuckoo encounters, and pulled out a card from the summer of 1993. Someone had called with a strange bird they'd found by a southeast Ohio roadside. The bird didn't seem to be hurt, but neither would it fly. I opened a shoebox to find a beautiful yellow-billed cuckoo sitting back as if slightly drunk. It voiced a guttural rattle and spread its wings in defense, leaning side to side. Checking it over, I found no broken bones, nor any explanation of its plight other than a distended abdomen. I installed it in a cage by a window in the basement and gave it bowls of live mealworms and water.

The cuckoo ate and moped on the bottom of its cage. It was bright enough, but I found it odd that it wouldn't try to attain the cage's higher perches. I took it in hand and blew on it to part the feathers on its abdomen. A naked brood patch was to be expected in June. The hard mass I could feel in its abdomen wasn't expected. It hit me

Yellow-billed Cuckoo
with a weird side-
and a clock-like

that this cuckoo could be a female suffering from egg binding, with an unlaid egg stuck somewhere on its descent. I fetched and warmed some baby oil and gently massaged it into the cuckoo's vent, a skill that has never made it onto my resumé. On my next check, I was elated to find the cuckoo on a high perch in the cage. An extremely large pale blue egg lay on the cage floor. I could hardly believe that monstrous egg came out of this slender bird. The cuckoo felt so much better after ridding herself of the massive egg that she made it clear she wanted *out*. Scrambling to the farm supply store for materials, I used chicken wire and a staple gun to construct a crude outdoor flight cage, about 6 × 10 feet, using our raised deck struts for a frame. The cuckoo gained strength quickly, and only four days later I was able to open the door, a huge smile on my face, and watch her arrow into the leafy canopy of our woods, free to fly and lay more enormous blue eggs.

I didn't know it then, but this odd event would be my first clue on a trail of discovery. As I watched the video I'd made of the newly hatched cuckoo chicks standing up in the nest, flapping their wing-paddles, and struggled to understand how any bird goes from egg to flight in only eight days, it occurred to me that it must take a big, well-fortified egg to make such a strong, well-developed chick. And I remembered the grounded female cuckoo. In fact, yellow-billed cuckoo eggs are among the largest in proportion to the female's body mass (14 percent) of any nidicolous bird (Hughes 2015). Nidicolous birds stay in the nest for some time after they hatch, while nidifugous birds are precocial, leaving the nest within hours after hatching.

Not only is a cuckoo egg large, but it develops quickly, too, hatching in as little as nine days. The other birds in my study average thirteen days of incubation, with the ruby-throated hummingbird needing sixteen, and the chimney swift nineteen. The last two species, being aerial foragers with aerodynamic weight restrictions, lay proportionately smaller eggs, which take longer to hatch. At least part of the puzzle was explained by the perilously large eggs a yellow-billed cuckoo lays.

Though I couldn't risk photographing chicks in the low and vulnerable cuckoo nest in our orchard, I burned to know what such an accelerated developmental arc might look like. This desire had only grown as I had drawn and painted my way through the sixteen species I *could* access. I found some images of yellow-billed cuckoo chicks online, and traced the best of them to field researchers at the Southern Sierra Research Station in Weldon, California. Shannon McNeil and Diane Tracy graciously lent dozens of their photos of nestling yellow-billed cuckoos, a species listed as Status 1 (Critically

Imperiled, Endangered) in California. Since 2008 Shannon and Diane have helped the Bureau of Reclamation monitor the response of cuckoos to riparian forest habitat creation on the lower Colorado River, a project managed under the Lower Colorado River Multi-Species Conservation Program. After large-scale modification of rivers throughout the West, little suitable breeding habitat remains, and habitat restoration will be essential to the cuckoo's recovery. In the course of their studies, Diane and Shannon measure, weigh, and photograph cuckoo chicks in the nest. Through their images, I could witness and share the stunning daily changes in the birds.

Another great boon was an article by Eloise Potter in the winter 1980 *Journal of Field Ornithology* (Potter 1980). In July of 1973, Potter found a yellow-billed cuckoo nest in her yard and spent almost sixty hours behind a spotting scope, observing without disturbing it. Think about what it took to sit for sixty hours, watching a nest, being present for everything that happened during daylight hours, seizing the moment, knowing that almost anything you recorded would be new to ornithology. With this one deceptively simple act, Potter contributed priceless knowledge to what little we know about yellow-billed cuckoos. Field ornithology happens in backyards and gardens.

The cuckoos began nest construction in Potter's yard on July 11. Their last nestling fledged July 30, only nineteen days later. In that breathlessly short space, the birds built a nest, laid eggs, incubated them, and the chicks developed enough to clamber-fly from

Sitting up already, the shards of their enormous eggs still beneath them. The vigor of these new chicks is incredible. 8-9 gm in weight.

Trying to show wing motion with multiple poses- maybe not so successful.

Day 1: When I jostle the nest they erupt with a sizzling rattle, waving their heads and wings frantically. I can't tell if it's begging or threat. They're so weird and snakelike! The bluish-white pearls on the roof of the mouth glow. The overall effect: startling.

the nest. After a nine-day incubation period, the newly hatched chicks were fed insects that had been pulverized, swallowed, and then regurgitated into their bills.

Only one day later, the chicks received whole live caterpillars, butterflies, and katydids. Having seen the small, soft larvae that chickadees and bluebirds bring their two-day-old hatchlings, I could not imagine any two-day-old chick gagging down a live katydid. But the enormous white-pearled scarlet maws of the day-old cuckoos I filmed in my orchard looked fit to receive just such fare. The birds' strength and vigor were simply astonishing. Potter theorized that the white pearly protuberances in the chicks' gapes might help them grip and subdue the "still-kicking" prey offered by the parents, describing a suction-cup effect of young birds latching on to and clinging to their providers' bills.

Interestingly, Potter did not observe the cuckoos feeding hairy tent caterpillars to their chicks. Adult cuckoos eat lots of caterpillars, often the noxious species other birds will not eat. The cuckoos carefully remove the toxic gut, then eat the rest, including the hairs and spines, with gusto. Their ability to exploit an irregularly abundant food source likely holds the key to cuckoos' elemental weirdness, as we shall see. They may

14-15 gm Day 2

Day 2. Startling display—this has to be a defensive reaction, rather than begging. Also startling is the growth of pinfeathers— especially on wings— in only 24 hours! Eyes wide open Day 2— doesn't happen in others. May climb to nest rim and snap at flies.

have a nomadic post-migratory phase where they wander, perhaps assessing the local food resources, before they settle in to breed.

Two-day-old chicks' eyes are wide open, and they perch on the nest rim, snapping at flies. When I read this in Janice Hughes's Birds of North America account, I blinked and read the sentence three more times. I thought of the eastern phoebes I'd raised, and the moment on Day 24 that one grabbed a moth off my forceps, rather than gaping to have me stuff it down its throat. And cuckoos snap at flies on Day 2? What could be going on here?

By Day 3, cuckoos are able to back up to the rim of the nest for their parents to take their fecal sacs. Wing quills are long and floppy by Day 3, while a same-age eastern bluebird is still naked, with tiny pink flippers for wings. Feedings increase from fifteen times a day around Day 3 to thirty-one times a day by Day 6 (Preble 1957). Caterpillars, grasshoppers, and katydids are the most frequently offered items.

By Day 4, the chicks are a mass of maturing quills, which take on a two-toned look as the sheath ends dry and begin to split.

Day 3 - Wing feathers are longer and tipped buff. Chicks can perch on rim of nest, eject fecal sacs onward.

18-19 gm Day 3

Day 4- Pinfeathers have a two toned look, lighter distally, as they begin to dry out and split. White chin and breast is evident. They're changing into birds!!

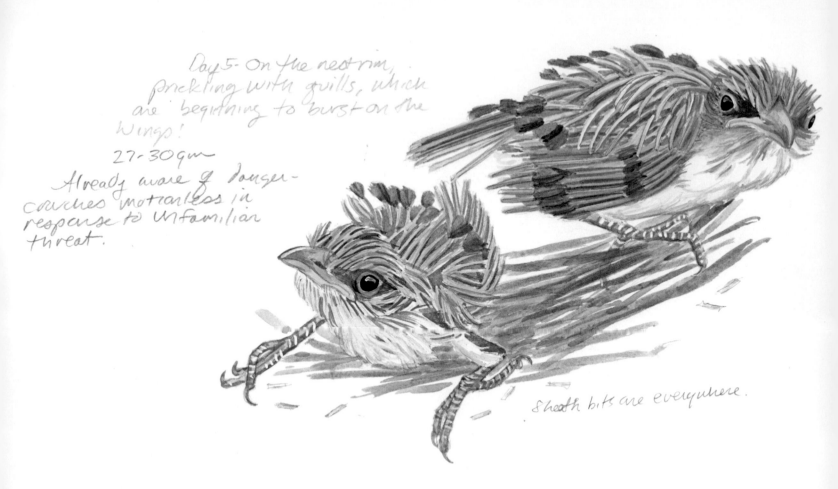

Day 5- On the nest rim, prickling with quills, which are beginning to burst on the wings!

27-30gm

Already aware of danger- crouches motionless in response to unfamiliar threat.

sheath bits are everywhere.

Long blue quills have paintbrush tips of brown on Day 5, a prelude to the explosion that will occur in the next two days. Sentience has taken root, and the birds crouch and freeze in response to perceived threats. Oddly, I have noted that this sentient behavior is presaged in other birds by loose, splattery feces, as if the birds discard their innocence along with their ability to produce neat fecal sacs. The same is true of a cuckoo, just much sooner than in other birds. Its brain and gut are ready to be grown up, at five days of age.

Day 6 is when it all happens for young yellow-billed cuckoos. The sudden transformation from pincushion to a feathered miniature of its parents takes place in a matter of hours. The event has been likened to popcorn popping, with feather sheaths falling everywhere. If there is a bigger mess than a six-day-old cuckoo, I have never painted it. I have met my Waterloo as a bird artist. I can't finish two in the same day. Trying to figure out the origin and direction of all those quills exhausts me; I can't imagine having to grow them. You couldn't feed me enough caterpillars to do that.

Making herself as big as possible

Day 6. If there's a bigger mess than a 6-day old Yellow-billed cuckoo, I haven't painted it. These chicks are exploding with new feathers. This defensive pose, exactly like the adult's- I couldn't resist the comparison! The feathers emerge in a matter of hours. And chicks can clamber away from the nest.

and small as possible... 26-29 gm Day 6

Day 7. In the space of
two hours, all feather
sheaths burst. Feces
became loose and
splattery. Chicks leave
the nest, running along
limbs to meet parent
incoming with food.
    May lose 3-5
gm making
these instant
feathers.

Day 8
32-34 gm
and gone from
the nest, clambering
through the foliage.

Day 7 sees a chick transformed to a stub-tailed, fully feathered miniature of an adult. It is able to run swiftly along limbs to meet an incoming parent, to clamber and flutter through vegetation. It leaves the nest area on this or Day 8. The more I marvel at the metamorphosis of cuckoo chicks, the more I wonder why it should be so. The most obvious answer is predation pressure. North American cuckoos build flimsy twig platforms low in brushy edge vegetation. Eggs can often be seen gleaming through the nests from below. The flat, hastily constructed nests are quite vulnerable to predation, and ratsnakes, jays, and crows take a heavy toll on eggs and chicks. The faster cuckoo chicks can get out of the nest, the better their chances of ultimate survival. Cuckoo chick development looks like a race for life, and it is. Studies have shown that up to 80 percent of yellow-billed cuckoo nests are lost to predation in some parts of the species' range (Nolan 1963).

I was fortunate to speak and bat about evolutionary theory in a rapid-fire conversation with Dr. Janice Hughes, biology professor at Lakehead University, Thunder Bay, Ontario, and preeminent authority on North American cuckoos. She studies the phylogenetics of cuckoos (how they're related to each other, and to other bird groups) and the evolution of their breeding behavior. She also works on conservation of western yellow-billed cuckoos, listed as Threatened on the Endangered Species List in late 2014.

There's a lot to consider when looking at the breeding behavior of *Coccyzus* cuckoos. The experience is much like peeling an onion. They belong, of course, to a family well known for brood parasitism; photos of tiny dunnocks feeding enormous European cuckoo fledglings are common. And oddly enough, Old World cuckoos—which are obligate brood parasites—lay proportionately small eggs, and their chicks develop much more slowly even than their host species' chicks! Somehow they fool the host species into investing weeks of effort feeding cuckoo chicks well after the hosts' chicks have fledged. So in considering cuckoos as a group, one must come prepared for some out-of-the-box behavior.

Suddenly abundant food, such as caterpillar outbreaks provide, is one likely keystone to a peculiar aspect of yellow-billed cuckoo reproduction. Although yellow-billed cuckoos build nests and raise their own young, they will also lay eggs in the nests of other yellow-billed cuckoos, a behavior known as intraspecific brood parasitism. Some Old World cuckoos are obligate brood parasites, and never raise their own young, so at first blush this behavior in our New World cuckoos could be interpreted as an evolutionary stab at brood parasitism. Certainly an egg laid in another cuckoo's nest, rather than that of an unrelated species, has the best chance of being successfully hatched and raised. But it may be that the same abundance of food that causes nest initiation also kicks female cuckoos into laying more eggs than they can handle themselves. Rather than dropping such a large and energetically expensive egg on the ground, it would be better to lay it somewhere it has a chance of hatching and carrying on her genes, to spread out one's output among a number of nests.

Harder to explain is the yellow-billed cuckoo that lays her egg in the nest of a black-billed cuckoo, American robin, gray catbird, or wood thrush, which constitutes interspecific brood parasitism. It is likely not coincidental that the just-listed species most often parasitized (of eleven total) also have unmarked blue eggs; in laying its eggs in these nests, the cuckoo reduces the chance that its blue egg will be ejected. Many of the cuckoo's most intriguing behaviors beckon one down a path of inquiry that dead-ends for lack of observational data. Successful hatching or fledging of yellow-billed cuckoo eggs has been recorded only in single black-billed cuckoo, northern cardinal, and red-winged blackbird nests (Bent 1940; Nickell 1954; Nolan and Thompson 1975). Interspecific brood parasitism is generally obligate, as it is in cowbirds; a cowbird lays its eggs only in the nests of other birds. Facultative interspecific brood parasitism, which is an occasional choice on the part of a bird that generally raises its own young, is found only in *Coccyzus* cuckoos (Janice Hughes pers. comm.).

In a telling point of light, a Pennsylvania study that looked at more than 10,000 songbird nests in an area with a high density of cuckoos found no evidence of interspecific brood parasitism (Dearborn et al. 2009). This led the researchers to conclude that the citations of cuckoos engaging in what appears to be brood parasitism of unrelated species might represent nothing more than a mistake by a bird intending to lay her egg in another cuckoo's nest. The fact that this occurs most often in nests with similar-looking eggs could bolster the theory that apparent interspecific brood parasitism in cuckoos is little more than an accident, or a glitch. "Maybe we're seeing a behavior that's not really cooked yet," Dr. Hughes observed.

Even more intriguing, she told me, is a recent discovery of facultative serial polyandry in two female yellow-billed cuckoos in Arizona. Each female mated with a male, laid eggs, then left her nest just prior to her young fledging, leaving the male to raise the young. Both females renested with other males within several days of leaving the first nest. Two males were also seen tending one California nest (Laymon 1998; Halterman 2009). Some populations of yellow-billed cuckoos have more males than females; serial polyandry might be a viable strategy for in-demand females, especially if other "floater" males are willing to help at the nest she leaves behind. Freeing a female of the enormous energetic cost of staying to tend a brood of chicks likely translates directly to greater egg production. Female brown-headed cowbirds, North America's predominant obligate nest parasite, can lay more than forty eggs in a single season, never lingering to incubate or feed the resulting young (Scott and Ankney 1980). All of this makes one wonder why more birds don't engage in brood parasitism or polyandry; why reproductive strategies that could be wildly successful are so rare.

In talking with Dr. Hughes, I learned a great deal about cuckoos both here and worldwide, strongly underscored by how much we don't yet know. I'm indebted to her for enlightening me to the probability that cuckoos are the most interesting birds in North America. Our slim, sneaky *Coccyzus* seem to do a little bit of everything: conventional brood rearing, egg dumping, nest parasitism of their own and unrelated species, helping at the nest, even polyandry. Shannon McNeil alerted me to the little-known fact that both sexes of yellow-billed cuckoo have a bare brood patch year-round, suggesting a readiness to reproduce at a moment's notice (Rohwer and Wood 2013). I was left thinking that there's little a cuckoo won't try in the great contest to reproduce; that this must be one of the most behaviorally plastic birds on the planet. I smiled at the thought that writers of another era might have questioned its morality had they known all the things a yellow-billed cuckoo is up to. But overall, I was left with the sneaky suspicion that all these behavioral quirks might trace back to an opportunistic tendency to produce more eggs when presented with more food: caterpillars, which tend to occur in outbreaks, resulting in a superabundance of available protein. Individual cuckoos have been found with more than 100 caterpillars in their stomachs! Inter- and intraspecific brood parasitism and especially serial polyandry might just be a female cuckoo's answer to the question of what to do with all these great big eggs she's suddenly making. Perhaps we're looking at several evolutionarily creative solutions to a single central issue.

But the breathtakingly short seventeen-day nesting period from placement of the first nest twig to fledging of the young is among the shortest for any bird, precocial or altricial, in North America. There is nothing about cuckoo biology that doesn't raise questions. We can come up with some theories, but without field observations that provide some data, we're just telling stories. In the end, all we can really do is bear slack-jawed witness to the nuptial hijinks and the dizzily accelerated process of becoming a cuckoo, that weird and wonderful phantom of the tangles.

Young yellow-billed cuckoo, virtually grown, still begs and is subsidized. Though they leave the nest around Day 8, they don't fly reliably until about Day 21, and they're doubtless fed at least that long. Cuckoos are so secretive that we can only guess. Yellow eyering is a sign of youth; adult (left) has grayish orbital ring.

Afterword

I DON'T WANT this project to end. So it won't. As I finished final edits for this book, three snooty-looking baby brown thrashers arrived in a shoebox, their Cincinnati hedgerow home having been cut down. I'd always dreamt of raising thrashers, such dashing and intelligent creatures. Through a phone tree, they found their way to me, clear on the other side of the state. I run out every hour to feed them, take notes, photograph them, sing to them, love them: these gifts that keep falling from their nests, right into an amazed and grateful heart. The stories keep coming, and I have to keep telling them.

References

Eastern Bluebird

Pinkowski, B. C. 1975. Growth and development of eastern bluebirds. *Bird-Banding* 46: 273–289.

European Starling

Crick, H. Q. P., R. A. Robinson, G. F. Appleton, N. A. Clark, and A. D. Rickard, eds. 2002. Investigation into the causes of the decline of Starlings and House Sparrows in Great Britain. BTO Research Report no. 290. Norfolk: British Trust for Ornithology. http://www.bto.org/sites/default/files/u32/researchreports/rr290.pdf.

Indigo Bunting

Westneat, D. F. 1987. Extra-pair fertilizations in a predominantly monogamous bird: genetic evidence. *Animal Behaviour* 35: 877–886.

Mourning Dove

Corliss, K. Flight lines: Urban wildlife often overlooked; observing nature without leaving the yard. *West Fargo Pioneer*, July 9, 2013.

The Natural Winning Ways, vol. 10. [n.d.]. Antwerp, Belgium: Natural Granen Co. This annual publication for pigeon racers is also useful for any pigeon breeder or rehabilitator.

Shetty, S., L. Bharathi, K. B. Shenoy, and S. N. Hegde. 1992. Biochemical properties of pigeon milk and its effect on growth. *Journal of Comparative Physiology* 162 (7): 632–636.

House Finch

Badyaev, A. V., V. Belloni, and G. E. Hill. 2012. House Finch (*Haemorhous mexicanus*), The Birds of North America Online (A. Poole, ed.). Ithaca: Cornell Lab of Ornithology; retrieved from The Birds of North America Online: http://bna.birds.cornell.edu/bna/species/046.

House Wren

Johnson, L. S. 1998. House Wren (*Troglodytes aedon*). The Birds of North America, no. 380 (A. Poole and F. Gill, eds.). Philadelphia, PA: The Birds of North America, Inc.

Pacejka, A. J., E. Santana, R. G. Harper, and C. F. Thompson. 1996. House Wrens (*Troglodytes aedon*) and nest-dwelling ectoparasites: mite population growth and feeding patterns. *Journal of Avian Biology* 27: 273–278.

Sabrosky, C. W., G. F. Bennett, and T. L. Whitworth. 1989. Bird blow flies (*Protocalliphora*) in North America (Diptera: Calliphoridae), with notes on the palearctic species. Washington, D.C.: Smithsonian Institution Press. http://archive.org/stream/birdblowfliespro00sabr/birdblow-fliespro00sabr_djvu.txt.

Yellow-billed Cuckoo

Bent, A. C. 1940. Northern cardinal raising a yellow-billed cuckoo. In *Life Histories of North American Cuckoos, Goatsuckers, Hummingbirds, and Their Allies*. U.S. National Museum Bulletin no. 176.

Dearborn, D. C., L. S. MacDade, S. Robinson, A. D. Dowling Fink, and M. L. Fink. 2009. Offspring development mode and the evolution of brood parasitism. *Behavioral Ecology* 20: 517–524.

Halterman, M. D. 2009. Sexual dimorphism, home range, detection probability, and parental care in the Yellow-billed Cuckoo. PhD diss., Univ. of Nevada, Reno.

Hughes, Janice M. 2015. Yellow-billed Cuckoo (*Coccyzus americanus*), The Birds of North America Online (A. Poole, ed.). Ithaca: Cornell Lab of Ornithology; retrieved from The Birds of North America Online: http://bna.birds.cornell.edu/bna/species/418.

Laymon, S. A. 1998. Yellow-billed Cuckoo (*Coccyzus americanus*). In *The riparian bird conservation plan: a strategy for reversing the decline of riparian-associated birds in California*. Bakersfield, CA: California Partners in Flight. http://www.prbo.org/calpif/htmldocs/species/riparian/yellow-billed_cuckoo.htm.

Nickell, W. P. 1954. Red-wings hatch and raise a Yellow-billed Cuckoo. *Wilson Bulletin* 66: 137–138.

Nolan, V., Jr. 1963. Reproductive success of birds in a deciduous scrub habitat. *Ecology* 44: 305–313.

Nolan, V., Jr., and C. F. Thompson. 1975. The occurrence and significance of anomalous reproductive activities in two North American nonparasitic cuckoos *Coccyzus* spp. *Ibis* 117: 496–503.

Potter, E. F. 1980. Notes on nesting yellow-billed cuckoos. *Journal of Field Ornithology* 51(1): 17–29.

Preble, N. A. 1957. Nesting habits of the Yellow-billed Cuckoo. *American Midland Naturalist* 57: 474–482.

Rohwer, S., and C. S. Wood. 2013. Abundant early-summer breeding in Sinaloa does not suggest post-migration breeding in three potential double breeders. *Wilson Journal of Ornithology* 125(2): 243–250.

Scott, D. M., and C. D. Ankney. 1980. Fecundity of the Brown-headed Cowbird in southern Ontario. *Auk* 97: 677–683.

Index

air sac problems, 30
altricial vs. precocial birds, xiv–xv
Audubon Magazine, xvi
Audubon Society, National, 34
aviary, nylon flight tent, 35, 87, 90, 111–12, 115, 148, 155, 259

Baby Bird Portraits by George Miksch Sutton: Watercolors in the Field Museum (Johnsgard), xv
Bates, Henry Walter, 74
Batesian mimicry
    birds and, 74–76, 80
    butterflies and, 74
    description/purpose, 74
Bird Observer, 36
Bird Watcher's Digest, 36, 176
birds
    ability to distinguish individuals, 36
    clutches per nesting season, xii
    helpers (previous year offspring) and, 226
    nesting near humans/predator protection and, 243–44
    nestling metabolism and, 165
    survival/nesting season and, 58
    See also specific species
Birds of North America (Golden Guide), 280
Birds of North America (reference), 72, 90, 117, 130, 311, 316
bluebird, eastern
    hyperproduction and, 55
    parasites in nest, 22, 27
    Pinkowski study on self-feeding schedule, 38
    post-fledging period, 34
    supplemental food from Zickefoose, 22–23, 55, 58
    survival/nesting season and, 58
    Zickefoose care/monitoring nest boxes, 22–24, 164
bluebird, eastern/orphan birds
    aviary for, 35–36
    food for/begging for food, 36–38
    Mil/Fran caring for, 34–35
    molting, 41

naming, 36
returning after fledging, 42–44
self-feeding, 38, 40
"soft release," 40–42
Zickefoose care of, 35–43, 45
bluebird, eastern/project
    adults behavior, 25, 28, 31
    air sac problem and, 30, 33
    behavior if starving, 32
    behavior when seeing human, 32
    "bluebird whistle" and, 24, 25, 26, 27, 31
    checking boxes before sunrise and, 24
    color and, 26, 28, 31–33
    consciousness and, 27, 32
    control and, 24–25
    development/activities, 24–33
    embryos hearing other embryo peeps and, 24
    gaping/feeding and, 24, 25, 26, 27, 28, 30, 31, 32
    gender distinction and, 32–33
    mites in nest/managing, 27
    obstruction in esophagus and, 28–29, 33
    pterylae/feathers and, 25, 26–27, 28, 30–31, 32–34
    thermoregulation/adult brooding ending, 28
Braunfield, Robert, 22
breeding strategy
    eastern wood-warblers, 192
    latitudinal food/predators and, 192
    northern cardinal, 192–93
brood parasitism
    cowbird, brown-headed, 249, 283–84, 322, 323
    New World cuckoos, 321–22
    Old World cuckoos, 321
bug omelets, 23, 112–13, 114, 144, 145, 178, 228
bunting, indigo
    breeding timing/adaptations, 244
    brown-headed cowbird eggs/young and, 249
    development comparison with northern cardinal, 198
    juvenile dependency period, 201
    male conspicuousness/predators and, 244
    molt, 254
    philandering by both sexes/male care and, 244–46

At Day Seven

A snapshot of all 17 species at Day 7. I've arranged them from slowest-to-fastest-developing. Most of the slower-developing birds are cavity nesters. Cavities are safer and harder for predators to reach, so the birds have the "leisure" to grow more slowly. By contrast, birds in open-cup nests, like cardinals and mourning doves, grow with dizzying speed, often leaving before they can fly well.

Chimney Swift
Fledges Day 29

Ruby-throated Hummingbird

Fledges Day 21

European Starling
Fledges Day 23

Tree Swallow - Fledges Day 20

Carolina Chickadee
Fledges Day 18

Tufted Titmouse
Fledges Day 19

Eastern Phoebe
Fledges Day 17

Eastern Bluebird
Fledges Day 18

House Finch
Fledges Day 16

Carolina Wren
Fledges Day 13

Mourning Dove
Fledges Day 12

House Sparrow
Fledges Day 13

House Wren
Fledges Day 13

Northern Cardinal
Fledges Day 10

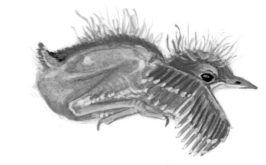

Prothonotary Warbler
Fledges Day 11

Indigo Bunting
Fledges Day 10

Yellow-billed Cuckoo
Fledges Day 8